Circumplex Model: Systemic Assessment and Treatment of Families

THE *JOURNAL OF PSYCHOTHERAPY & THE FAMILY* SERIES:

- *Computers and Family Therapy*
- *Divorce Therapy*
- *Family Therapy Education and Supervision*
- *Marriage and Family Enrichment*
- *Treating Incest: A Multiple Systems Perspective*
- *Depression in the Family*
- *The Use of Self in Therapy*
- *The Family Life of Psychotherapists: Clinical Implications*
- *Chronic Disorders and the Family*
- *Women, Feminism and Family Therapy*
- *Circumplex Model: Systemic Assessment and Treatment of Families*

Circumplex Model: Systemic Assessment and Treatment of Families

David H. Olson
Candyce S. Russell
Douglas H. Sprenkle
Editors

The Haworth Press
New York • London

Circumplex Model: Systemic Assessment and Treatment of Families, has also been published as *Journal of Psychotherapy & the Family*, Volume 4, Numbers 1/2 1988.

The Haworth Press, Inc., 12 West 32 Street, New York, NY 10001
EUROSPAN/Haworth, 3 Henrietta Street, London WC2E 8LU England

Library of Congress Cataloging-in-Publication Data

Circumplex model.

"Has also been published as Journal of psychotherapy & the family, volume 4, numbers 1/2 1988"–T.p. verso.

Includes bibliographies and index.

1. Circumplex Model of Marital and Family Systems. 2. Family psychotherapy. I. Olson, David H. L. II. Russell, Candyce Smith. III. Sprenkle, Douglas H.

RC488.53.C57 1988 616.89'156 88-30151

ISBN 0-86656-776-3

Circumplex Model: Systemic Assessment and Treatment of Families

CONTENTS

ABOUT THE EDITORS

David H. Olson, PhD, is Professor of Family Social Science at the University of Minnesota. He developed the "Circumplex Model of Marital and Family Systems," which is being used as the theoretical foundation for over 600 studies nationally and internationally. This model is also being used widely in marital and family therapy and in preventive programs for couples and families. He has also developed over ten inventories that are used extensively for research and clinical work with couples and families. His best known self-report instruments include FACES, PAIR, PREPARE, and ENRICH.

Candyce S. Russell, PhD, is Professor in the Department of Human Development and Family Studies at Kansas State University. She is past secretary of the American Association for Marriage and Family Therapy and a frequent contributor to professional journals in the marriage and family field.

Douglas H. Sprenkle, PhD, Professor of Marriage and Family Therapy, is also Director of the Marriage and Family Therapy Program and Center at Purdue University in West Lafayette, Indiana. Dr. Sprenkle is a frequent author on marriage and family therapy issues. His associate editorships include the *Journal of Divorce*, the *Journal of Psychotherapy & the Family*, the *Journal of Marital and Family Therapy*, and *Family Relations.*

Circumplex Model: Systemic Assessment and Treatment of Families

EDITORIAL NOTE

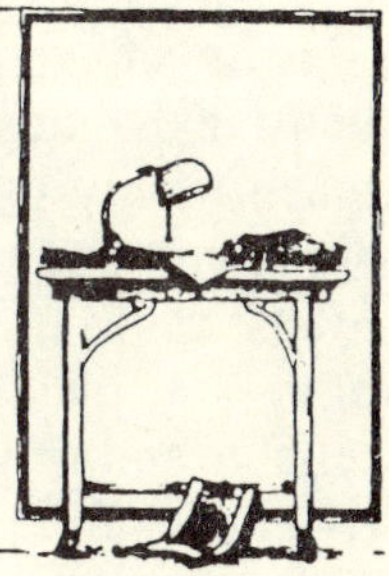

The *Journal of Psychotherapy & the Family* is pleased to present this special issue focusing on the Circumplex Model of family assessment and treatment. As subscribers already know, the purpose of the *Journal* is to provide the practicing psychotherapist with a comprehensive array of well-written, accurate, authoritative, and relevant information vital to working with clients about interpersonal and family-related issues. This issue, with its concern about the integration of theory, research, and treatment, fits this mission extremely well.

Developed nearly a decade ago, the Circumplex Model of Family Systems has been one of the most respected and widely used approaches of its kind in family studies. It has evolved from a rather simple and undeveloped conceptualization of family functioning to a model that is useful in the diagnosis and treatment, as well as theorizing about a wide variety of systems, including the family.

The Editorial Board of the *Journal* challenged the guest editors and contributors to show that the Circumplex Model is the state of the art. It is rare that a theory of systemic intervention, such as the Circumplex Model, not only articulates a theory, but also provides specific methods of both assessment and intervention. Ideally, this collection would provide a single-source handbook for the practitioner, along with the sufficient warnings that the approach/model has its limitations. In both these ways, it is our belief that they have exceeded our expectations.

Efforts have been under way for some time to develop a comprehensive diagnostic schema for family systems. This comes at a time when family psychotherapists envy the diagnostic power, relative simplicity and generally universal acceptance of the Diagnostic and Statistical Manual of Mental Disorders applied to individual pathology. Yet, the Circumplex Model, in contrast to others, provides a reliable and valid methodology for measuring and categorizing family clients and guiding their treatment.

This set of papers is unique. It is the first time, within the same collection, that the architects of this Model fully explicate the Model and provide a comprehensive overview and illustrations of its use in a wide variety of contexts. It should serve as a primary reference for practitioners for some time, if not a classic for all time.

The guest editors are internationally-known scholar clinicians. David H. Olson is Professor in the Department of Family Social Sciences at the University of Minnesota and incoming President of the National Council on Family Relations. Candyce S. Russell is Professor in the Department of Human Development and Family Studies at Kansas State University and currently serves as Secretary of the Board of Directors of the American Association for Marriage and Family Therapy. Douglas H. Sprenkle is Professor and Director of the Marriage and Family Therapy Program in the Department of Child Development and Family Studies at Purdue University and a member of the Commission on Marital and Family Therapy Education.

The *Journal* welcomes comments about this and other published issues and suggestions regarding future ones.

Charles R. Figley, PhD
Editor

Introduction

David H. Olson
Candyce S. Russell
Douglas H. Sprenkle

This collection is designed to perform two functions. The first is to introduce the Circumplex Model of Marital and Family Systems to readers who may be unfamiliar with it. The second function is to update those readers already familiar with the model with recent work which extends the model and describes its use with specific client populations and social systems beyond the nuclear family unit (e.g., family of origin and the system of helpers involved with symptomatic families).

In the opening paper, David H. Olson reviews the development of the Circumplex Model, the empirical data which supports it, and the various measurement tools which are now available for assessment of families and for hypothesis testing. Each subsequent paper presumes knowledge of the material Olson presents here.

Froma Walsh teams up with Olson in the next paper to discuss ways in which the Circumplex Model and associated assessment tools can be used in guiding the treatment of severely dysfunctional family systems. They suggest specific categories of interventions which are especially effective with systems located in extreme regions of the Circumplex Model. The authors identify types of systems where such interventions as circular questioning, use of paradox or direct assignment of tasks are most effective.

In the next paper, Candyce S. Russell conceptualizes presenting problems as the family's attempt to bring the polarities of separateness versus connectedness and stability versus change into balance. This understanding is used to help couples and families reframe their experience and to identify alternative strategies for achieving balance. Although symptoms can be conceptualized as shifting the balance along both the cohesion and adaptability dimensions, Russell suggests choosing *one* theme (either distance or change) as a focus in the therapy of a particular couple or family. She suggests that symptoms which arise during periods of critical transition are easily framed as attempts to regulate change while symptoms which are chronic in nature can often be understood as regulating distance.

Terry S. Trepper and Douglas H. Sprenkle use the Circumplex Model and corresponding measurement tools to assess and plan the treatment of families referred for child sexual abuse. The paper is especially useful in providing a clear, calm, and organized response to a presenting problem which typically activates anxiety in the community and helping professionals as well as in the client family. Careful attention is given to several subsystem levels (including individual, nuclear family, family of origin) as well as the family's location in its community. In their description of the various family styles associated with intrafamily child sexual abuse, the authors offer especially useful observations on the interface between individual perceptions, personality and family organization.

The Circumplex Model provides the foundation for a psychoeducational approach to the treatment of sexual addictions, as described in the paper by Patrick Carnes. Carnes defines sexual addiction as a *family* illness in that family members observe the addict's behavior, attempt to control it and thus intensify the behavior of the addict. The program Carnes developed uses the Circumplex Model to provide family members with a vocabulary to talk about their problems and to create avenues for effecting change within their own system.

In the next paper, James W. Maddock and Carol G. Lange offer a new method of treating difficult families by broadening the original focus of the Circumplex Model to the entire therapeutic community. They provide input from a Milan-type team to balance the positions of multiple helpers involved with multiproblem families. Recognizing that the "balance" within the larger ecosystem is in a dynamic relationship with the "balance" managed within a smaller sub-system, these authors use input from team members to capitalize on the dialectical process of structural transformation within the multiple layers of an ecosystem. The team's interventions are designed to encourage a series of small changes which permit structural transformations without threatening organizational autonomy and identity or the family's "fit" to its ecosystem. Data collection is guided by three well-established principles of Milan-style systemic therapy: hypothesizing, circular questioning and neutrality. Information collected in this manner is then used to decide from which quadrant of the Circumplex Model the team's "balancing" message should come. This is an innovative use of the Circumplex Model, and the authors continue to collect impressionistic data on its impact on several system levels.

Howard L. Barnes uses the FACES III pencil and paper instrument to illustrate how the clinician can make use of discrepant reports of family process by individual family members. In particular, he presents data to document the problematic nature of cross-generational coalitions, but finds no support for the hypothesis that cross-gender parent-child coalitions are any more destructive than same gender coalitions.

Carol E. Woehrer addresses the issue of families which are an exception to the general rule of "balance," and which operate well in more extreme regions of the Circumplex Model. She hypothesizes that certain *intergenerational* systems, contrary to nuclear family systems, operate well at higher levels of cohesion since they can offer kin a richness in resources which families at lower levels of cohesion may lack. Furthermore, she suggests that when nuclear families are a part of a larger extended family, family members do regard otherwise rigid authority structures more flexibly. That is, while spouses may not have a tradition of much negotiation between themselves, discussion of issues often takes place with extended family members. Woehrer also suggests that the effects of low adaptability are considerably diminished when extended family relationships are high in cohesion by offering multiple role models and "dispensing" supervision among a larger number of adults.

Woehrer's paper extends the Circumplex Model by offering additional *hypotheses* based on published clinical and ethnographic sources. Maria J. Flores and Sprenkle, though operating without prior knowledge of Woehrer's paper, present empirical data on a large sample of one of the ethnic groups included in Woehrer's review: Mexican Americans. It is important to note, however, that respondents in the Flores and Sprenkle study were describing their *nuclear* families, not their intergenerational family systems. They found these nuclear systems to be generally described as balanced. However those families which were located in more extreme regions of the model were twice as likely to describe themselves as disengaged as they were to describe themselves as enmeshed. The most extreme scores came from families living in the most economically depressed areas.

The treatment of families of adjudicated youth is addressed in the paper by P. E. Maynard and A. Hultquist. The authors explain how the Circumplex Model has been used to help staff make the transition to family level assessment treatment goals and interventions. The authors provide a detailed case study in which pencil and paper (FACES II) and clinical rating scales were used to track the movement of the family within the Circumplex Model. Maynard and Hultquist also document discrepancies among the self-reports of family members and offer initial speculations on how they can be used in treatment planning.

The family-school ecosystem is the focus of Don-David Lusterman's contribution. He suggests that in assessing cases where school performance is part of the presenting problem, the clinician include information on the nature of interaction between the family and the school. This information can be used to begin the construction of a "circumplex ecomap" that describes the way the home and school interact. Based on the mapping of school-family interaction, the author illustrates treatment designed to move both the school system and the family to the same quadrant within the balanced regions of the Circumplex Model.

The Circumplex Model, which was first introduced in 1979, has stimulated a large number of dissertations and research projects, many of which have used the measurement tools developed by Olson and his colleagues at the University of Minnesota. The model has also been used by a group of creative clinicians to systematically approach the treatment of specific clinic populations. Thirdly, the hypotheses of the model have been extended and elaborated through the efforts of both researchers and clinicians. The papers included in this volume represent each of these three continuing developments.

Circumplex Model of Family Systems VIII: Family Assessment and Intervention

David H. Olson

SUMMARY. This paper describes how the Circumplex Model can be used to provide a systematic assessment of a marital and family system and for planning treatment intervention. The three dimensions in the Circumplex Model of cohesion, change (adaptability) and communication are described. This paper also reviews a variety of hypotheses that have been derived and tested which validate the Circumplex Model. It is recommended that both the self-report scales, Circumplex Assessment Package (CAP), and the Clinical Rating Scale (CRS) be used for family assessment and treatment planning. The paper reflects the continuing attempt to further develop the Circumplex Model and more adequately bridge research, theory and clinical practice.

The Circumplex Model of Marital and Family Systems was developed in an attempt to bridge the gap that typically exists between research, theory and practice. One major approach used to bridge this gap has been the systematic development of both a self-report and clinical rating scale based on the Circumplex Model. Both the self-report scale, called the Circumplex Assessment Package (CAP), and the Clinical Rating Scale (CRS) have been revised several times to increase their reliability, validity and clinical utility.

David H. Olson, PhD, is Professor, Family Social Science, University of Minnesota, 290 McNeal Hall, St. Paul, MN 55108.

A variety of hypotheses have been developed and tested using the Circumplex Model. Some of the research has focused on the relationship between family symptoms and types of family systems. Recent studies are investigating changes in family types before and after treatment and change during the treatment process.

In addition to its value in research projects, the Circumplex Model can also be used in clinical practice. Clinically, it can be used for assessing marital and family systems and for planning treatment intervention. In addition to identifying types of family systems, work is currently being done to describe the type of therapeutic techniques and interventions that are most and least effective with various types of systems.

BRIEF REVIEW OF THEORETICAL MODELS OF FAMILY SYSTEMS

Family cohesion, adaptability, and communication are three dimensions of family behavior that have emerged from a conceptual clustering of over fifty concepts developed to describe marital and family dynamics. Although some of these concepts have been used for decades (power and roles, for instance), many of the concepts have been developed recently by individuals observing problem families from a general systems perspective (pseudomutuality, double binds).

A variety of other theoretical models have focused independently on variables related to the *cohesion, adaptability*, and *communication* dimensions. Most of these models have been developed in the last ten years by individuals having a systems perspective on the family. Evidence regarding the value and importance of these three dimensions is the fact that these theorists have quite independently concluded that these dimensions were critical for understanding and treating marital and family systems.

Table 1 summarizes the work of eleven theorists who have worked on describing marital and family systems. Most of the recent theorizing about family dynamics and intervention has been strongly influenced by general systems theory. Current work has focused on

Table 1: Theoretical Models Using Cohesion, Adaptability, and Communication

	Cohesion	Adaptability	Communication
Beavers & Voeller (1983)	Centripetal Centrifugal	Adaptability	Affect
Benjamin (1977)	Affiliation	Interdependence	
Epstein, Bishop & Levin (1978)	Affective Involvement	Behavior Control Problem-Solving Roles	Communication Affective Responsiveness
French & Guidera (1974)		Capacity to change Power	
Gottman (1979)	Validation	Contrasting	
Kantor & Lehr (1975)	Affect Dimension	Power Dimension	
L'Abate (1985)	Intimacy	Power	
Leary (1957) & Constantine (1986)	Affection Hostility	Dominance Submission	
Leff & Vaughn (1985)	Distance	Problem Solving	
Parsons & Bales (1955)	Expressive Role	Instrumental Role	
Reiss (1981)	Coordination	Closure	

describing both clinical and nonclinical families or has been concerned with clinical intervention with families.

Marital and Family Cohesion (Togetherness)

Family cohesion is defined as the emotional bonding that family members have toward one another. Within the Circumplex Model, some of the specific concepts or variables that can be used to diagnose and measure the family cohesion dimensions are: emotional bonding, boundaries, coalitions, time, space, friends, decision-making, and interests and recreation.

There are four levels of cohesion, ranging from *disengaged* (very low) to *separated* (low to moderate) to *connected* (moderate to high) to *enmeshed* (very high) (see Figure 1). It is hypothesized that

Figure 1: CIRCUMPLEX MODEL - Couple & Family Map

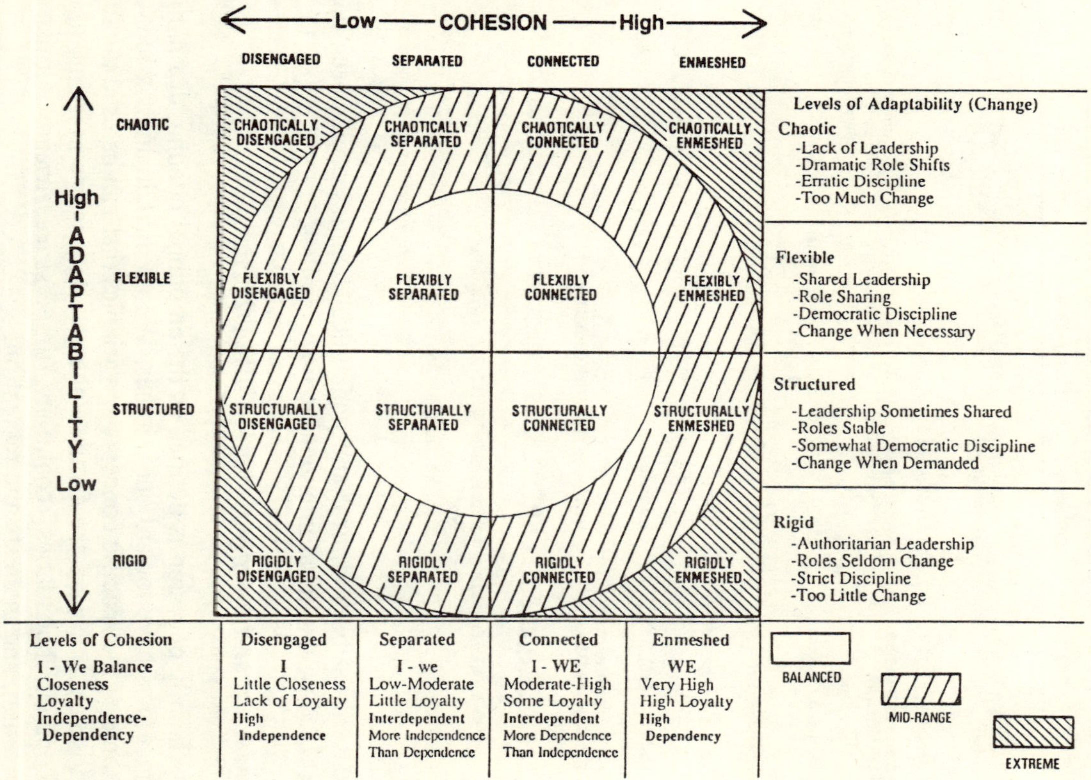

the central levels of cohesion (separated and connected) make for optimal family functioning. The extremes (disengaged or enmeshed) are generally seen as problematic.

Many couples and families that come for treatment often fall into one of these extremes. When cohesion levels are high (enmeshed systems), there is too much consensus within the family and too little independence. At the other extreme (disengaged systems), family members "do their own thing," with limited attachment or commitment to their family. In the model's central area (separated and connected), individuals are able to experience and balance these two extremes and are able to be both independent from and connected to their families.

A disengaged relationship often has extreme emotional separateness. There is little involvement among family members and there is a lot of personal separateness and independence. People often do their own thing and have separate interests.

A separated relationship has some emotional separateness but it is not as extreme as the disengaged system. While time apart is important, there is some time together and some joint decisions. Activities and interests are generally separate but a few are shared. A connected relationship has some emotional closeness and loyalty to the relationship. Time together is more important than time apart to be by oneself. There is an emphasis on togetherness. While there are separate friends, there are also friends shared by the couple. There are often shared interests.

In the enmeshed relationship, there is an extreme amount of emotional closeness and loyalty is demanded. Persons are very dependent on each other and reactive to one another. There is a general lack of personal separateness and little private space is permitted. The energy of the persons is mainly focused inside the marriage or family and there are few outside individual friends or interests.

Based on the Circumplex Model, high levels of cohesion (Enmeshed) and low levels of cohesion (Disengaged) might be problematic for relationships. On the other hand, relationships having moderate scores (Separated and Connected) are able to balance being alone versus together in a more functional way. Although there is no absolute best level for any relationship, some may have problems if they always function at either extreme of the Map (Disengaged and Enmeshed).

Marital and Family Adaptability (Change)

Family adaptability is defined as the ability of a marital or family system to change its power structure, role relationships, and relationship rules in response to situational and developmental stress. In order to describe, measure, and diagnose couples and families on this dimension, a variety of concepts have been taken from several social science disciplines, with heavy reliance on family sociology. These concepts include: family power (assertiveness, control, discipline) negotiation styles, role relationships and relationship rules.

The four levels of adaptability range from *rigid* (very low) to *structured* (low to moderate) to *flexible* (moderate to high) to *chaotic* (very high) (see Figure 1). As with cohesion, it is hypothesized that central levels of adaptability (structured and flexible) are more conducive to marital and family functioning, with the extremes (rigid and chaotic) being the most problematic for families as they move through the family life cycle.

Basically, adaptability focuses on the ability of the marital and family system to change. Much of the early application of systems theory to families emphasized the rigidity of the family and its tendency to maintain the status quo. Until the work of recent theorists, the importance of potential for change was minimized. Couples and families need both stability and change and the ability to change when appropriate distinguishes functional couples and families from others.

Marriages and families can range from having a rigid and authoritarian leader to being chaotic with erratic or limited leadership. A rigid relationship is where one person is highly controlling. The roles are strictly defined and the rules do not change. A structured relationship is overall less rigid. Leadership is somewhat less authoritarian and controlling, and is shared between the parents. Roles are stable, but there is some sharing of roles. There are a few rule changes, but not a lot of change. A flexible relationship is even less rigid. Leadership is more equally shared. Roles are sometimes shared and rules could change. A chaotic relationship has erratic or limited leadership. Decisions are impulsive and not well thought out. Roles are unclear and often shift from person to person.

Based on the Circumplex Model, very high levels of change (chaotic) and very low levels of change (rigid) might be problematic for a marriage and family. On the other hand, relationships having moderate scores (structured and flexible) are able to balance some change and some stability in a more functional way. Although there is no absolute best level for any relationship, many relationships may have problems if they always function at either extreme of the Map (rigid and chaotic).

Marital and Family Communication

Family communication is the third dimension in the Circumplex Model, and is considered a facilitating dimension. Communication is considered critical for facilitating couples and families to move on the other two dimensions. Because it is a facilitating dimension, communication is not graphically included in the model along with cohesion and adaptability.

Positive communication skills (i.e., empathy, reflective listening, supportive comments) enable couples and families to share with each other their changing needs and preferences as they relate to cohesion and adaptability. Negative communication skills (i.e., double messages, double binds, criticism) minimize the ability of a couple or family members to share their feelings and, thereby, restrict their movement on these dimensions.

CIRCUMPLEX MODEL: COUPLE AND FAMILY MAP

Another way to consider the Circumplex Model is as a map of sixteen types of couple and family relationships, in other words a Couple Map and a Family Map. The Couple Map is used to describe sixteen Types of Marriages. The Family Map is used to describe a person's Family of Origin.

The Family Map is important because people often use their own family of origin as a reference for the type of marriage and family they either want or do not want. People often either recreate the type of family system they had as a child or they sometimes react by doing the opposite. Thus, if a couple came from two quite different family systems or they like different types of family dynamics, this may create a challenge for them as a couple.

The Type of Marriage, as illustrated on the Couple Map, is important for the individual and relationship development of a couple. Couples need to balance their levels of separateness-togetherness on cohesion and their levels of stability-change on adaptability. These levels can be adjusted by a couple to achieve a level that is acceptable to each person.

There are several ways couples can have difficulty in balancing these levels of cohesion and adaptability. First, couples might disagree on how they actually see their marriage. One might see their marriage on cohesion as disengaged and the other might see it as connected. In terms of adaptability, one person might see their marriage as rigid and the other might see it as flexible. If a couple disagrees too much, it will often reflect dissatisfaction with their current relationship.

Second, one or both partners might not like the levels of cohesion or adaptability they currently have in their relationship. That is, one person might feel the relationship is too low on cohesion (separated type) and the other might feel their partner is too smothering (enmeshed type).

Couples can make deliberate attempts to change their marriage on cohesion and adaptability. This is important to do to keep the marriage more satisfying. Couples may find it helpful to discuss how they each see the relationship and to explore how satisfied they are with their current level of functioning on these three dimensions. If they are dissatisfied, they can use the model to explore possible directions for change and help them set goals to make their marriage more mutually satisfying.

Balanced versus Extreme Types

An important distinction in the Circumplex Model is between balanced and extreme types of couple and family relationships. There are four balanced types that are "separated" or "connected" levels on cohesion and "structured" or "connected" on adaptability. The four extreme types are "disengaged" or "enmeshed" on cohesion and "rigid" or "chaotic" on adaptability. Figure 2 describes in some detail the characteristics of the four balanced relationships and a description of the four extreme relationships: chaotically disengaged, chaotically enmeshed, rigidly disengaged and rigidly enmeshed.

Figure 2: CIRCUMPLEX MODEL - Balanced and Extreme Types

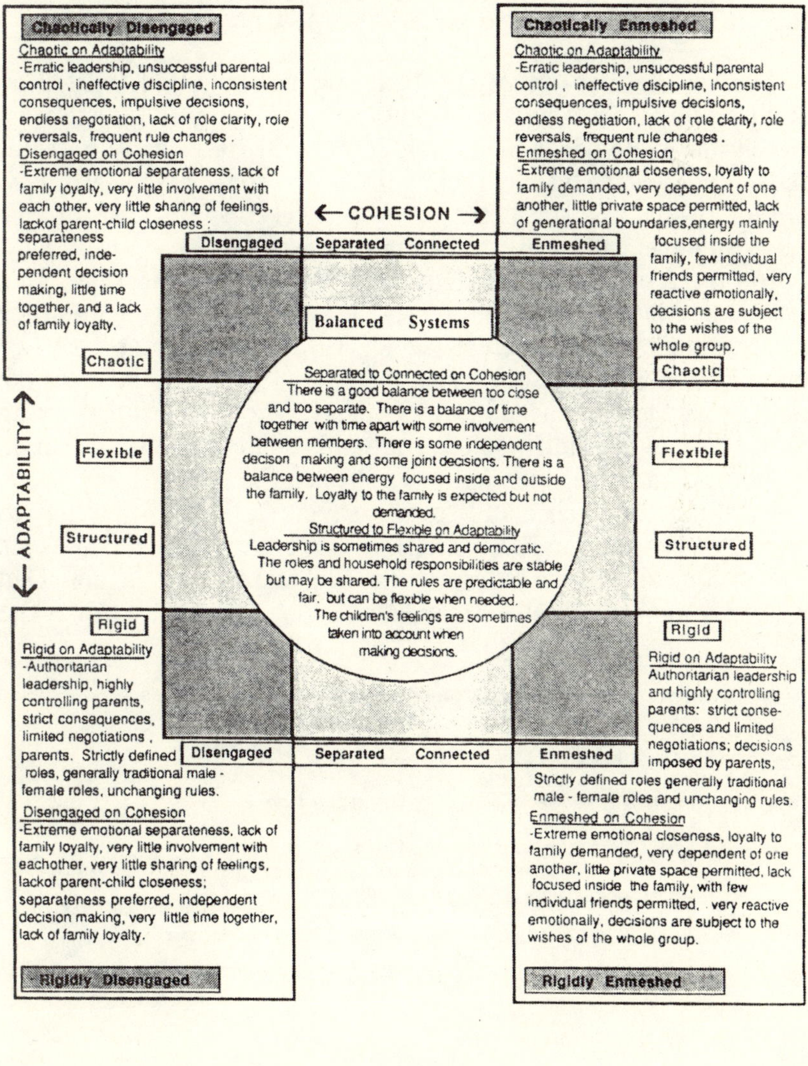

Circumplex Types as Illustrated by the Movies

Movies often provide excellent examples of extreme types of couple and family relationships because these are more dynamically and dramatically interesting than balanced types. Table 2 lists movies that illustrate the four extreme types and the Cosby TV show which illustrates how balanced families operate. A brief description of each movie and extreme type is given below.

A. "The Great Santini": Rigidly Enmeshed

This is a military family, both inside and out. Dad (played by Robert Duvall) is a colonel in the Marines and wants to run his family the same way. He is rigidly enmeshed especially with his oldest son, who he wants to follow in his footsteps into the Marines. On top of that, the son is supposed to excel in sports. For him the son's achievement means his achievement.

But the father cannot just cheer his son from the sidelines. In a one on one home basketball game, the son beats the father and the father cannot take the defeat, saying he must win by at least two points. He bullies the son, trying to get him to cry. He bounces the ball off the kid's forehead in a mocking, confrontive manner, trying to get his son to admit weakness after his son has just beaten him.

None of the other kids have ever beaten the father at any sport, not at ping-pong, checkers, cards, anything. Dad always has to win. So when the son beats him, Dad can't take it. He ridicules his son, trying to get him to cry so he will feel superior again. Dad primarily ignores his two daughters and his youngest son. The

Table 2: **Circumplex Types As Illustrated By Movies**

Circumplex Types	Movies/TV
Rigidly Enmeshed	Great Santini
Rigidly Disengaged	Ordinary People
Chaotically Disengaged	Shoot the Moon
Chaotically Enmeshed	Who's Afraid of Virginia Woolf?
Balanced Type	Cosby TV Show

mother acts in a co-dependent way. She makes excuses for him, defends him to the kids, and is careful not to cross him.

This is also a very enmeshed system. Loyalty is demanded. The son's achievements are a reflection on Dad and an extension of Dad's ego. He is the center of the family; he sets the tone. If he is up, the family is up, if he is down, the family better watch out. This is an enmeshment based on intimidation, not on affection or even feigned affection. But the intimidation works. This family has a very rigid system. Rules are set down and strictly enforced by Dad. There will be no deviance from them, no whimpering or complaining.

B. "Ordinary People": Rigidly Disengaged

The other extreme of the cohesion dimension is the disengaged family from the movie, "Ordinary People." There is rigidity in this pleasant suburban family with mother (played by Mary Tyler Moore) and husband (played by Donald Sutherland). Unlike the angry, authoritarian rigidity of the Meechams in "The Great Santini," this is a passive and subtle rigidity.

This rigidity occurred after the loss of the oldest son in a boating accident on Lake Michigan. Their son, Buck, was the star of the family: handsome, charming, excellent student, star athlete, and now tragically gone. His death has left an emptiness in the family which moves them toward rigidity and disengagement.

There is a good deal of emotional controlling, strictly defined roles and unchanging rules, especially the rules about what feelings can be openly discussed. The surviving son, who has attempted suicide over his guilt surrounding the boating accident, cannot talk about his feelings in the family because of the implicit rules forbidding such intimate and painful self-disclosure.

Likewise, the disengagement in this family is painfully apparent. Feelings are not discussed and a distance is carefully maintained to prevent any future grief. Near the end of the movie, the mother wakes up in the middle of the night and finds her husband not at her side. She goes downstairs and finds him sitting in the dining room, in the dark, crying softly to himself. He says he doesn't think he knows her anymore. She is so distant and when Buck died, a part of her also seemed to die. He does not know the woman who is left behind. And he is not sure he loves her anymore. Without another word, she goes upstairs and begins packing her suitcase to leave. There is a brief moment when she gasps, and nearly cries. She regains control, resumes packing and leaves.

Both of these families are rigid and the rigidity effects the degree of emotional closeness in these families. In "The Great Santini," the rigidity serves the purpose of controlling the level of enmeshment. The demands for family loyalty, the lack of individuation, and emotional reactivity are thrust upon the system by the power they give to the father who dictates the rules of the family: what people should do, how they should perform, and what their level of importance should be within his rigid view of the family. In "Ordinary People," the rigidity serves the purpose of maintaining emotional disengagement in order to prevent the surfacing of the grief and guilt over the loss of the oldest son.

C. "Shoot the Moon": Chaotically Disengaged

This is a family falling apart. Because of the crises this family is under, their family system moved to the extremes of a chaotically disengaged family from one that was typically a flexible separate type. Dad (played by Albert Finney) has been having an affair. He's been trying to keep it from the family, but his oldest daughter is suspicious and listens in on a conversation he has with his lover from an extension at home. He has never called his lover from a phone at home before. But he is desperately in love and beginning to get careless.

His wife (played by Diane Keaton) has been suspicious for some time, but has not confronted him on it. However, his excuses for "working late" wear pretty thin and she finally does confront him and a dish-breaking fight ensues. He suggests he should leave and she says she packed his bag last night.

This couple has been disengaged for some time. And the dad is also disengaged from his daughters. The mom has been close to her daughters before the separation, but even she gets disengaged from them through her depression. The rules and roles are all up for grabs in this family. The father has left, the mother is depressed and unable to function, and the oldest daughter has taken over some of the parenting roles, while still wanting to have a mother and father care for her and be in charge.

The disengagement of the couple really shows in these early scenes of the movie. They have not been connected in a long time as their estrangement has become more extensive. When he finally does move out, the chaos in the family system increases.

The oldest daughter, Julie, takes over Mom's role. Mom sleeps late, buries her head under the pillow, moans, and turns over to try to escape her pain. This happens to a woman who before was never tired and was always patient and had time for her four daughters. In a scene typical of the family chaos, the oldest daughter is trying to make breakfast, talk on the phone to a doctor's office to make an appointment for one of her sisters who sprained her foot, and at the same time yelling upstairs at her sisters to get downstairs for breakfast, while the toast is burning. The sisters yell back down that they don't want her breakfast (that she so carefully has tried to prepare) and so she yells back at them that she doesn't need this, throws the frying pan of scrambled eggs into the kitchen sink and heads out to the school bus.

Dad is waiting at the end of the driveway to pick them up in his car to take them to school. He is trying to overcome his guilt and spend some time with his daughters at the same time. The oldest, parentified daughter just walks around his car and gets onto the bus without saying a word to him. The bus pulls out and she can be seen looking through the bus window crying.

D. "Who's Afraid of Virginia Woolf?": Chaotically Enmeshed

This is a good example of a classical chaotically enmeshed alcoholic system. George (Richard Burton) and Martha (Elizabeth Taylor) have a dependent, love-hate relationship bound together by powerful forces of mutual dependence and kept tolerable through the numbing and disorienting properties of alcohol.

George is an associate professor of English at a small college and Martha is the president's daughter. Martha and her father were impressed with George at first, but have become increasingly disenchanted with him over time. Martha thinks he's a "nothing," a wash-up and an enormous disappointment. And George thinks Martha is a monster, who he said used to howl and claw at the turf outside his window when he first came to the college. So he married her, he said, in order to get some work done.

They cannot let go of each other. They know where to attack each other's vulnerability and don't hesitate to do so. To George, Martha is a promiscuous, liquor-ridden monster who never hesitates to make a fool of herself. To Martha, George is a weak-willed, pretentious, academic flop. They even share a secret, a mutual fantasy of a son. Since they were never able to have children, they created one.

But one night, in an extended drunken battle when two guests come over after a faculty party, the secret gets disclosed. And for a while it looks like their enmeshed relationship will come unraveled through the chaotic fighting during the course of an endless nightmare of fighting. They break mutually-agreed-upon rules, but manage to stick together in the end, even though it looks as though they will destroy each other.

Their extreme enmeshment and dependency keeps them together when it looks like their system chaos will tear them apart. But they survive the pain of their enmeshment dependency by using alcohol or fantasy when the pain gets too intolerable.

HYPOTHESES DERIVED FROM THE CIRCUMPLEX MODEL

One of the assets of a theoretical model is that hypotheses can be deduced and tested in order to evaluate and further develop the model. The following are hypotheses derived from the model.

I. Couples/families with balanced (two central levels) cohesion and adaptability will generally function more adequately across the family life cycle than those at the extreme of these dimensions.

An important issue in the Circumplex Model relates to the concept of balance. Even though a balanced family system is placed at the two central levels of the model, it should not be assumed that these families always operate in a "moderate" manner. Being balanced means that a family system can experience the extremes on the dimension when appropriate but that they do not typically function at these extremes for long periods of time.

Families in the balanced area of the cohesion dimension allow family members to experience being both independent from and connected to their family. Both extremes are tolerated and expected, but the family does not continually function at the extreme. Conversely, extreme family types tend to function only at the extreme and are not encouraged to change the way they function as a family. This leads to Hypothesis II.

II. Balanced family types have a larger behavioral repertoire and are more able to change compared with extreme family types.

Integrating Normative Expectations of Families

Although a curvilinear relationship is generally predicted, some important qualifications must be made in terms of the normative expectations and cultural bias of Hypothesis I. Hypothesis III states:

III. If the normative expectations of a couple or family support behaviors extreme on one or both of the Circumplex dimensions, they will function well as long as all family members are satisfied with these expectations.

The normative expectations in our culture provide two conflicting themes that can create problems for couples and families. One theme is that family members are expected to do things together as a family. Yet, the second theme encourages individuals to "do their own thing" and develop autonomy. The theme of independence becomes more prominent as children approach adolescence and it has taken on greater importance for increasing numbers of women in our culture. As a result, many American families find that balancing these two themes has become a difficult issue.

Families in our culture still vary greatly in the extent to which they encourage family closeness and individual development. Although most parents would prefer their children to develop values and ideas similar to theirs, most parents also want their children to become somewhat autonomous and differentiated from the family system.

A sizable minority of families, however, have normative expectations that strongly emphasize family togetherness in both the nuclear and extended families. Their family norms emphasize emotional and physical togetherness, and they strive for high levels of consensus and loyalty. Some ethnic groups in this country such as Slovak-American, Puerto Rican, and Italian families, and religious groups such as the Amish and Mormons have high expectations regarding family togetherness.

These expectations are also common, but less predominant, in many other American families regardless of ethnic or religious orientation. Many of these families could be described as extreme on the cohesion dimension (i.e., enmeshed), and they function well as long as all family members are willing to go along with those expectations. Problems occur when a family member, often an adolescent or mother, becomes frustrated with these extreme family systems (i.e., rigidly enmeshed). It is, therefore, important to assess not only the type of family system but how satisfied each family member is with that type of family.

Family Communication as a Facilitating Dimension

Communication is a critical dimension related to the Circumplex Model because it facilitates movement on the two dimensions. This leads to two specific hypotheses linking communication to balanced types and to change on cohesion and adaptability.

IV. Balanced couples/families will tend to have more positive communication skills than extreme families.

V. Positive communication skills will enable balanced couples/families to change their levels of cohesion and adaptability more easily than those at the extremes.

In general, positive communication skills are seen as helping marital and family systems facilitate and maintain a balance on the two dimensions. Conversely, negative communication skills impede from moving into the central areas and thereby increase the probability that extreme systems will remain extreme.

Positive communication skills include the following: sending clear and congruent messages, empathy, supportive statements, and effective problem-solving skills. Conversely, negative communication skills include the following: sending incongruent and disqualifying messages, lack of empathy, nonsupportive (negative) statements, poor problem-solving skills, and paradoxical and double-binding messages. Although many studies have investigated communication and problem-solving skills in couples and families, these studies have not specifically tested the relationships of these skills to the hypotheses derived from the Circumplex Model.

Family Development and the Circumplex Model

VI. To deal with situational stress and developmental changes across the family life cycle, families will change their cohesion and adaptability to adapt to stress.

This hypothesis deals with change in the family system to deal with stress or to accommodate changes in family members, particularly as family members change their expectations. The Circumplex Model is dynamic in that it assumes that couples and families will change types, and it hypothesizes that change can be beneficial to the maintenance and improvement of family functioning.

When one family member desires change, the family system must somehow deal with that request. For example, increasing numbers of married women want to develop more autonomy from their husbands (cohesion dimension) and also want more power and equality in their relationships (adaptability dimension). If their husbands are unwilling to understand and change in accordance with these expectations, the marriages will probably experience increasing levels of stress and dissatisfaction. Another common example of changing expectations occurs when a child reaches adolescence. Like the wife in the previous example, adolescents often want more freedom, independence, and power in the family system.

The Circumplex Model allows one to integrate systems theory with family development, a proposal made more than a decade ago by Reuben Hill (1970). Building on the family development approach, it is hypothesized that families must change as they deal with normal transitions in the family. It is expected, therefore, that the stage of the family life cycle and composition of the family will have considerable impact on the type of family system.

It is first of all hypothesized that at any stage of the family life cycle, there will be a diversity in the types of family systems as described in the Circumplex Model. In spite of this diversity, it is predicted that at different stages of the family life cycle many of the families will cluster together in some types more frequently than in others. For example, it would be predicted that pre-marital couples would tend toward the high range on cohesion (enmeshed and connected) and toward the lower range on adaptability (structured and rigid). In other words, they would fall into the lower right quadrant of the Circumplex Model.

The model is dynamic in that it assumes that changes can occur in family types over time (Olson et al., 1983). Families can move in any direction that the situation, stage of the family life cycle, or socialization of family members may require. A look at couples illustrates the dynamic nature of the model.

> Fred and Mary were married and developed a flexibly enmeshed marriage. Three years after their marriage, they became parents, and Mary resigned from her teaching job. Because of the dependency needs of their son and their own desire for mutual support in this transition period, their family became structurally connected.
>
> However, when Mary and Fred's son became a teenager, their family moved from being connected to being more separated on cohesion. Mary started pursuing a career, and both parents experienced a good deal of "consciousness raising" about sex roles through the media and through involvement in several growth groups. Because of their son's needs for more autonomy at this age, as well as the parents' separate career interests, they began operating at a lower level of cohesiveness.
>
> Furthermore, the family power structure shifted from being husband-dominant to a more shared pattern. They moved on adaptability from a structured type to a flexible type. Mary exercised much more control in the relationship than previously, and the couple were struggling, almost on a weekly

basis, to redefine the rules and role definitions that will govern their relationship. Although they occasionally yearned for the security of their earlier, more structured relationship, both found the challenge in this more flexible relationship style.

In short, their family could be described as flexibly separated at the adolescent stage of the family life cycle. This brief case history illustrates the dynamic nature of the model, which allows for movement within reasonable limits. It also seeks to recognize diverse values and legitimize the diverse organizational ideals of families. None of the four balanced types in the inner circle is designated as "the ideal" at any given stage of the family life cycle, but all are more functional than the extreme types, especially with families at the adolescent stage.

STUDIES VALIDATING THE CIRCUMPLEX MODEL

Balanced versus Extreme Families

A central hypothesis derived from the model is that balanced couples/families will function more adequately than extreme couples/families. This hypothesis is built on the assumption that families extreme on both dimensions will tend to have more difficulties functioning across the life cycle. This assumes a curvilinear relationship on the dimensions of cohesion and adaptability. This means that too little or too much cohesion or adaptability is seen as dysfunctional to the family system. However, families that are able to balance between these two extremes seem to function more adequately.

To test the major hypothesis that balanced family types are more functional than extreme types, a variety of studies has been done focusing on the range of emotional problems and symptoms in couples and families. A recent study by Clark (1984) focused on families with schizophrenics, neurotics, families who had therapy sometime in their past, and a no-therapy control group (see Figure 3). He used FACES II, a self-report scale which assesses family cohesion and adaptability. In general, he found a very high level of extreme families in the neurotic and schizophrenic groups compared to the no-therapy group. Conversely, he found a significantly

Figure 3: Problem Families

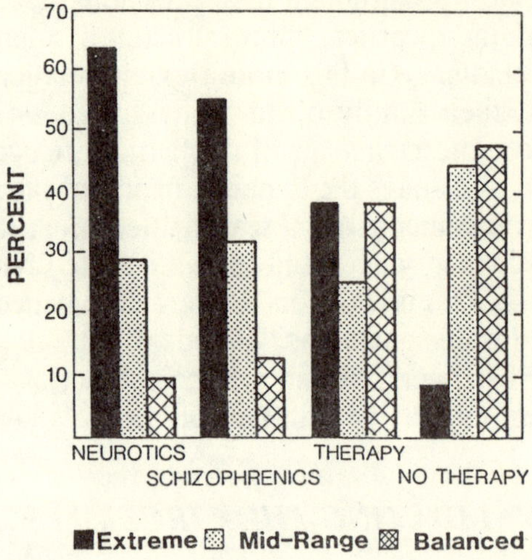

higher level of balanced families in the no-therapy group compared to the other groups.

Figure 3 illustrates the differences in the levels of cohesion and adaptability between these groups. While the percentage of extreme family types decreased dramatically from the symptomatic to no-therapy groups (neurotic, 64%; schizophrenic, 56%; therapy, 38%; no therapy, 7%), the percentage of balanced families increased (neurotic, 8%; schizophrenic, 12%; therapy, 38%; no therapy, 48%) as hypothesized.

Other studies have focused on alcoholic families in which the identified patient was the mother or father. Using the original FACES, Olson and Killorin (1984) found significant differences between the chemically dependent families and the nondependent families. As hypothesized, alcoholic families had a significantly higher level of extreme families compared to the nondependent family. Over 20% of the chemically dependent families were extreme types, while only 4% of the nondependent families were extreme types. Conversely, about two-thirds (65%) of the nondependent families were balanced, while about one-third (32%) of the dependent families were balanced.

A study of alcoholics in treatment by Bonk (1984) assessed 20 families before treatment (pre), after treatment (post), and one month after treatment (follow-up). While no changes occurred over time on cohesion and adaptability, significant changes did occur between pre/post and pre/follow-up on the family satisfaction scale (27), which measures satisfaction on cohesion and adaptability.

A recent study by Carnes (1987) that used FACES II investigated the family systems in sex offenders and found high levels of extreme family types in both their family of origin and their current families (see Figure 4). While about half (49%) had extreme family types in their family of origin and about two-thirds (66%) of their current families were extreme types, only 19% of the nonoffender families were extreme. Conversely, while only 11% of their families of origin and 19% of their current families were balanced types, about half (57%) of the nonoffender families were balanced.

Comparing 27 high risk families with 35 low risk families, Garbarino, Sebes, and Schellenbach (1985) focused on the type of family systems using the original FACES scale. Using intact families, both parents and one adolescent completed FACES and a variety of other scales that were used to assess family stress, parenting, and family conflict. As hypothesized by the Circumplex Model, they found the majority of the low risk families were balanced types

Figure 4: Sex Offenders

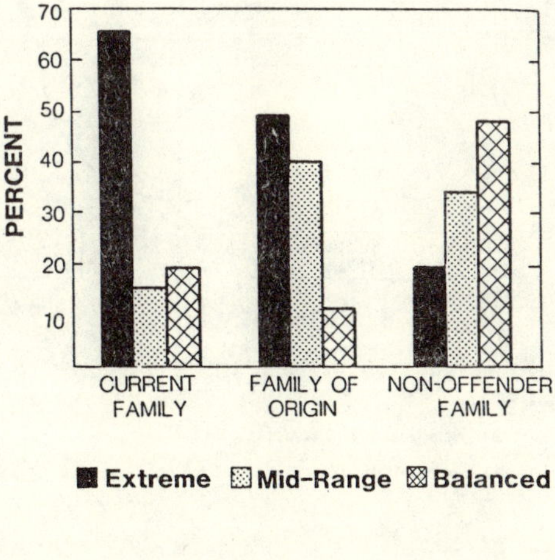

(mainly flexibly connected) while the majority of the high risk families were an extreme type (mainly chaotically enmeshed).

A recent study by Rodick, Henggeler, and Hanson (1986) compared 58 mother-son dyads from father-absent families in which half (29) had an adolescent juvenile offender and the other half (29) had adolescents with no history of arrest or psychiatric referral. As graphically illustrated in Figure 5, only 7% of the delinquents were balanced while 93% of the delinquent families were mid-range or extreme types. In contrast, 69% of the nondelinquent families were balanced while 31% were mid-range or extreme.

In summary, these studies of clinical samples clearly demonstrate the discriminant power of the Circumplex Model in distinguishing between problem families and nonsymptomic families. There is

Figure 5: Delinquent Families

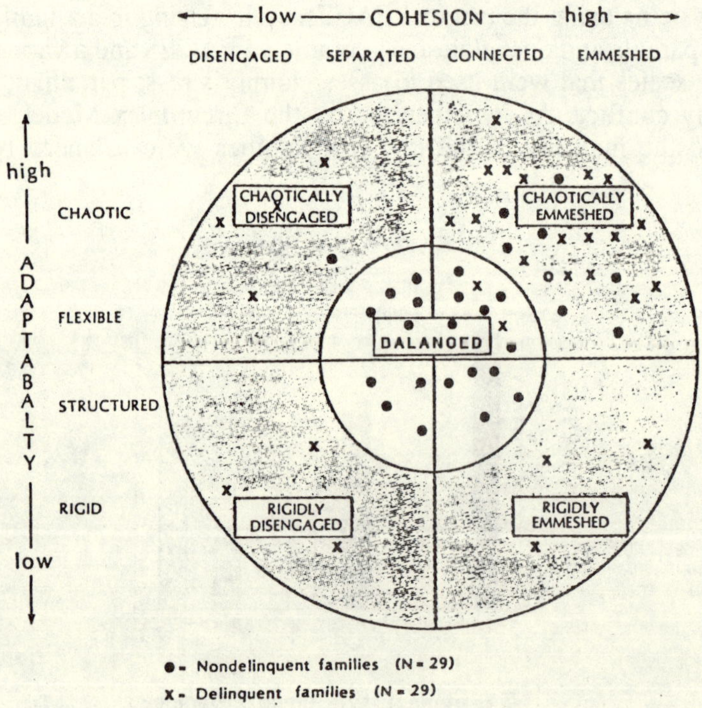

strong empirical support for the hypothesis that balanced types of families are more functional than extreme family types. There is, however, a lack of evidence that any of these symptoms are specifically linked with a specific type of family system, for example, chaotically enmeshed. This was the hope of early family research linking family symptoms (a schizophrenic offspring) and family systems.

In contrast to the curvilinear relationship found on these dimensions among problem families, there appears to be a linear relationship between cohesion and change (adaptability) in family functioning among "normal" families. More specifically, higher levels of cohesion and change seem to be associated with better family functioning.

These results were found in the national survey of 1,000 families across the life cycle, which was reported in the recent book by Olson and colleagues (1983), *Families: What Makes Them Work*. A primary reason for this finding is that normal families represent only a narrow spectrum of the range of behavior on these two dimensions. As a result, there are very few of the "normal" families that legitimately fall into the extreme types.

Balanced Families and Communication

Another hypothesis is that balanced families will have more positive communication skills than extreme families. Communication can be measured at both the marital and family level. Using data from the national survey of 1,000 families, Barnes and Olson (1982, 1983) investigated parent-adolescent communication and family functioning. Using "nonproblem" families, the hypothesis that balanced families would have better communication skills was supported when relying on data from the parents. However, this hypothesis was not supported for adolescents. Future research is needed to test hypotheses at both the marital and family level with both normal and problem families.

In addition to testing the hypothesis regarding balanced versus extreme families reviewed earlier, Rodick et al. (1986) found strong support for the hypothesis that balanced families have more positive communication skills. Using observational measures of mother-adolescent interaction, they found that mothers in the balanced group had significantly higher rates of supportive communication, explicit information, and positive affect than did the mother in the extreme type with the majority of problem dyads (chaotically enmeshed).

Accounting for Cultural and Ethnic Diversity Using Family Satisfaction

In order to make the Circumplex Model culturally relevant to a variety of families with different ethnic and cultural backgrounds, a hypothesis was developed to reflect this diversity. Hypothesis III states that if normative expectations of families support behavior extreme on one or both of the dimensions, families will function well as long as all family members are satisfied with these expectations. In this way, the family serves as its own norm base.

This approach necessitates measuring family satisfaction of each family member. A 14 item Family Satisfaction Scale (Olson & Wilson, 1982) taps the Circumplex dimensions. While it might be more difficult to observe behavioral change in cohesion and adaptability (and related family types) related to treatment, family satisfaction might be more sensitive to treatment change. This was demonstrated in a recent treatment outcome study of alcoholics by Bonk (1984). While he found no change in mean scores on cohesion or adaptability, significant increases in family satisfaction occurred between pre-post and pre-follow-up assessments.

INVENTORIES FOR CLINICAL ASSESSMENT AND RESEARCH

In order to adequately assess the three major dimensions of the Circumplex Model and other related concepts, Olson and colleagues (1982) have developed a variety of self-reports assessment tools. These assessment tools were designed to provide an "insider's perspective" on their own family system, but also an "outsider's perspective." The self-report instrument called the Circumplex Assessment Package (CAP) provides the insider's perspective, whereas the Clinical Rating Scale (CRS) provides the outsider's perspective. Both perspectives are useful and often provide conflicting data. Used together, however, it was discovered they help capture the complexity of marital and family systems (Olson, 1977).

Assessment Criteria: Multi-Method, Multi-Trait, Multi-System Level

The multi-method approach utilizes both self-report scales, which provide an "insider's perspective" on their own relationship, and the therapist's or observer's ratings which provide an "outsider's perspective" on that same system. Both clinical work and research with families have indicated that there is often a discrepancy between these two perspectives and related methodologies (Olson, 1977; Olson et al., 1983). Because these two methodologies often provide different perspectives, this provides an important rationale why both approaches should be used in work with families.

If a therapist only relies on his/her own perception of the system (an outsider's perspective), our data indicates that this will often differ in significant ways from one or more of the family members' perceptions. It is also problematic to rely on only one family member because family members often do not agree with each other in describing their family system (Olson, 1983). Assessment using multiple family members, therefore, provides a more complete picture of how each family member sees the system and the level of agreement or disagreement between them.

Multi-trait assessment is based on the three central dimensions of the Circumplex Model: cohesion, adaptability and communication. Although there are other traits that can be incorporated into couple and family assessment, these three dimensions provide the foundation and central core of these relationship systems.

Multi-System assessment ideally focuses on the individual, the marital system, parent-child system and total family, including extended family relationships. One important question to ask family members is who they each consider to be members of their family. It is surprising to us how often family members disagree regarding who is currently in their family system. This raises important questions about boundary issues and who is psychologically and/or physically present in a given family system (Boss & Greenberg, 1984).

Reliability, Validity and Clinical Utility

In developing assessment tools it is essential that the scientific criteria of reliability and validity be met at acceptable levels. The more rigorous the reliability and validity, the greater the accuracy and value of the instrument for making individual assessment of a specific couple or family system.

Too often, the clinical utility of the tool is not considered or assessed. In order for an instrument to have high clinical utility it must be easy for family members to complete and must provide information that can help the therapist understand the system from each individual's perspective. Assessment should also be efficient; and it should facilitate the family's involvement in the therapeutic process.

Circumplex Assessment Package (CAP)

The Circumplex Assessment Package (CAP) is the latest in a series of self-report assessments developed which are based on the Circumplex Model. This assessment procedure is multi-dimensional in that it assesses the three Circumplex dimensions of cohesion, adaptability and communication, and also includes the satisfaction dimension.

It is also multi-system level in that assessment procedures focus on both the marital system and the family system. More specifically, each of the four dimensions are assessed at the couple and family level (see Table 3). Two parent households (nuclear or blended) would complete both the marital and family scales. Single parent families would complete the family scales and would complete the marital scales if the single parent has a significant other. Couples (married or cohabitating) would complete the couple scales.

FACES III is an acronym for Family Adaptability and Cohesion Evaluation Scales and MACES III is an acronym for Marital Adaptability and Cohesion Evaluation Scales. The communication di-

Table 3: Circumplex Assessment Package (CAP)

Dimensions	Couple System	Family System
Cohesion Adaptability	MACES III	FACES III
Communication	Couple Communication	Family Communication
Satisfaction	Couple Satisfaction	Family Satisfaction

mension is assessed at the couple level using a sub-scale from the ENRICH instrument (Olson, Fournier, & Druckman, 1986) and family communication is based on the Parent-Adolescent Communication scale (Barnes & Olson, 1982, 1983). The satisfaction dimension is assessed at the couple level using a sub-scale from ENRICH instrument (Olson, Fournier, & Druckman, 1986) and the Family Satisfaction scale (Olson & Wilson, 1982) which is based on the Circumplex dimensions.

The reliability of these scales has been assessed in a variety of studies and the most comprehensive summary is provided in the volume entitled, *Family Inventories* (Olson et al., 1983). As indicated in Table 4, both the internal consistency and test-retest reliability of these scales are consistently high (r = .80). In terms of validity, therapists and researchers have evaluated the items in terms of face validity and find them to meet acceptable criteria. The scales also demonstrated have also discriminate validity in that they distinguish between clinical and non-clinical families (Olson, 1986).

In studies of normal families (non-clinical), there is a linear relationship on all of these dimensions. More specifically, higher levels of cohesion, adaptability, communication and satisfaction at both the marital and family level is associated with better functioning. In clinical families, the Circumplex hypothesizes a curvilinear relationship between cohesion and adaptability and effective functioning, but a linear relationship on communication and satisfaction. More specifically, clinical families would be more extreme on co-

Table 4: Reliability of Circumplex Assessment Package (CAP)

	Reliability Coefficients	
	Internal	Test
FACES III (Family)	Consistency	Re-Test
Cohesion	.77	.83
Adaptability	.62	.80
MACES III (Marital)		
Cohesion	.79	.83
Adaptability	.73	.80
Communication		
Marital Communication (ENRICH)	.82	.90
Parent-Adolescent Communication	.88	.78
Satisfaction		
Marital Satisfaction (ENRICH)	.86	.86
Family Satisfaction	.92	.75
Average	**.80**	**.82**

hesion and adaptability than non-clinical families. The hypothesis most often tested is that clinical families will tend to fall into the extreme types of the Circumplex Model, whereas non-clinical families tend to fall into the more balanced areas. This hypothesis is supported in some studies but not in others (Olson, 1986). Studies using FACES II, which has a high correlation between cohesion and adaptability, have tended not to support the curvilinear hypothesis (Green, Kolevgon, & Vosler, 1985). However, clinical studies using FACES I and III do find support for this curvilinear idea.

Clinical Rating Scale for the Circumplex Model

The Clinical Rating Scale (CRS) was developed by Olson and Killorin (1984) in order to do clinical assessment on cohesion, change and communication. The actual Clinical Rating Scale (CRS) is presented in Appendix A, which illustrates the specific clinical indicators for each level of the three dimensions. This scale is a useful training device for helping therapists learn more about the Circumplex Model and its clinical usefulness (see Appendix A).

Complete instructions for using and scoring the CRS can be obtained by writing the author.

A Family Profile is used to summarize the ratings on these three dimensions. The CRS can be used for rating the behavior of a family system based on semi-structured interview with an individual family member or several members. One useful format to generate information and dynamics about these dimensions is to ask the family member(s) to describe and discuss how they handle daily routines, what a typical weekend is like, and what they do separately and together and how they make decisions.

It has been found that the CRS is easy for practitioners to learn and use in their clinical practice. Inter-rater reliability with this scale has been assessed at rather high levels ($r = .75 - .85$) in a study by Olson and Logacz (1985). In general, there has been less agreement between therapists and raters on the cohesion dimension often because of coalitions and social isolates in a family. For example, there might be an enmeshed mother-son relationship with a disengaged father. In many cases, it is important to distinguish subunits within the family system.

In order to obtain more detailed information regarding coalitions within a family, a new scale has been developed called the Family Closeness Scale (Olson, 1987). This simple scale asks each person to first list the various members in their family system and, secondly, to rate how close they feel to each of these people on a one to eight scale. The data from other family members is summarized into a matrix which provides a more comprehensive picture of family closeness and identifies coalitions and members that are social isolates.

Clinical Assessment of a Chaotically Disengaged Family

Using the Clinical Rating Scale (CRS), the three dimensions of cohesion, change and communication are organized into eight-point scales. The Family Profile is used to summarize the global ratings on these three dimensions and the numerous concepts related for each of the dimensions. The ratings for the following family were based on the first semi-structured interview with them after they were referred for treatment.

The Kelly family was referred to a family therapist because of a court referral for physical abuse between the father, Harold, and the 14-year-old stepdaughter, Elaine. The mother, Margaret, also had experienced some physical abuse and had no other children. The final assessment was that the family was chaotically disengaged with very poor communication skills. The results of the clinical assessment are summarized on the Family Profile in Figure 6.

On family cohesion, the global assessment for the family was 2, indicating that they were a disengaged family. This global evaluation was based on their overall functioning after looking at the six major areas related to cohesion. In regard to emotional bonding, the family had extreme levels of emotional separateness and lacked family loyalty. In terms of family involvement, members had very little interaction with each other. Even though the affective responsiveness was infrequent, when it occurred it was often intense. The marital relationship was also characterized by extreme emotional separateness. Regarding parent-child coalitions, there was a lack of closeness between the father and daughter, but a rather strong closeness between the mother and adolescent. The internal boundaries were characterized by high separateness in that family members seldom spent time with each other and usually shared separate space in their home. Their external boundaries were mainly focused outside the family where they saw their separate friends and participated in separate interests and recreation. In conclusion, this family across most of the concepts related to cohesion could best be characterized as a "disengaged" family system (see Figure 6).

In regard to family change (adaptability), the family generally functioned as a "chaotic" family system. Regarding leadership, neither the father nor the mother exercised much leadership in the family. The discipline of the daughter was often very lenient and the parents were inconsistent in their punishment. The negotiation regarding problems was often endless and while they agreed on decisions, they rarely carried them out. The roles in the household were characterized by a great deal of role ambiguity since no one felt responsible for taking

Figure 6: Family Profile of a Chaotically Disengaged Family

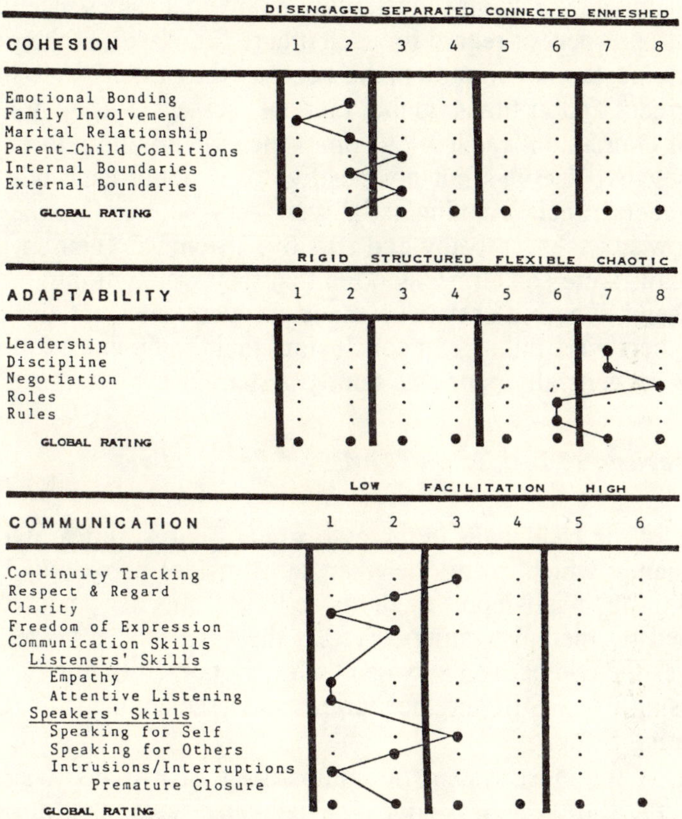

FAMILY SOCIAL SCIENCE 290 McNeal Hall, University of Minnesota, St. Paul, MN 55108

care of the most routine responsibilities. The family rules frequently changed and were inconsistently enforced. As a result, the Kelly family tended to function as a "chaotic" family system (see Figure 6).

The family communication was generally very poor and it did not facilitate understanding or movement on either cohesion or adaptability dimensions. After observing their family interaction, it was apparent that their continuity of tracking was generally good but sometimes was inconsistent in that members would make distracting nonverbal asides. There was little respect or regard for each other. The clarity of their communication was problematic because they often made incongruent and at times double binding messages. Their freedom of expression was low. At times they were willing to express negative feelings but not positive ones about each other. In general, their listening skills were very poor in that they had low levels of empathy and attentive listening. Their speaking skills were sometimes good in that they were willing to assert themselves but they also made frequent interruptions when others were talking. In conclusion, their communication skills were generally poor as a family system.

Comparison of Insider and Outsider Perspectives

One of the challenges in the assessment field is to deal with the discrepancy which occurs between the "insider perspective" obtained through self-report methods and the "outsider perspective" obtained by therapist ratings. Within the Circumplex Model, this involves the comparison between the self-report from family members using FACES III and the therapists assessment using the Clinical Rating Scale.

One of the most systematic comparisons of FACES II and the Clinical Rating Scale was done by Friedman, Utada, and Morrissey (1987) in which they compared drug abusing adolescents and their parents. Family members each completed FACES II and the therapists completed the Clinical Rating Scale. As in past studies (Olson, 1983), the Friedman et al. study found a higher correlation between parents (r = .50 for cohesion and .53 for adaptability) then the correlation between either parent and the adolescent. More specifically the mothers' and adolescents' description of their family correlated .39 for cohesion and .34 for adaptability. The correlations between fathers and their adolescents was .26 for cohesion and .33 for adaptability. In general, the adolescents saw their families as more rigid on adaptability and more disengaged on cohesion than their parents.

In general, there was little agreement between family members' ratings and therapists' ratings of the family. Most of the correlations were non-significant and near zero. The exception was that fathers' ratings on adaptability correlated .40 with the therapists' ratings and the adolescents' ratings on cohesion correlated .31 with the therapists' ratings.

The most dramatic finding was that most of the family members rated themselves in the lower left hand quadrant of the model (low cohesion, low adaptability) but only 19% of the therapists rated the family in this quadrant. While family members tended to rate their families as disengaged, therapists tended to rate these same families as enmeshed. On the adaptability dimension, families tended to rate themselves as rigid whereas therapists tended to see them as structured or chaotic.

This significant difference between family member and therapist ratings could occur for a variety of reasons. Part of the problem could be the lack of similarity in the two instruments and the differing methodological procedures by which data were collected. Differences can also occur because family members and therapists disagree on how they understand closeness. Family members might feel conflict means that they are disengaged while therapists might see conflict as a sign of being too close, i.e., enmeshed (Hoffman, 1981).

Another possibility is that both of these are important realities of the family that are, in fact, different. Studies in other fields, such as social psychology, have also consistently demonstrated the lack of congruence between self-report and observational data. While the self-report methodology emphasizes the phenomenological approach, the observational approach emphasizes the behavioral tradition. More details on the philosophical and empirical discrepancy between these two approaches are described elsewhere (Olson, 1977).

Because of the discrepancy in self-report and observational assessment, it is highly recommended that assessment be done using both self-report and observational procedures. In this way, a more comprehensive and, hopefully, more realistic description of the family system can be obtained.

GOALS OF FAMILY THERAPY

While family therapists have as a central goal reduction of the presenting problems and symptoms of family members, this is achieved by intervention focused on changing the type of couple and/or family system. The basic assumption is that the current family system dynamics are helping to maintain these symptomatic behaviors. In other words, the current pattern of interaction in the family needs to be changed before the symptoms or presenting problems will be alleviated.

Table 5 summarizes the specific goals of family therapy based on the Circumplex Model. The first goal is to ultimately reduce any problems and symptoms. Because most of these dysfunctional families coming for therapy represent mid-range or extreme types on the Model, it often means trying to shift the system one level on cohesion and one level on adaptability towards the balanced types. It is, therefore, typically assumed that the family will function more

Table 5: Goals of Marital & Family Therapy

Based on Circumplex Model

Goal Regarding Symptoms

- Reduce presenting problems and symptoms

Goals Regarding System (Marital and/or Family)

- Change system one level on cohesion and adaptability toward Balanced Types
- On cohesion, balancing separateness and togetherness
- On adaptability, balancing stability and change
- Improve communication skills

Meta-Goal Regarding System (Preventive)

- Increase ability to negotiate system change over-time

adequately if the marital and/or family system is moved toward the balanced types.

Because the Model is dynamic, intervention on cohesion or adaptability often has a ripple effect in that it influences the system on the other dimension. In terms of cohesion, problems in couples and families often occur because of their inability to balance separateness (autonomy) and togetherness (intimacy). In couples coming for therapy, often there is a difference in the amount of separateness and togetherness a couple experiences or desires. For example, in disengaged couples, both individuals have emphasized looking out for themselves and thus, they have not maintained their emotional bond of intimacy.

In families, the dynamics on cohesion are often more complicated. One type of problem family might have an enmeshed mother-adolescent coalition with a disengaged father. In this case, the marital dyad would not be emotionally close. Increasing their marital intimacy is one strategy for breaking up the strong parent-child coalition.

In terms of adaptability, couples and families with problems often have difficulty balancing stability and change. Often these relationships are either too rigid or too chaotic. With rigid systems, often their behavioral repertoire is very narrow. When they are confronted with increasing stress, they tend to become more rigid and inflexible. These families can often benefit from learning and using more democratic decision-making and better problem-solving skills. On the other hand, chaotic relationships often need increasing structure and they can also benefit from improved problem-solving skills.

Increasing the positive communication skills of couples and families can also facilitate system change. Individuals in problem families often need to learn how to be more assertive in expressing their wants and desires. They also can usually benefit from learning how to express their feelings in a constructive manner and how to listen and give empathic feedback to each other.

However, improving the communication skills in a family is a necessary but not sufficient condition for change on the dimensions of cohesion and adaptability. Communication skills can help increase awareness of current needs and preferences. However, system change on cohesion and adaptability is more difficult and complex. Having good communication skills enables families to express more clearly the type of relationship they would like to have on cohesion and adaptability.

One goal of couple and family therapy is ultimately to teach the couple not only to deal with their current issues, but to provide them with the necessary skills to negotiate system change over time. It is an assumption of the model that couples and families need to change their system as their individual needs and preferences change.

Being able to articulate and negotiate these changes on cohesion and adaptability will also enable the couple or family to more adequately cope with stress and the other problematic issues that they encounter over time. This is an important preventive goal that moves beyond dealing with presenting the current and presenting symptoms. Unfortunately, this meta-goal is rarely achieved in therapy because families and therapists are typically too focused with reducing the current presenting problems.

Diagnostic and Outcome Assessment

A diagnostic assessment of a couple or family is an essential first step in the treatment process. Assessment achieves several important functions. First, it helps provide a more comprehensive picture of the couple and/or family system. It has also been found that this assessment can be an effective way of engaging families in the therapeutic process. Many families feel that they learn a great deal about their family dynamics from the assessment process and they also are often surprised by the differences between family members in how they see their family.

Therapy and assessment are often two sides of the same coin. Assessment is often therapeutic for family members and therapeutic intervention is also diagnostically useful. The interplay between diagnosis and intervention is a constant one for therapists. They continually assess the family in order to select which intervention to use, which is later evaluated in terms of its effectiveness. If interventions are not successful in producing change, then new interventions are sought which are based on this assessment process.

Assessment is an ongoing procedure that is done throughout the therapeutic process. It is assumed that effective interventions will produce system change. This assessment-intervention cycle is a process that is repeated continually throughout the course of therapy.

Outcome assessment of marital and family system change is also important, but it is seldom done in a systematic manner. Ideally, post-assessment should be completed at the end of the therapy process. This would enable a therapist to compare pre- and post-evaluations in order to identify the amount of change that has occurred on the various dimensions at the couple and family level. It also provides the therapist with the possibility of determining what specific treatment technique does and does not work with what type of family system. This linkage between treatment strategies and type of family system is an important step in the professional growth of therapists.

Treatment Planning and Intervention Strategies

An important intervention question is what type of therapeutic interventions work most effectively with what type of family systems. There is currently some clinical support for the idea that certain types of intervention approaches seem to work better with certain types of families. A more detailed description of linkages between therapeutic intervention and system change are described in another paper (Walsh & Olson) in this volume.

Effective therapeutic intervention involves integrating three important systems (Adolphi, 1986). The three systems are the current marital and family system, the therapeutic goals for that system and the therapist's personal skill level. Because of the interaction of these three systems, it is difficult to specify a one to one correspondence between technique and system change.

However, there are some types of intervention strategies that do, in fact, seem to work better with certain types of systems. In working with a disengaged system, a more directive approach seems to be more effective than a nondirective approach. Circular questioning techniques seem to work well with enmeshed systems. Working with chaotic systems, therapists have often found that being more structured with these families helps them make beginning steps towards change. Paradoxical techniques often work well to reduce rules and loosen up rigid systems.

In closing, there are currently projects under way which attempt to more systematically assess what are the most effective and ineffective treatment interventions for various types of couple and family systems. It is hoped that clarifying effective and ineffective treatment strategies for various types of families will increase the effectiveness and efficiency of family therapy. Increasing the specificity between therapeutic techniques and family type increases the importance of an accurate and useful diagnostic assessment both at the beginning and throughout the process of therapy. Bridging theory, assessment and intervention will also help move the field of family therapy from a therapeutic art toward a therapeutic science.

REFERENCES

Adolphi, M. (1986). *Behind the family mask*. New York: Brunner/Mazel.

Barnes, H., & Olson, D. H. (1982). Parent adolescent communication scale. In D. Olson, H. I. McCubbin, H. Barnes, A. Larsen, M. Muxen, & M. Wilson (Eds.), *Family inventories*. St. Paul, MN: Family Social Science, University of Minnesota.

Barnes, H., & Olson, D. H. (1983). Parent adolescent communication and the Circumplex Model. *Child Development, 56*, 438-447.

Beavers, W. R., & Voeller, M. N. (1983). Family models: Comparing and contrasting the Olson Circumplex Model and the Beavers Systems Model. *Family Process, 22*, 250-260.

Benjamin, Lorna S. (1977). Structural analysis of a family in therapy. *J. Counsel. Clin. Psychol., 45*, 391-406.

Bonk, J. (1984). Perceptions of psychodynamics during a transitional period as reported by families affected by alcoholism. Unpublished doctoral dissertation, University of Arizona.

Boss, P. G., & Greenberg, J. (1984). Family boundary ambiguity: A new variable in family stress theory. *Family Process, 23*, 535-546.

Carnes, P. (1987). *Counseling sexual abusers*. Minneapolis: CompCare Publications.

Caron, W., & Olson, D. H. (1984). *Family satisfaction and perceived-ideal discrepancy on FACES II*. St. Paul, MN: Family Social Science, University of Minnesota.

Clarke, J. (1984). The family types of schizophrenics, neurotics and normals. Unpublished doctoral dissertation. St. Paul, MN: Family Social Science, University of Minnesota.

Constantine, L. (1986). *Family paradigms*. New York: Guilford Press.

Epstein, N. B., Bishop, D. S., & Lewis, S. (1978). The McMaster Model of family functioning. *Journal of Marriage and Family Counseling, 4*, 19-31.

French, A. P., & Guidera, B. J. (1974). The family as a system in four dimensions: A theoretical model. Paper presented at the American Academy of Child Psychology, San Francisco, CA.

Friedman, Alfred S., Utada, Arlene, & Morrissey, Margaret R. (1987). Families of adolescent drug abusers are rigid: Are these families either disengaged or enmeshed or both? *Family Process, 26*, 131-148.

Garbarino, J., Sebes, J., & Schellenbach, C. (1985). Families at risk for destructive parent-child relations in adolescents. *Child Development, 55*, 174-183.

Gaughan, L. D. (1982). Structural theory of family mediation. In L. Messinger (Ed.), *Therapy with remarriage families*. Rockville, MD: Aspen System Corporation.

Gottman, J. M. (1979). *Marital interaction*. New York: Basic Books.

Green, R. G., Kolevzon, M. S., & Vosler, N. R. (1985). The Beavers-Timberlawn Model of family competence and the Circumplex Model of family adaptability and cohesion: Separate but equal? *Family Process, 24*, 385-398.

Hill, R. (1970). *Family development in three generations*. Cambridge, MA: Schenkman.

Hoffman, L. (1981). *Foundation of family therapy*. New York: Basic Books.

Kantor, D., & Lehr, W. (1975). *Inside the family*. San Francisco: Jossey-Bass.

L'Abate, L. (1987). The emperor has no clothes! Long live the emperor! A critique of family systems thinking and a reductionist proposal. *American Journal of Family Therapy, 15*, 19-33.

Leary, T. (1957). *Interpersonal diagnosis of personality*. New York: Ronald Press.

Leff, J., & Vaughn, C. (1985). *Expressed emotion in families*. New York: Guilford Press.

Olson, D. H. (1977). Insiders' and outsiders' view of relationships: Research strategies. In G. Levinger and H. Rausch (Eds.), *Close relationships*. Amherst, MA: University of Massachusetts Press.

Olson, D. H. (1987). *Family closeness scale*. St. Paul, MN: Family Social Science, University of Minnesota.

Olson, D. H., Fournier, D. G., & Druckman, J. M. (1986). *PREPARE, PREPARE-MC & ENRICH Inventories*. Minneapolis, MN: PREPARE/ENRICH.

Olson, D. H., & Killorin, E. (1984). *Clinical rating scale for Circumplex Model*. St. Paul, MN: Family Social Science, University of Minnesota.

Olson, D. H., & Logacz, E. (1985). *Reliability of the clinical rating scale (CRS) for the Circumplex Model*. St. Paul, MN Family Social Science, University of Minnesota.

Olson, D. H., McCubbin, H. I., Barnes, H., Larsen, A., Muxen, M., & Wilson, M. (1982). *Family inventories*. St. Paul, MN: Family Social Science, University of Minnesota.

Olson, D. H., McCubbin, H. I., Barnes, H., Larsen, A., Muxen, M., & Wilson, M. (1983). *Families: What makes them work*. Los Angeles: SAGE Publishing.

Olson, D. H., Portner, J., & Lavee, Y. (1985). *FACES III*. St. Paul, MN: Family Social Science, University of Minnesota.

Olson, D. H., Russell, C. S., & Sprenkle, D. H. (1983). Circumplex Model VI: Theoretical update. *Family Process, 22*, 69-83.

Olson, D. H., & Wilson, M. (1982). Family satisfaction. In D. Olson et al. (Eds.), *Family inventories*. Family Social Science, University of Minnesota.

Olson, D. H. (1986). Circumplex Model VII: Validation studies and FACES III. *Family Process, 25*, 337-351.

Parsons, T., & Bales, R. F. (1955). *Family socialization and interaction process*. Glencoe, IL: Free Press.

Reiss, D. (1981). *The family's construction of reality*. Cambridge: Harvard University Press.

Rodick, J. D., Henggler, S. W., & Hanson, C. L. (1986). An evaluation of Family Adaptability and Cohesion Evaluation Scales (FACES) and the Circumplex Model. *Journal of Abnormal Child Psychology, 14*, 77-87.

Appendix A: Clinical Rating Scale - Family Cohesion

	COUPLE/ FAMILY SCORE	DISENGAGED (Very Low) 1 2	SEPARATED (Low to Moderate) 3 4	CONNECTED (Moderate to High) 5 6	ENMESHED (Very High) 7 8
EMOTIONAL BONDING		Extreme emotional separateness. Lack of family loyalty.	Emotional separateness. Occasional family loyalty.	Emotional closeness. Loyalty to family expected.	Extreme emotional closeness. Loyalty to family is demanded.
FAMILY INVOLVEMENT		Very low involvement or interaction between members. Infrequent affective responsiveness between members.	Involvement acceptable but personal distance preferred. Some affective responsiveness is demonstrated.	Involvement emphasized but personal distance allowed. Affective interactions encouraged and preferred.	Very high symbiotic involvement, members very dependent on each other. Affective dependency is demonstrated.
MARITAL RELATIONSHIP		Extreme emotional separateness.	Emotional separateness.	Emotional closeness.	Extreme emotional reactivity.
PARENT-CHILD COALITIONS		Lack of parent-child closeness.	Clear sub-system boundaries some p/c closeness.	Clear sub-system boundaries with parent-child closeness.	Parent-child coalition. Lack of generational boundaries.
INTERNAL BOUNDARIES		Personal separateness predominant.	Some personal separateness encouraged.	Need for separateness respected but less valued.	Lack of personal separateness.
TIME (physical & emotional)		Time apart from family maximized. Rarely time together.	Time alone important. Some time together.	Time together important. Time alone permitted.	Time together maximized. Little time alone permitted.
SPACE (physical & emotional)		Separate space needed and preferred.	Separate space preferred; sharing of family space.	Sharing family space. Private space respected.	Little private space permitted.
DECISION MAKING		Independent decision making.	Individual decision making but joint possible.	Joint decisions preferred but not necessary.	Decisions subject to wishes of entire group.
EXTERNAL BOUNDARIES		Mainly focused outside the family.	More focused outside than inside family.	More focused inside than outside family.	Mainly focused inside the family.
FRIENDS		Individual friends seen alone.	Individual friendships seldom shared with family.	Individual friendships shared with family.	Family friends preferred with limited individual friends.
INTERESTS		Disparate interests.	Separate interests.	Joint interests preferred.	Joint interests mandated.
RECREATION		Mainly separate recreation.	More separate than shared. recreation.	More shared than individual recreation.	
GLOBAL COHESION RATING (1-8)					

Appendix A: Clinical Rating Scale - Family Adaptability

	COUPLE OR FAMILY SCORE	RIGID (Very Low) 1 2	STRUCTURED (Low to Moderate) 3 4	FLEXIBLE (Moderate to High) 5 6	CHAOTIC (Very High) 7 8
LEADERSHIP (Control)		Authoritarian leadership. Parent(s) highly controlling.	Primarily authoritarian but some equalitarian leadership.	Equalitarian leadership with fluid changes.	Limited and/or erratic leadership. Parental control unsuccessful, rebuffed.
DISCIPLINE (For Families Only)		Autocratic, "law & order". Strict, rigid consequences. Not lenient.	Somewhat democratic. Predictable consequences. Seldom lenient.	Usually democratic. Negotiated consequences. Somwhat lenient.	Laissez-faire and ineffective. Inconsistent consequences. Very lenient.
NEGOTIATION		Limited negotiations. Decisions imposed by parents	Structured negotiations. Decisions mainly made by parents.	Flexible negotiations. Agreed upon decisions.	Endless negotiations. Impulsive decisions.
ROLES		Limited repertoire; strictly defined roles.	Roles stable, but may be shared.	Role sharing and making. Fluid changes of roles.	Lack of role clarity, role shifts and role reversals.
RULES		Unchanging rules. Rules strictly enforced	Few rule changes. Rules firmly enforced	Some rule changes. Rules flexibly enforced.	Frequent rule changes. Rules inconsistently enforced.
GLOBAL ADAPTABILITY RATING (1-8)					

Appendix A: Clinical Rating Scale - Family Communication

LOW ---------FACILITATING --------- HIGH

	COUPLE OR FAMILY SCORE	1 — 2	3 — 4	5 — 6
CONTINUITY TRACKING		Little continuity of content; Irrelevant/distracting non-verbals and asides frequently occur; Frequent/inappropriate topic changes;	Some continuity but not consistent across time or across all members; Some irrelevant/distracting non-verbals and asides; Topic changes not consistently appropriate;	Members consistently tracking; Few irrelevant/distracting non-verbals and asides; facilitative non-verbals; Appropriate topic changes;
RESPECT & REGARD		Lack of respect for feelings or message of other(s); possibly overtly disrespectful or belittling attitude;	Somewhat respectful of others but not consistent across time or across all members;	Consistently appears respectful of others' feelings and message;
CLARITY		Inconsistent and/or unclear verbal messages; Frequent incongruencies between verbal and non-verbal messages;	Some degree of clarity, but not consistent across time or across all members; Some incongruent messages;	Verbal messages very clear. Generally congruent messages;
FREEDOM OF EXPRESSION		Infrequent discussion of self, feelings and relationships;	Some discussion of self, feelings and relationships;	Open discussion of self, feelings and relationships;
COMMUNICATION SKILL				
Listeners' Skills				
Empathy		Seldom evident	Sometimes evident	Often evident
Attentive Listening		Seldom evident	Sometimes evident	Often evident
Speakers' Skills				
Speaking for Self		Seldom evident	Sometimes evident	Often evident
Speaking for Others		Often evident	Sometimes evident	Seldom evident
Intrusions/Interruptions Premature Closure		Often evident	Sometimes evident	Seldom evident
GLOBAL FAMILY COMMUNICATION RATING (1-6)				

Utility of the Circumplex Model with Severely Dysfunctional Family Systems

Froma Walsh
David H. Olson

SUMMARY. This paper demonstrates the clinical utility of the Circumplex Model for assisting therapists to effectively assess the type of family system and plan treatment intervention with severely dysfunctional families. The Model helps the therapist move beyond focusing on the presenting problems or symptoms and facilitates movement into intervention. The inter-related concepts of balance and curvilinearity are described. Clinical intervention aimed at moving families extreme on the Circumplex dimension towards more balanced levels is concretely demonstrated.

The Circumplex Model of Marital and Family Systems is finding increasing application in clinical assessment and treatment. The model is particularly useful in treatment planning with severely dysfunctional and multi-problem families who present the most difficult challenges in therapy. This paper will discuss the relevance of the model for work with these families and suggest intervention guidelines and strategies that can be most effective.

ASSESSMENT: FAMILY SYSTEM TYPE AND PRESENTING PROBLEMS

Traditionally, family treatment with severe disorders was based on an assumption that families could be typed by the presenting

Froma Walsh, PhD, is Associate Professor, School of Social Science Administration and Department of Psychiatry, University of Chicago, IL 60637.
David H. Olson, PhD, is Professor, Family Social Science, University of Minnesota, St. Paul, MN 55108.

problem or diagnosis of the family member identified as the patient. From our research and clinical experience, we become concerned by several troubling issues raised by that approach to families. In the most prevalent practice, any family with a member diagnosed with schizophrenia, for example, was categorized and labeled as "schizophrenogenic family" and presumed to have a particular set of characteristics that contributed to the etiology of the schizophrenic disorder or to its ongoing maintenance. Generally these attributes were unspecified and remained undocumented by empirical research.

The diagnosis of an individual patient has not been found to be a reliable indicator of family diagnosis. There is no simple one-to-one correlation between individual symptoms and the family system (Russell et al., 1983). While certain family interaction patterns have been found to be commonly associated with a particular individual diagnosis, not all families with the same individual problems have the same transactional style. For example, Killorin and Olson (1984) found that, although there was a typical (modal) pattern of chaotic disengagement among families with an alcoholic member, some families operated at the other extremes, highly enmeshed and rigid. Moreover, no single family trait or style has been found to differentiate families containing a member with one diagnosis, such as schizophrenia from families of patients with other disorders. Families across diagnostic categories share many common features that are not linked specifically to one disorder (Walsh & Anderson, 1987; Rolland & Walsh, 1987).

Furthermore, in cases of severe and chronic individual disorder, not all families are severely dysfunctional. Families with a specific individual diagnostic category, such as schizophrenia, exhibit a range of functioning, from families with varying degrees of dysfunction to some families coping remarkably well (Hatfield & Lefley, 1987). When type and degree of patient and family disorder are equated, families may be erroneously categorized and pathologized by a diagnostic label carrying assumptions of a particular dysfunctional pattern and attribution of lineal causality.

When families are labeled by the diagnosis of the individual patient, they feel blamed by the implicit message that they are the "real" problem underlying the patient's symptoms. Family strengths and coping efforts may not be recognized.

In cases where dysfunction is present, clinicians need to maintain a biopsychosocial perspective, recognizing the circularity of influences including the impact of chronic stress on family functioning. Given the reciprocal impact of patient, family and larger systems, dysfunctional family patterns may be, at least in part, a product of unsuccessful attempts to cope with stresses associated with very disturbed and destructive patient behavior and with the experience of repeated hospitalizations and treatment failures (Anderson et al., 1986; Walsh & Anderson, 1987). Thus, the term "severely dysfunctional" families is used here to refer descriptively to a set of interactional processes that are not working for a family, with the assumption of multiple circular causality.

A serious problem is that treatment approaches based on the assumption that all families with the same patient diagnosis have the same transactional patterns and degree of dysfunction may err in setting therapeutic objectives and strategies that are inappropriate to particular families. Another clinical dilemma arises in the case of multiproblem families, in which more than one member may be "diagnosable," frequently with different disorders, and the family may be struggling with many serious problems, such as substance abuse, violent or suicidal behavior, and chaotic organization.

Families with multiple, pervasive problems present challenges in clinical assessment and treatment because it is difficult to identify transactional patterns, to determine treatment priorities, and to focus interventions toward specific, reachable objectives. Too often, therapist and family set vague, unrealistic goals that only reinforce the family's sense of overwhelm and deficiency, that contribute to therapist burnout, and that result in repeated experience of treatment failure.

Some family therapists have responded to these dilemmas by disregarding individual diagnosis and biochemical processes altogether (Haley, 1980), by limiting interventions narrowly to immediate symptom reduction, and by devising one set of objectives and techniques for all families, such as the invariant prescription of Selvini Palazzoli (1986). We would contend, instead, that a true systems orientation requires attention to both individual symptom and family system. We would argue against any invariant family approach that is driven either by patient diagnosis or by intervention technique.

In order to respect and respond to the diverse characteristics as well as the commonalities among families, we see the importance of assessing each family's strengths and deficits in order to set appropriate intervention objectives and effective strategies for family system change. In our view, therapeutic goals are twofold: to achieve problem reduction and a more functional family system. Family interventions are aimed to strengthen the functioning of the family system as it is (reciprocally) linked to improve functioning of symptomatic individual members. Efforts to strengthen the family are essential in cases of severe and chronic dysfunction in an individual and/or the family, where problems are not simply resolved and are likely to recur, especially in biologically-based disorders or multiproblem families with constant stress, limited resources, and ineffective coping patterns.

CIRCUMPLEX MODEL: A BRIEF OVERVIEW

The Circumplex Model was developed in order to integrate family system theory, family research and family therapy. This was facilitated in part because the three dimensions of *family cohesion, family adaptability* and *family communication* were deduced from the fields of family theory, family research and family therapy.

The two dimensions build directly into the Model are family cohesion and adaptability. These dimensions are related in a curvilinear way to family functioning in that too much or too little is seen as problematic if families are stuck at these extremes. The third dimension is family communication which facilitates movement on the other two dimensions. This dimension has a linear relationship to family functioning which means that higher levels of good communication facilitate better family functioning.

Family cohesion is defined as the emotional bonding that family members have toward one another. Within the Circumplex Model, some of the specific components of this dimension are: emotional bonding, boundaries, coalitions, time, space, friends, decision-making, and interests and recreation. The four levels of cohesion range from *disengaged* (very low) to *separated* (low to moderate) to *connected* (moderate to high) to *enmeshed* (very high) (see Figure 1).

It is hypothesized that the central levels of cohesion (separated and connected) make for optimal family functioning. Individuals are able to experience and balance being both independent from and connected to their families. The extremes (disengaged or enmeshed) are generally seen as problematic.

Family adaptability (change) is defined as the ability of a family system to change its power structure, role relationships, and relationship rules in response to situational and developmental stress. The four levels of adaptability range from *rigid* (very low) to *structured* (low to moderate) to *flexible* (moderate to high) to *chaotic* (very high). It is hypothesized that central levels of adaptability (structured and flexible) are more conducive to family functioning, with the extremes (rigid and chaotic) being the most problematic for families as they move through the family life cycle.

Well-functioning families maintain a balance between structure and flexibility. Families require enough stability and continuity in their organization to maintain integration as a family unit. At the same time there has to be enough flexibility in the system for adaptation in response to changing external conditions or to internal developmental demands as the family progresses through the life cycle.

Figure 1 illustrates the four levels of cohesion and four levels of adaptability. At the most basic level, this is a descriptive model with sixteen types of marital and family systems. These sixteen types are grouped into three more general types: four balanced types, eight mid-range types and four extreme types. The four balanced types are those where there are balanced levels on both cohesion and adaptability, while the extreme types represent extremes of both dimensions. Mid-range types are those that are extreme on one dimension and balanced on the other dimension.

Balance and the Curvilinear Dynamics of the Circumplex Model

There are two central and interrelated aspects of the Circumplex Model and these relate to the concepts of balance and curvilinearity.

Figure 1: CIRCUMPLEX MODEL - Couple & Family Map

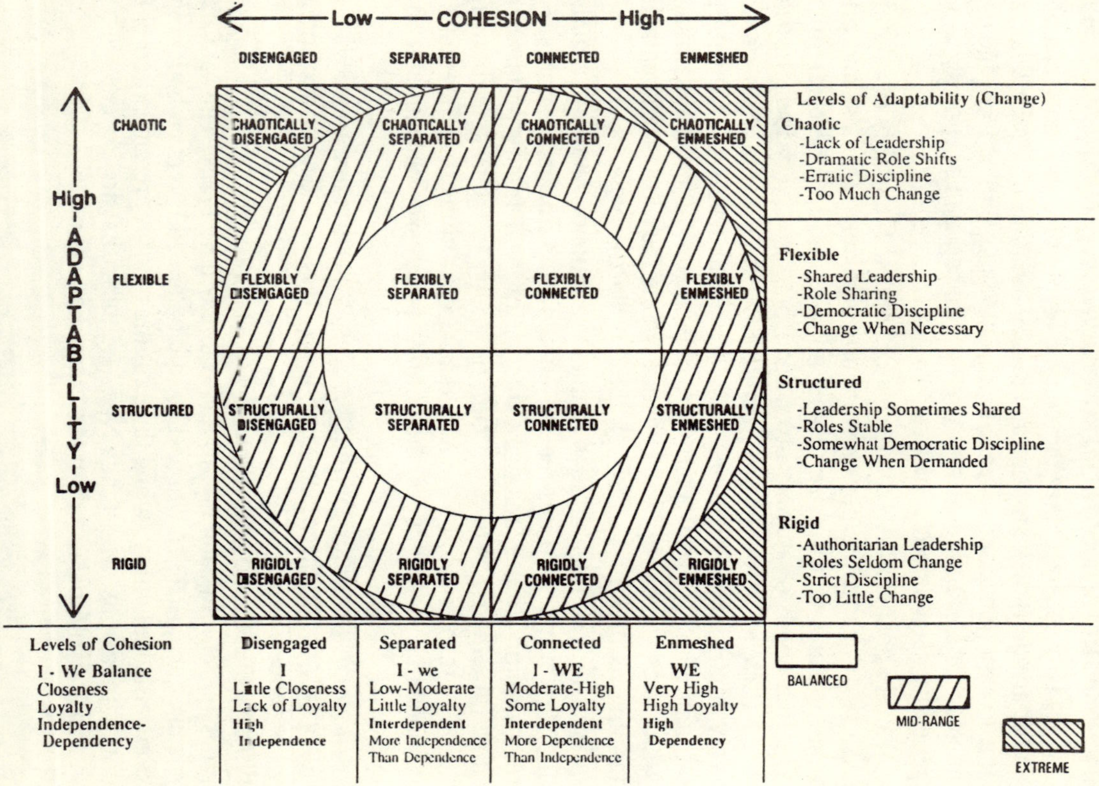

On the cohesion dimension, it involves balancing the amount of separateness versus togetherness, where too much separateness can lead to a disengaged system and too much togetherness can lead to an enmeshed system. On the adaptability dimension, balance involves maintaining the amount of stability versus change, where too much stability can lead to a rigid system and too much change can lead to a chaotic system.

The model postulates that a balance on these dimensions is related to more adequate functioning. Even though a balanced family system is placed at the two levels of the Model, it should not be assumed that these families always operate in a moderate way. Being balanced means a family can experience the extremes on the dimensions in some situations, but they do not typically function at these extremes for long periods of time.

A balanced system on cohesion assumes that individuals can both be autonomous and intimate with their other family members. It means that the family members can both be independent from and connected to their family. On adaptability, it means that the family provides a basic level of stability but are able to change when necessary.

In other words, in balanced families both extremes can be tolerated and expected provided the system does not operate at that extreme for an excessive period of time. Also, it means that balanced families are not stuck at these extremes like is typical of severely dysfunctional families.

The curvilinear aspects of cohesion and adaptability are illustrated in Figure 2 where the extreme levels of cohesion (disengaged and enmeshed) and adaptability (rigid and chaotic) are at the lowest level of the arch and are the most dysfunctional. These extreme types are dynamically related to each other and there is a tendency for extreme families to swing between these two extremes. This short-circuiting process is illustrated by the dotted line between the extreme types. When these dimensions are laid out in a flat surface, extreme types are at opposite sides of the Model (see Figure 1).

Dynamically, there is a greater similarity between the four balanced types with each other and four extreme types with each other than between any of the balanced or extreme types. This is graphically illustrated in Figure 3 where the four extreme types are

FIGURE 2: CURVILINEAR DYNAMICS OF THE CIRCUMPLEX MODEL

<u>FAMILY COHESION</u>

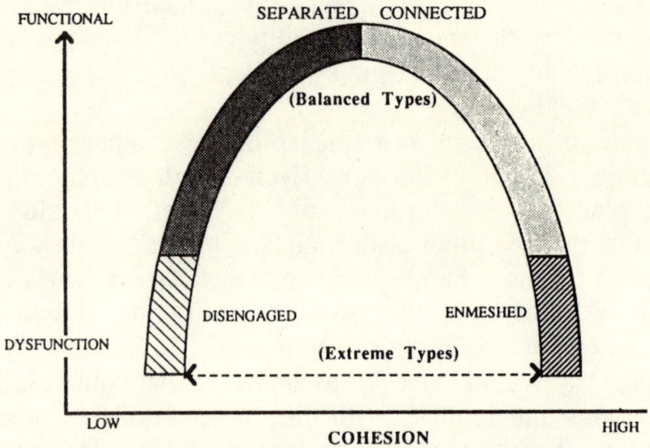

FAMILY ADAPTABILITY

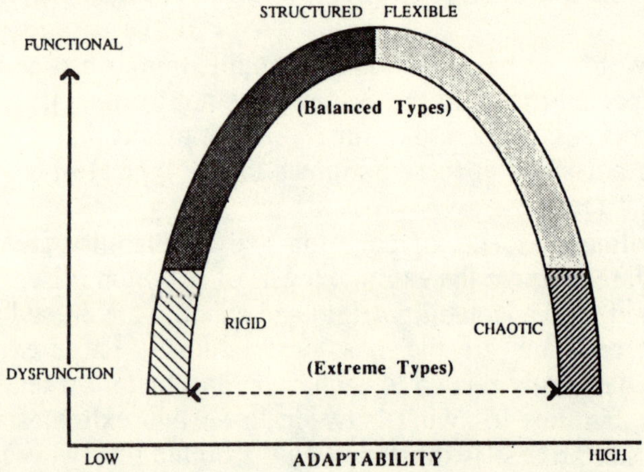

FIGURE 3: DYNAMIC INTER-RELATION OF EXTREME TYPES AND OF BALANCED TYPES ON THE CIRCUMPLEX MODEL

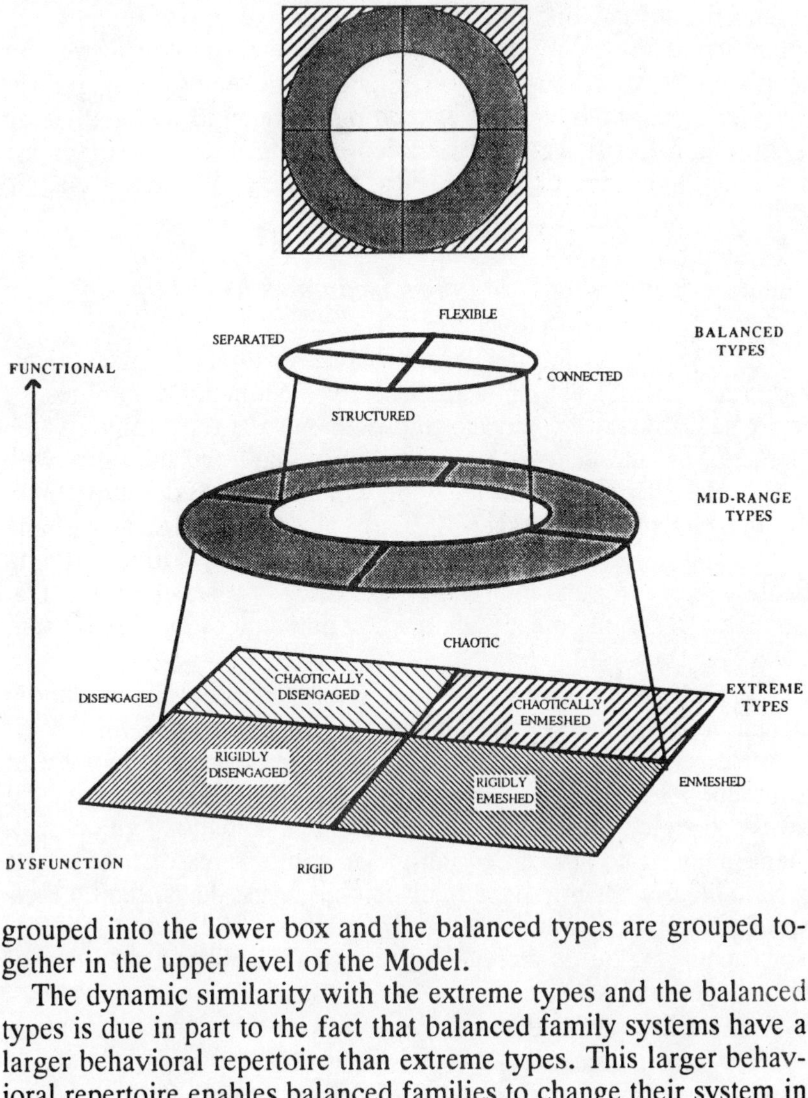

grouped into the lower box and the balanced types are grouped together in the upper level of the Model.

The dynamic similarity with the extreme types and the balanced types is due in part to the fact that balanced family systems have a larger behavioral repertoire than extreme types. This larger behavioral repertoire enables balanced families to change their system in smaller increments in order to cope with stress and presenting problems.

Conversely, extreme types often operate on an "all-or-none" principle whereby if their current family system does not work, their first reaction is to become more extreme on those dimensions. If this does not work, they often assume the opposite approach might work. For example, if a family system encounters a stressful family event like an adolescent child being picked up by the police, the family might first react by getting more rigid and setting up additional rules. If that does not seem to help, they might then assume that they should drop all rules, becoming more like a chaotic system.

Treatment Planning Using the Circumplex Model

The Circumplex Model is a valuable resource in assessment-based treatment planning with severely dysfunctional families. A major task for family therapy and outcome is to determine which elements of intervention are most appropriate and effective with which presenting problems and with which elements of family functioning (Gurman & Kniskern, 1978). The Circumplex Model and accompanying self-report scale (FACES III) and Clinical Rating Scale (CRS) offer an empirically-based family assessment tool that can be used for treatment planning and outcome evaluation (Olson, 1986).

The model provides a conceptual framework for assessing family system functioning on two fundamental dimensions of family organization: cohesion and adaptability. This descriptive typology of transactional patterns can be used to determine a family's current level and style of functioning on each dimension and to guide treatment planning to strengthen particular components of functioning toward clearly specified and realistic objectives. Thus, family therapy is not limited to reduction or interruption of extreme dysfunctional patterns, but is directed systematically toward promotion of more functional patterns.

For families assessed at either extreme on the dimensions, intervention strategies can be targeted to fit their particular pattern of organization and to guide change, in a stepwise progression, toward a more balanced system. In most cases of severe and chronic dysfunction, a reachable therapeutic goal would be the achievement of higher functioning at the next, adjacent pattern, such as a shift from disengaged to separated or from enmeshed to connected. It would be unrealistic to attempt to change family patterns to a quite different type of organization, such as pushing a disengaged family to be strongly connected, or an enmeshed family to become separated. Such goals might even be inappropriate to a family's values relative to their socio-economic context, or to demands in their life cycle stage. A common therapeutic error with severely dysfunctional families is to assume either that patterns are unchangeable or that change toward the opposite pattern is necessary and desirable.

In our experience, severely dysfunctional families often assume such extreme all-or-none positions regarding change. They are likely to alternate between feelings of hopelessness that any change can occur and unrealistic expectations for goals that are unlikely to be met. They commonly fluctuate between extremes of enmeshed/disengaged and extremes of rigidity/chaos. An enmeshed family may resist a clinician's efforts to promote physical separation, such as leaving home at launching, when they hold catastrophic expectations that any separation will result in a total cut-off.

Opposite extremes may also be found in different subsystems within a family. In many enmeshed families, some siblings may disengage completely from the family in order to avoid fusion, assuming positions of pseudo-autonomy that dissolve in contact with the family. Clinicians must be cautious not to collude with presuppositions of either all-or-none position. Fears of runaway change or loss of patterns considered to be essential to individual or family survival are common sources of "resistance" to change and therapy drop-out. Clinicians need to be alert to prevent extreme family oscillation that can occur much like a "short-circuiting" process, as diagrammed in Figure 2.

A therapist must be active in structuring and monitoring family interaction to block or interrupt the all-or-none tendency in these families to flip to the other extreme from their current organizational pattern. In work with families with extreme patterns, it is essential to set modest, concrete objectives to be reached through small increments of change in order to reduce anxiety to a manageable level, to prevent extreme fluctuations, and help the family to modulate and moderate changes than can be maintained over time.

In the following section of this paper, characteristics of families at each extreme on the Circumplex Model will be described, with interaction objectives and guidelines suggested to fit the challenges of each system pattern and to shift interaction to a more functional level. Based on clinical and research experience with a range of severely dysfunctional families (Walsh, in press; Walsh & Anderson, 1987), we will recommend and illustrate the sorts of intervention strategies that we would expect to be most effective with each pattern.

CLINICAL INTERVENTION ON FAMILY ADAPTABILITY

Moving Families from Rigid to Structured Systems

In families with extremely rigid interactional patterns, leadership tends to be authoritarian, with one or both parents highly controlling. Discipline is typically autocratic, based on a simplistic principle of "law and order," and consequences are strict, and even harsh, without leniency. Negotiations tend to be limited, with decisions imposed by parents, often arbitrarily, or by applying a single solution to all problems regardless of its applicability. Rigid families have a very limited repertoire of roles, which are strictly defined and inflexible. Rules are unbending and strictly enforced. These tendencies prevent the family from making adaptive changes when confronted by new circumstances and demands.

Applying the Circumplex Mode, we would propose that therapy with rigid families target interventions to shift their organization to the structured range on the family adaptability dimension. Leadership, while still primarily authoritarian, would become less controlling and more egalitarian. Discipline would become somewhat more democratic, with consequences predictable, although still seldom lenient. Roles would be stable, with somewhat greater flexibility and sharing. Rules would allow for few changes and be firmly, yet less strictly, enforced.

The chief therapeutic task with rigid families is to promote the interaction flexibility that is lacking (see Table 1). Tasks that facilitate more open communication, negotiated decision making, and

TABLE 1: FAMILY CHANGE: GOALS AND TECHNIQUES - RIGID TO STRUCTURED

COMPONENTS	CURRENT SYSTEM: RIGID →	GOAL: STRUCTURED	INTERVENTION TECHNIQUES
LEADERSHIP (Control)	Authoritarian leadership. Parent(s) highly controlling	Primarily authoritarian but some egalitarian leadership.	Model & promote more flexible, equalitarian leadership without (feared) loss of control.
DISCIPLINE (For Families Only)	Autocratic, "law & order". Strict, rigid consequences. Not lenient.	Somewhat democratic. Predictable consequences. Seldom lenient.	Increase democratic process. Negotiate more flexible, yet predictable consequences.
NEGOTIATION	Limited negotiations, solutions. Decisions imposed by parents.	Structured negotiations. Decisions mainly made by parents.	Increase flexibility, experiment-ation. Expand repertoire of solutions.
ROLES	Limited repertoire; strictly defined rules.	Roles stable, but may be shared.	Increase role flexibility.
RULES	Unchanging rules. Rules strictly enforced.	Few rule changes. Rules firmly enforced.	Increase flexibility of rules and enforcement.

experimental problem solving can be useful. At the same time, it is crucial to maintain stability in the family. A common clinical error with extremely rigid families is to push for too much change too fast, which typically only heightens the family's resistance to change.

An approach that simplistically attempts to loosen up or shake up a rigid family may have dramatic success in some cases but have destructive impact with others. Families with rigid patterns typically hold a catastrophic expectation that any change will destabilize the family, resulting in total loss of control and disintegration into chaos. Frequently, such fears are based on previous overwhelming crisis experiences in the marital family or families of origin. Concrete objectives, in small increments of change, are therefore most likely to be successful. Paradoxical techniques involving retraining, such as instructions to slow down or do more of the same, can be highly effective, as they respond to the family's need to maintain a sense of stability in the midst of change.

The metaphor of skiing is useful here. A good skier going down the mountainside maintains a stable, but not rigid, stance. When a skier stiffens up out of fear of losing control, the risk of falling and serious injury is increased. A good ski instructor first teaches novices how to stop and how to fall to minimize injury. Next the skier learns how to maintain a dynamic balance of steadiness and flexibility, that requires a constant adjustment of minor fluctuations between maintaining stability and adapting as the terrain changes. Achieving a more functional balance between family system stability and change is the therapeutic task that guides the use of specific intervention techniques.

Moving Families from Chaotic to Flexible Systems

Families at the chaotic extreme on the adaptability dimensions are characterized by a lack of structure, order, and predictability in their interactions. Leadership tends to be limited and erratic. Decisions are impulsive, with a lack of consistent follow-through in actions. Roles and rules are unclear and shifting. Loss of control is frequently experienced in escalating conflict and run-away change. Chaotic families tend to be crisis-prone, as unanticipated and unresolved problems pile up to overwhelming proportions and members rebound from one crisis into the next.

We propose that therapy with chaotic families be aimed to shift their organizational pattern toward the flexible range on the family adaptability dimension (see Table 2). Objectives would include stronger and more consistent parental leadership and control of the family process, with authority shared by parents and changes fluid but not erratic. Discipline, while somewhat lenient, would become more democratic and effective, with consequences more often negotiated and consistent. Negotiation would be flexible, yet with more careful consideration, agreement and closure. Greater clarity and consistency of roles and rules would be an important objective.

The chief therapeutic task with chaotic families is building structure. The extreme disorganization makes it imperative for therapists to assume an active and at times even authoritarian position of leadership in the initial phase of therapy, gradually strengthening the leadership capacities of parents and family. The therapist needs to take charge of the therapy rather than follow the family process, which is likely to become diffuse or spiral out of control. This involves establishing clear and consistent groundrules and limits for the structure of the therapy, setting concrete problem-solving objectives with the family, and defining therapist and family roles and mutual expectations.

One meta-rule is to set whatever rules are needed to be able to work productively toward objectives, both in session and between sessions. Because constant interruptions and distractions interfere with shared focal attention and effective problem solving in chaotic families, a therapist may need to set a rule that only one family member may speak at a time during sessions so that the work of therapy can be accomplished. A second meta-rule is to be prepared to follow through on rules and consequences, since limits will likely be breached and the structure of therapy can easily disintegrate. The therapist will need to take charge to interrupt distractions and redirect focus productively. Families with chaotic organization tend to respond well to such active structuring, finding it helpful to experience therapy as a context that provides and promotes stability and effective leadership in the family.

A therapeutic stance that is somewhat rigid, and even authoritar-

TABLE 2: FAMILY CHANGE: GOALS AND TECHNIQUES - CHAOTIC TO FLEXIBLE

COMPONENTS	CURRENT SYSTEM: CHAOTIC →	GOAL: FLEXIBLE	INTERVENTION TECHNIQUES
LEADERSHIP (Control)	Limited and/or erratic leadership. Parental control unsuccessful, rebuffed.	Egalitarian leadership with fluid changes.	Model & promote strong leadership and control.
DISCIPLINE (For Families Only)	Laissez-fairre and ineffective. Inconsistent consequences. Very lenient.	Usually democratic. Negotiated consequences. Somewhat lenient.	Set clear limits, appropriate consequences. Follow through consistently.
NEGOTIATION	Endless negotiations without closure; impulsive decisions.	Flexible negotiations. Agreed upon decisions.	Increase ability to reach compromise, closure.
ROLES	Lack of role clarity, role shifts and role reversals.	Role sharing and making. Fluid changes of roles.	Increase role clarity, stability, and continuity.
RULES	Frequent rule changes. Rules inconsistently enforced.	Some rule changes. Rules flexibly enforced.	Increase predictability of rules & enforcement.

ian may be necessary initially in therapy with chaotic families, especially in situations where loss of control can precipitate or exacerbate a crisis resulting in very destructive or even life threatening actions. Where structure, leadership, and controls are lacking, the clinician may need to lean to the other extreme to establish minimal order, predictability, and safe limits. A useful analogy might be that of a sailboat keeled over in a severe storm, when the captain orders the crew to lean to the other side of the boat, literally using their weight to prevent capsizing and restore stability.

CLINICAL INTERVENTION ON FAMILY COHESION

Moving Families from Disengaged to Separated Systems

A disengaged relationship is characterized by extreme emotional and physical separateness. The paradigmatic rule in disengaged families tends to be: everyone for him/herself. There is little interest, involvement, or sense of mutual caring between family members. Each member goes his or her own way, with limited attachment or commitment to the family. There is little expectation that others can be counted on to support a member in distress.

While extreme separateness may be confused with autonomy, in fact, genuine autonomy involves the maintenance of self in the context of relationships with others, as is found in the balanced levels of cohesion. Disengagement, instead, is a distancing or total cut-off from family relationships, resulting in an isolated pseudo-autonomous position.

We would propose that therapy with disengaged family systems aim toward the separated level of family cohesion (Table 3). A separated relationship (low to moderate cohesion) has a good deal of emotional and physical separateness, yet it is more balanced with some connectedness among family members. Family loyalty and affective responsiveness are occasionally demonstrated. While time and space apart may be preferred, there is some time together and some joint decisions. Activities, interests, and friendships tend to be separate, but a few are shared.

A chief therapeutic goal with disengaged families is to promote connectedness through shared problem solving. Intervention is of-

TABLE 3: FAMILY COHESION: GOALS AND TECHNIQUES - DISENGAGED TO SEPARATED

COMPONENTS	CURRENT SYSTEM: DISENGAGED →	OBJECTIVE: SEPARATED	TASKS & TECHNIQUES
EMOTIONAL BONDING	Extreme emotional separateness. Lack of family loyalty.	Emotional separateness. Occational family loyalty and connectedness.	Increase some connectedness, mutality. Restrain from over closeness. Model caring, commitment with limits.
FAMILY INVOLVEMENT	Very low involvement or interaction. Infrequent affective responsiveness between members. Pseudo-independent.	Involvement acceptable but personal distance preferred. Some affective responsiveness is demonstrated.	Increase structured involvement or shared problem solving.
MARITAL RELATIONSHIP	Extreme emotional separateness. Fear of intimacy (blocks closeness).	Emotional separateness with limited closeness.	Strengthen marital/parental coalition. Respect limits of intimacy.
PARENT-CHILD COALITIONS	Lack of appropriate parent-child closeness. Neglect, abuse common. Protective boundaries lacking.	Clear sub-system boundaries some p/c closeness.	Increase parental nurturance and protection from abuse.

COMPONENTS	CURRENT SYSTEM: DISENGAGED →	OBJECTIVE: SEPARATED	TASKS & TECHNIQUES
EMOTIONAL BONDING	Extreme emotional separateness. Lack of family loyalty.	Emotional separateness. Occational family loyalty and connectedness.	Increase some connectedness, mutality. Restrain from over closeness. Model caring, commitment with limits.
INTERNAL BOUNDARIES			Increase tolerance for shared time, space, decision-making.
TIME (physical & emotional)	Personal separateness predominent. Time apart from family maximized. Rarely time together.	Some personal separateness encouraged. Time alone important. Some time together.	
SPACE (physical & emotional)	Separate space needed and preferred.	Separate space preferred; sharing of family space.	Respect needs for separateness.
DECISION MAKING	Individual decision making, reactive, oppositional, or without regard for others.	Individual decision making some joint possible.	
EXTERNAL BOUNDARIES	Mainly focused outside the family.	More focused outside than inside family.	Strengthen family unit boundary. Increase sense of family identity and belonging.
FRIENDS	Individual friends seen alone.	Individual friends occasionally shared with family.	Increase sharing friends/family.
INTERESTS	Disparate interests.	Separate interests.	Increase some joint interests and activities. Tasks: plan shared "time-off" from problems.
RECREATION	Mainly separate recreation.	More separate than shared recreation.	Frame as reward for efforts, refueling. Celebrate success.

ten problematic from the start because it is difficult even to convene members at the same time and place. A major therapeutic challenge is to engage family members to work together on behalf of a symptomatic member. The therapist needs to frame treatment as a collaborative effort: valuing the input of each member, and offering potential benefit to all who participate.

It is unrealistic to expect all members to be present for all therapy sessions. It would be an error, however, to get locked into working with only one member or parent-child dyad with the vague hope that eventually the other spouse or children would become involved. That structure of therapy unproductively replicates the fragmentation of the system. While it may be necessary to meet occasionally with separate parts of the family system, the therapist must keep the total system in mind, and work actively as a connecting link, gradually (and loosely) knitting members together.

Often family members in disengaged systems fear becoming dependent on others because of previous experiences of physical abuse, neglect or abandonment. In other cases, they are fearful of intimacy: that too much closeness could lead to fusion or incest. They may resist change out of such catastrophic fears of loss of boundaries to enmeshment. Therapists need to recognize and respect such concerns, taking care not to push for more closeness than is tolerable, and upholding appropriate individual and generational boundaries. Concrete shared tasks, with clear focus, rewards, and limits are useful. Therapy should not be framed as aiming for more closeness and intimacy, which are anxiety provoking for disengaged families. Instead, families are more receptive to interventions aimed at strengthening their capacity as a mutual caring and support network for one another, specifically focused on resolution of presenting problems.

Moving Families from Enmeshed to Connected Systems

Enmeshed relationships are characterized by an extreme amount of emotional closeness and demands for loyalty and consensus. The paradigmatic rule operating in enmeshed family systems is, "All for one and one for all." Individual needs are sacrificed for the group. Members are highly dependent and emotionally reactive to one another. There is a general lack of personal separateness and little private space or time is permitted. Individual boundaries are blurred to the extreme of fusion, with members poorly differentiated, lacking a coherent sense of self as distinct from family role expectations. Generational boundaries are breached, with children treated as parents or mates (at times sexualized) as parents. Attention is focused inside the family, with a paucity of outside friendships or interests. Members are unable to tolerate separation from the family, with developmental transitions involving launching or loss especially problematic.

We would propose that therapy with enmeshed family systems aim at shifting the family organization toward the connected level of the cohesion dimension of family functioning (see Table 4). Emotional closeness, while high, is better balanced with tolerance and respect for separateness. Loyalty and involvement are expected, yet some personal choice and separate time, space, friendships, and interests are allowed. Social markers of independence, such as leaving home, may not be emphasized, as family members are likely to remain in close emotional and physical contact over the course of the life cycle.

The major goal of therapy with enmeshed family systems is to encourage a tolerance for some separateness and boundaries in relationships, while respecting needs for maintaining high connectedness. Unlike disengaged families, enmeshed families are likely to come together for therapy, even when individual sessions are scheduled. Because of difficulties with separation, they are more likely to have difficulty leaving therapy, both at the end of a session and at termination. They are likely to become overinvolved and helplessly dependent on the therapist, expecting unrealistic amounts of all-giving attention and responsibility for rescuing them. They often call in the middle of the night, invite the therapist home to dinner, and even express the wish that the therapist could move in with them. Clinicians need to guard against becoming overcommitted and overresponsible in ways that do not strengthen the family, but instead contribute to therapist burnout. Therapists need to communicate clear expectations for their own roles and boundaries, to model a balanced position of caring involvement with limits (Walsh, 1983).

TABLE 4: FAMILY COHESION: GOALS AND TECHNIQUES - DISENGAGED TO SEPARATED

COMPONENTS	CURRENT SYSTEM: ENMESHED ⟶	OBJECTIVE: CONNECTED	TASKS & TECHNIQUES
EMOTIONAL BONDING	Extreme emotional closeness, Poor differentiation. Loyalty to family is demanded. Fear separateness & disengagement.	Emotional closeness. Loyalty to family expected. Some separateness allowed.	Increase tolerance for some separateness with limits. Restrain from cut-off.
FAMILY INVOLVEMENT	Fusion, over dependency Responsibility for others; controlled by others. Extreme emotional reactivity.	Involvement emphasized but personal distance allowed. Affective interactions encouraged and preferred.	Increase differentiated interdependence and responsibility for self; Interrupt emotional reactivity, attempts to control others.
MARITAL RELATIONSHIP	Fused or united front (pseudomutual). Fear runaway conflict & violent or divorce.	Emotional closeness, with limited separateness.	Promote some separateness while maintaining connectedness.
PARENT-CHILD COALITIONS	Parent-child coalition. Lack of generational boundaries. Child assumes parental or mate role, threat of incest.	Clear sub-system boundaries with parent-child closeness.	Increase clarity, firmness of generational boundaries. Restructuring tasks.

COMPONENTS	CURRENT SYSTEM: ENMESHED →	OBJECTIVE: CONNECTED	TASKS & TECHNIQUES
INTERNAL BOUNDARIES	Lack of personal separatness.	Need for separateness respected but less valued.	Increase differentiation of self; personal boundaries.
TIME (physical & emotional)	Time together maximized. Little time alone permitted.	Time together important. Time alone permitted.	Increase tolerance for some separate time.
SPACE (physical & emotional)	Little private space permitted.	Sharing family space. Private space respected.	Increase tolerance for some separate space.
DECISION MAKING	Individual needs sacrificed for group; consensus sensitivity.	Joint decisions preferred but not necessary.	Stuctured tasks promoting joint decisions with respect for individual needs, differences.
EXTERNAL BOUNDARIES	Mainly focused inside the family. Closed boundary; mistrust of outsiders.	More focused inside than outside family.	Increase family boundary permeability: members can exit and re-enter.
FRIENDS	Family friends preferred with limited individual friends. Lack social support.	Some connections.	Increase structured contacts for companionship and increased support network.
INTERESTS	Joint interests mandated.	Joint interests preferred. Some separateness tolerated.	Increase separate interests.
RECREATION	Separate friends, interests viewed as disloyal or abandonment.	More shared than individual recreation.	Increase separate activities.

In the family, individual differentiation and responsibility for self can be promoted by communicating directly to each member, blocking other members' mind reading attempts or interruptions to speak for or control one another. To decrease family isolation from community resources, increased permeability of family boundaries with the outside world is a crucial therapeutic task, achieved by building linkages with friends and neighbors, schools and religious affiliations. Tolerance for separation should be encouraged through small, gradual steps, whereby members feel freer to exit and reenter the family.

It may be necessary to interrupt the "short-circuiting" that may occur whereby any separation attempt generates fears of total cutoff. It is useful to reemphasize the integrity and continuity of the family unit and the strengthening of relationships that occurs in healthy families as members can also develop more independence. Individual and generational boundaries can be strengthened through tasks between sessions that promote separate space, time and activities by individuals and by parents, apart from the children. Normative reframing, such as in terms of typical needs and preference of teenagers, helps to shift negative connotations of family disloyalty, rejection, or abandonment that are paradigmatic in enmeshed family systems.

CASE ILLUSTRATION: A CHAOTICALLY ENMESHED FAMILY

This household consisted of a separated mother and four teenagers. There were two "identified patients" presented for treatment: the middle sons, aged 15 and 16, who were reported to the police on several occasions for neighborhood vandalism, and most recently for firesetting. Notably, they had just set Mother's bed on fire.

The initial interview was disorganized. It was difficult to gather information or remain focused on any topic due to repeated disruptions by the two "bad boys," who talked over other family members, hurled insults, punched each other, and got up out of their seats, roaming the room and picking up objects from the therapist's desk. Mother sat by helplessly, almost not noticing the clamor. When asked, she said the behavior was pretty typical, that the boys were impossible to control. Mother had to work full-time, with no support from the father, and was exhausted by the demands of work and children. She was too embroiled in intense conflict with her extended family to gain support from them and had no time for friends or activities for herself.

Inquiry around the burning bed revealed that, since Father's departure, the parental bed was occupied by the eldest son, who had quit school to get a job to help support the family. Mother reported that she was sleeping on the living room sofa. There were only two other beds in the apartment for the other three children. The two problem sons and their 13-year-old sister slept together, wherever they happened to fall asleep. The daughter, sitting with her arm around her mother in the session, assumed a role of caretaker to her mother.

A genogram was used to obtain a more coherent picture of the family. The father, with a history of alcohol abuse accompanied by paranoid psychotic episodes and violence, had been forced by Mother to leave the home a year earlier and had "disappeared." It was also learned that Mother had a sister who, in fact, had become overwhelmed by responsibility, lost control, and killed her two small children. Clearly, boundaries and limits were lacking in this family system, leadership was ineffectual, and anything could happen, including the possibility of murder and incest.

Two major therapeutic goals were imperative: to shift the family system from chaotic toward a flexible level of organization; and from an enmeshed pattern toward a connected level. Interventions were directed toward two chief objectives. First was to increase structure, especially parental leadership, controls, and limits. Second was to promote separateness, in particular, establishing clear and firm individual and generational boundaries; increasing Mother's connectedness with other adult supports; decreasing the high level of emotional intensity and reactivity. Two examples of interventions will be given here.

The therapist immediately seized control of the run-away process in the therapy room, setting clear and consistent rules for how the therapy would be conducted. To enforce those rules, she physically separated the children in conflict by moving her chair between them, and used time-out techniques, such as having any child who repeatedly interrupted the therapy focus sit for a specified time in the corner of the room while attention returned to those who were working productively. While perhaps sounding simplistic, such techniques, when communicated with clarity and enforced consistently, did have a calming and ordering effect.

Another task focussed on changing the chaotic and inappropriate sleeping arrangements. The therapist made the task game-like, drawing a floorplan of the apartment with the family in a session. They made cut-out beds and moved them around to arrive at a more functional arrangement. It was framed normatively that Mother, because she was the parent and worked so hard to provide for her family, deserved to have her own room back, where she should close the door and have time for peace and quiet. Also, now that the children had reached adolescence, it was important for each of them to have their own space, if only a corner, and for the daughter to have privacy from the boys.

With the therapist's suggestion that all the children pitch in and help, the family managed to buy two more beds and set up a curtain for the daughter to have her own room in the enclosed porch. Spontaneously the children took the task a step further, each arranging their possessions around their bed, and putting up their own posters and pictures. This concrete restructuring furthered a healthier differentiation as it created more appropriate boundaries.

CONCLUSION

In conclusion, this paper illustrates the clinical utility of the Circumplex Model in the assessment and treatment of severely dysfunctional families. The particular advantages of the model in meeting therapeutic challenges with this population are that it provides a useful framework for clinical assessment of the type of family system, aids in treatment planning and helps focus clinical intervention.

The Model helps the therapist move beyond focussing on the presenting problems to the clinically relevant dynamics of family cohesion, family adaptability and family communication. Treatment goals based on the Model focus on moving families extreme on one or both dimensions to more balanced levels of functioning.

The interrelated concepts of balance and curvilinearity are discussed. The curvilinearity on cohesion and adaptability are based on the premise that too much or too little cohesion or adaptability are dysfunctional to families in the long run. Families need to learn how to balance their separateness versus togetherness on cohesion and their stability versus change on adaptability without getting stuck at the extreme levels.

Specific therapeutic techniques are illustrated for helping move families from extreme levels of cohesion and adaptability to more balanced levels. Intervention approaches that work with dealing with rigid versus chaotic and disengaged versus enmeshed are described. The interrelated dynamics of the extremes and the treatment process of moving families towards balanced levels is clearly described.

REFERENCES

Anderson, C. M., Reiss, D. J., & Hogarty, G. E. (1986). *Schizophrenia and the family*. New York: Guilford Press.

Gurman, A., & Kniskern, D. (1978). Research on marital and family therapy: Progress, perspective and prospect. In S. Garfield & A. E. Bergin (Eds.), *Handbook of psychotherapy and behavior change* (2nd ed.). New York: John Wiley.

Haley, J. (1980). *Leaving home*. New York: McGraw-Hill.

Hatfield, A., & Leffley, H. (Eds.). (1987). *Families of the mentally ill*. New York: Guilford Press.

Killorin, E., & Olson, D. H. (1984). The chaotic flippers in treatment. In E. Kaufman (Ed.), *Power to change: Alcoholism*. New York: Gardner Press.

Olson, D. H., & Killorin, E. (1985). *Clinical rating scale for the Circumplex Model of marital and family systems*. Rev. Ed. St. Paul, MN: Family Social Science, University of Minnesota.

Olson, D. H., Russell, C. S., & Sprenkle, D. H. (1980). Marital and family therapy: A decade review. *Journal of Marriage and the Family, 42*, 973-993.

Rolland, J. S., & Walsh, F. (1987). Longterm physical and psychiatric disorders: Toward a unified systems framework. Paper presented at 45th Annual Meeting, American Association for Marriage and Family Therapy, Chicago.

Russell, C. S., Olson, D. H., Sprenkle, D. H., & Atilano, R. B. (1983). From family symptom to family system: Review of family therapy research. *American Journal of Family Therapy, 11*, 3-14.

Selvini Palazzoli, M. (1986). *Journal of Marriage & Family Therapy, 12*, .

Walsh, F. (in press). *Treating severely dysfunctional families*. New York: Guilford Press.

Walsh, F. (1987). New perspectives on schizophrenia and families. *Journal of Psychotherapy & the Family, 3*(3), 19-31.

Walsh, F. (1987). The clinical utility of normal family research. *Psychotherapy, 24*, 496-503.

Walsh, F., & Anderson, C. M. (1987). Chronic illness and families: An overview. *Journal of Psychotherapy & the Family, 3*(3), 3-18.

Symptoms as Regulators of Distance and Change

Candyce S. Russell

SUMMARY. Symptoms are conceptualized as attempts to bring the polarities of separateness versus connectedness and stability versus change into balance. The author suggests choosing one theme (either distance or change) and returning to that theme repeatedly during the family's therapy. Symptoms which occur at periods of critical transition can generally be linked to the regulation of change while symptoms which are chronic in nature often appear to regulate distance.

A theoretical model offers the clinician a way of attending to and organizing the vast amount of data a couple or family presents. In the process of using theory, certain pieces of information will be highlighted while others will recede.

The Circumplex Model of Marital and Family Systems (Olson, Russell & Sprenkle, 1983) provides a theoretical framework which organizes the family's experience around issues of *distance* (from disengagement to enmeshment) and *change* (from chaos to rigidity). Family systems are thought to function best when these polarities are "balanced" in styles labeled "separate," "connected," "flexible" or "structured." Yet the balance is often disturbed, not in a pathological sense, but from the demands of maturation and change in the environment. The theory suggests that symptoms are likely to occur when the balance between stability and change or separateness and connectedness is threatened. Furthermore, the symptoms can be conceptualized as attempts to bring these polarities into balance.

Candyce S. Russell, PhD, is Professor, Department of Human Development and Family Studies, Kansas State University, Manhattan, KS 66506.

Identifying the function of symptoms in balancing separateness with connectedness, and stability with change, provides the therapist with an "organizing frame" which is reiterated in therapy as the couple or family comes to understand its dilemma differently and to explore new alternatives. Child conduct problems or marital conflict begin to be understood in relation to distance between family members and/or change within the family as a group.

Each family's struggle to cope with issues of relative distance and change, though familiar to the therapist in form, is unique in its content. An effective response to the unique content of each family's struggle requires that the therapist listen carefully to that family's language and understanding of its experience. The art in therapy involves "speaking the family's language" and connecting it to the theory of the therapist. Four case studies will be described to illustrate the process of connecting the family's experience to the therapist's theory in such a way that the family is able to identify new alternatives.

The first two case studies are conceptualized as attempts to regulate change in rigidly enmeshed and rigidly disengaged (see Olson, Russell & Sprenkle, 1983) systems. Both involve responses to progression of the family life cycle and the losses that inevitably entails. Therapy in both cases could also have been organized around the theme of regulating distance. However, in the author's experience, therapy generally proceeds more effectively if one theme is identified and returned to repeatedly in the family's therapy. Symptoms which appear at critical transitions in the family life cycle can generally be linked to the regulation of change with great clarity. The life cycle change may be within the nuclear family or within the family of origin. The regulation of distance is an especially helpful frame when symptoms are presented which have no clear onset or are chronic in nature.

SYMPTOMS AS REGULATORS OF CHANGE

Both of the families described below presented with symptoms at critical transition periods. The first family presented at the time launching of children was to be completed, which is an expected and predictable transition. The second family presented when the task of launching was just beginning. However, its task was complicated by co-occurrence with a death in the extended family and potentially life-threatening disease in one of the parents.

Case I: "My Daughter's Mother-in-Law Is a Witch"

Mrs. A asked for therapy following the premature birth and subsequent death of twin granddaughters. She was concerned that her daughter's mother-in-law had caused the babies to be born prematurely through witchcraft. Furthermore, Mrs. A was concerned about her daughter living with her husband's parents in the home of a witch.

The therapist explained to Mrs. A that she had no experience with witchcraft, but that it might be useful to get some information about what had been happening in the two families recently. In providing information for a genogram, Mrs. A explained that within the past three months all three of her children had left home: the oldest daughter got her own apartment after returning to her mother during a marital separation, the youngest child, a son, left home to join the Navy, and the pregnant middle daughter left home to live with her husband's family. In addition, Mrs. A suffered the death of the family dog.

Mrs. A went on to explain that her husband was the children's stepfather, and although the children could remember having no other father, he was a "loner" and generally kept his distance from both her and the children. Mrs. A described herself as chaotically enmeshed with her children but rigidly disengaged with her husband. Her goal was to become less upset about her daughter's problems (dead babies, intensive in-laws, "irresponsible" husband, etc.).

The therapist suggested to Mrs. A that she had suffered many losses in a very short period of time and that it would be understandable if she felt that her daughter's mother-in-law had "stolen" her daughter from her and perhaps had a strong influence on her. This prompted Mrs. A to talk about the focus her children had provided in her life following abandonment by her first husband. This overfocus on children was eventually connected to the difficulty each of the children was having in "staying launched." Though the son had not yet returned home, both daughters called home whenever they had fights with their husbands. The therapist suggested to Mrs. A that she had raised loving, loyal children who were helping her to stay employed in the job she did best—being a mother. They were helping her to slow down change. Perhaps she needed to continue being a mother for a while longer before learning how to live alone in the same house with Mr. A—something they had never done before.

The therapist asked Mrs. A to bring her husband into therapy. He refused, but Mrs. A did bring the daughter who had lost the twin babies. By that time the daughter had returned home to her mother once again, and therapy took a playful, strategic direction. The therapist asked each woman what she could do to ensure that the daughter, at 35, would still be living with mother and keeping her employed. Each laughed and rapidly developed a long list of concrete ways each could sabotage the other in becoming more separate and becoming more involved with their own husbands. They were sure, however, that they did not want to continue living in the same home and each eventually requested marital therapy. The family's goal in therapy became helping the daughter to establish a separate household and helping Mrs. A get closer to her husband. In other words, the family was requesting help in making the changes necessitated by the launching phase of the family life cycle.

Over the course of therapy, Mrs. A found a way to give less to her children and to be less critical of her husband, "the loner." They eventually went into a business together—providing her with a new job and him with more freedom since he was his own boss. Both daughters eventually had one more child each, divorced their husbands and established separate households.

Both daughters continue to have crises from time to time. However, Mrs. A is generally able to avoid over-responding and to keep her loyalty to her husband primary. Her relationship with her children at termination was one of flexible connectedness while she was structurally separate from her husband. The family had successfully accomplished launching.

The original fear that her daughter had fallen into the hands of a "witch" functioned to keep Mrs. A protectively involved with at least one of her children during a period of very rapid change. The symptom slowed the launching process and functioned to make it more manageable.

Case II: "We're Always Late"

The B family initially asked for therapy because their children were always making them late. The middle two children, both girls, were primary offenders. The family denied having any other problems, though the oldest child, a son, had recently been arrested during a "joy ride" and was not brought to therapy. Mother and both of the girls were strikingly attractive. Mother sold cosmetics and also taught modeling. The older daughter (aged 14) was very attentive to her own grooming, and the family attributed her tardiness to "primping." The younger daughter had developed a morning ritual which required that her mother stand in the doorway and be visible while waving good-bye and throwing kisses as the daughter walked to the school bus. It was not acceptable to the little girl (aged eight) to have Mom say good-bye from another room. Mom had to be visible in the doorway. The children described the family on the FACES scale as *rigidly disengaged*. The parents described the family as *separated* and *structured*. The family's goal was to get the family to arrive at functions "on time." The problem the family presented seemed to the therapist to be a small one; one not typically warranting the help of a therapist. Family history was collected as a way of helping the therapist to understand the concern the parents focused on, tardiness.

Genogram information revealed deaths in both extended families, but especially in Mom's, where her mother and sister both died of cancer. Mrs. B had already had two mastectomies herself and numerous smaller operations for cancerous skin growths. The parents vigorously denied concern about Mrs. B's health. Mrs. B, in particular, cited her and her husband's religious belief as reason for lack of concern. However, the oldest daughter was able to admit that she sometimes worried about her mom—and about her own likelihood of developing cancer. The parents quickly jumped in to reassure their daughter and once again avidly denied any concern on their own parts. After several ineffective sessions of dealing with the family's focus on tardiness, the oldest son, who never came to sessions, had a big fight with his father. The fight followed another one of Mom's "small skin surgeries" and ended with the son angrily driving off in his car, declaring that his dad would "no longer have him to kick around." This terrified the parents, who heard the son's declaration as a suicide threat. This was a turning point in therapy and allowed the family to begin to consider the possibility that the children (if not the parents) were worried about unspoken issues of death and were concerned that they would lose their mother prematurely. Thus the symptoms functioned to respect the parents' wish not to speak of cancer in the family by providing them with a new focus that either slowed down changes in the daily routine (e.g., being late for school) or threatened to accelerate it (a child dying before a parent). It was the oldest son's threat of accelerating change that enabled the family to talk about the children's fears that they might lose their mother prematurely and that they, too, might die prematurely. After opening this toxic issue for discussion, the presenting problem of tardiness was no longer a problem, and the parents chose to terminate therapy. At post-test, the children reported movement from *disengaged* on the FACES scale to *separated* and from *rigid* to *structured*. The parents continued to report a *structuredly separate* style. A three-month phone follow-up revealed that the family was continuing to arrive at events promptly and that the eight-year-old was leaving for school with less need for ritual. However, the oldest son continued to get into arguments with his father, mostly about use of a car. It is possible that the father-son arguments functioned to distract the family from a continuing fear of loss. It is also possible that the arguments were simply functioning to further facilitate the oldest son's launching. The parents' view was that the latter was the correct interpretation.

SYMPTOMS AS REGULATORS OF DISTANCE

The presenting problems of the couples described below were of relatively long-standing duration, and while issues of stability and change could also be identified, the regulation of distance between the marital pair was chosen as the organizing theme. The first is a family with two pre-school children. The second is a large remarried family with three children (aged ten, 14 and 15) from the wife's earlier marriage and two (aged four and six) from the present marriage.

Case III: "We Argue"

Mr. C was an engineering student who worked long hours and achieved high grades. Mrs. C was a full-time wife and mother who felt her abilities were inferior to her husband's, but also felt resentful of the greater burden she carried in caring for the couple's two pre-school children. Their presenting problem was generally marital conflict around the issue of time – his time spent away from the family and her time spent with little adult stimulation. Both spouses described themselves as *disengaged*, though the wife reported somewhat more *flexibility* in their relationship than the husband, who saw their relationship as *structured*. The couple's goal was to argue less and to feel closer to one another.

Mr. C came from a family where men were either "leeches" or over-responsible "workaholics." His father, as patriarch of a family business, was a "workaholic." His uncle, who was in the employ of his father, was seen as a "leech." Mr. C had gone through an earlier period of irresponsibility, during which he had gotten Mrs. C pregnant. However, since making the decision to marry Mrs. C, he has followed the pattern of his father, feeling a heavy burden to support others and to achieve great success in his chosen field.

Mrs. C's family was less educated than Mr. C's family. It was also a family where women were pregnant at marriage, married young, and were not easily assured of their value to their husbands. Women in this family redeemed themselves by sacrificing for their children and asking little from their husbands.

Mr. C "encouraged" Mrs. C to go back to school and to do something on her own, but in so doing implied that she was less adequate than he and was in need of his guidance. Mrs. C complained about her confined, unstimulating life but resented her husband's "pushing" her into school – an arena where he had been so successful.

The therapist suggested to the couple that each was being loyal to his/her own family of origin and that that loyalty was protecting them from having a relationship that was closer than the one either of their parents had. When the husband spoke for his wife in the session or analyzed her situation, the therapist pointed to the similarity between Mr. C and his father and suggested that Mr. C might want to consider taking on a less burdensome role in this family. When Mrs. C acted helpless and confused, the therapist asked how her mom might feel if she (Mrs. C) were to achieve a more equal relationship with Mr. C than Mrs. C's mom had achieved with her husband.

In the process of each partner taking responsibility for his/her own career, while avoiding attempts to control or manipulate the other's, Mr. and Mrs. C were able to experience greater intimacy in their marriage. Mr. C eventually chose a job in another state rather than returning to the family business. Mrs. C chose to stay at home with the children, at least until the family got settled in their new location. But she planned to become involved in the community through volunteer work and held in reserve the possibility of returning to school herself. At termination, the couple had moved from a *disengaged* position to a *separate* but *structured* style and reported both more closeness and less arguing.

Case IV: "He's Like One of the Kids"

In this remarried family, Mr. D was a skilled laborer and Mrs. D was a secretary. Mr. D was a small man, of slight frame, who avoided eye contact, slouched as he walked or sat and was unable to read. Mrs. D was a more robust woman, though not overweight. She was energetic (though getting very tired), an excellent organizer and attentive to each of her five children. Mrs. D's initial complaint was discord between her husband and her daughter (14) by a previous marriage. However, Mrs. D also made it clear that her husband was very little help to her in managing the family and that, in fact, he was like "one of the kids." Both parents described the family as *structured* and *disengaged*. Mrs. D was the responsible parent, and Mr. D avoided the family whenever possible. The family's goal was to decrease conflict between Dad and stepdaughter and to get Mom some help in her job as parent.

The therapist joined with Mr. D and attempted to elevate him in the family by commenting that he must be very clever to have risen to position of foreman without knowing how to read. Mr. D was allowed to talk about how he taught his skill to less experienced men. The therapist then asked how it was that a man who was such a skillful teacher had not developed that role with his own children.

After several failed attempts at getting Mr. D to become more involved at home, the couple reported a playful incident the previous week where the husband had found a set of directories that had been lost, after which the couple shared a long laugh about the husband's inability to read them. The therapist suggested that actually Mr. and Mrs. D enjoyed their "mother/son" relationship and did not want to change it even though it meant more work for Mrs. D at home and meant that Mr. D suffered some humiliation. The therapist asked the couple to develop a list of advantages to staying in their current mother/son relationship. One advantage for the wife was that she didn't have to share control and could avoid thinking about some of her own unmet needs and whether or not she deserved to be cared for. The current pattern also allowed her to demonstrate to the children from her first marriage that no one, including Mr. D, would ever be as close to her as they are. The major advantage for the husband in maintaining the current pattern was avoidance of failure. If he didn't try to be more responsible, he wouldn't fail. He had a long history of failure with women (mother, teachers), and he didn't want to fail in still another task.

The couple seriously considered divorce, believing that the costs in changing the mother/son relationship and becoming "closer in age" were possibly too great. However, Mr. D did become more involved with the two younger children he and Mrs. D shared biologically, and while Mr. D and the older children failed to rework their relationship, Mrs. D was able to acknowledge and support her husband's developing relationship with the younger children. Mr. D requested individual sessions and explored his fantasies about relationships with less powerful women than his wife. But he never felt confident enough of his ability to get close to a woman that he wanted to risk leaving the relationship with Mrs. D.

While their marital relationship pattern changed little, Mr. and Mrs. D saw more clearly the advantages in maintaining a relatively distant relationship. They understood their mother/son relationship differently. The family had reorganized with greater connectedness between Dad and his biological children, but continued disengagement between husband and wife, and Dad and stepchildren. Thus, the family operated in both *structurally separate* and *structuredly disengaged* patterns at termination. The family's goals had been partially met in that Mom and Dad shared more parenting with their joint children, but Dad and stepdaughter continued a conflictual relationship, and Mom continued to be the primary parent to her children.

FREQUENT CATEGORIES OF SYMPTOMS WHICH REGULATE DISTANCE AND CHANGE

The symptoms presented by each of the families described above could have been framed in more than one way to provide an organizing theme in therapy. The theme must be familiar to the family and yet invite them to take a fresh look at the symptom. The framing of the problem must also fit the therapist's theory and help her organize the vast amount of data presented by the family into a meaningful whole. There is no way of knowing whether the frame the therapist chooses is "true" in an absolute sense. However, if the frame provides the therapist with a map and leads the family to new alternatives, it has served a useful purpose. Table 1 summarizes each case described above and the way in which the concepts of *distance* and *change* were used to organize therapy. More general categories of symptoms which can be conceptualized as the family's attempt to regulate distance or change are listed in the following section.

Symptoms Which Regulate Distance

– *Conflict* may provide a "safe" or "familiar" mode of contact and thus allow for closeness with the assurance that the partners won't appear to be "too close."
– *An Extra-marital Affair* may "heat up" a relationship thermostat set too low (see e.g., Whitaker, in Neill & Kniskern, 1982) in an otherwise stale and boring marriage.
– *A Child Behavior Problem* may draw an absent member into increased involvement in the family. The most frequent exam-

ple of this occurs in divorcing families where a child's behavior problem is the occasion for parents (and former marital partners) to re-contact one another.

– *Psychosomatic Behavior* may provide a "polite" way to protect personal boundaries from other intrusive family members. Anorexia in a teenage family member frequently functions in this way (see e.g., Minuchin, Rossman & Baker, 1978).

– *"Over-Functioning"/"Under-Functioning" Behavior* may protect partners from deeper levels of intimacy by using only part of a "self" in the relationship (see e.g., Kerr, 1981).

Ways in Which Symptoms May Regulate Change

– By reworking an unresolved loss, as in the addict family with a history of early loss and where the addiction of a young adult child repeatedly provides the family with opportunities to confront death defying behavior (see e.g., Stanton, 1977).

– By avoiding the next stage in the family life cycle.

– By forcing movement into the next family life cycle stage.

– By slowing down change in a time of flux.

These are not the only possible frames for these symptoms; however, they may be helpful in offering the therapist a consistent theme for intervention and the family alternative ways of understanding their problem. By shifting the focus from the symptom to the regulation of *distance* or *change* in their relationship(s), the family is often able to find new solutions to its own problems. Finding ways to move "in" or "out," "faster" or "slower" is often easier than finding ways to get a child to go to school or to get a wife to stop complaining. A focus on regulation of distance or change takes the blame off any one person and broadens the problem to include a relationship partner who is attempting to be helpful in organizing the family as a group.

Table 1

Family Style, Presenting Symptom, Therapeutic Theme, Family's Goal and Therapeutic Outcome

CASE	PRE CIRCUMPLEX STYLE	PRESENTING SYMPTOM	THERAPEUTIC THEME	FAMILY'S GOAL	POST CIRCUMPLEX STYLE
1	Chaotically enmeshed Mother/Child Subsystem ------- Rigidly Disengaged Marital Subsystem	Conflict with Daughter's Inlaws	Regulation of change: slow down launching	Become less upset about daughter's problems	Flexible Connectedness In Mother/Child Subsystem ------- Structured Separateness In Marital Subsystem
2	Rigidly Disengaged	Tardiness	Regulation of Change: Avoid Potential Loss (Death)	Punctuality	Structured Separateness
3	Structuredly Disengaged	Marital Discord	Regulation of Distance: Loyalty to Family of Origin Above Spouse	Less Conflict and Greater Perceived Closeness	Structured Separateness
4	Structuredly Disengaged	Father/ Step-daughter	Regulation of Distance: Avoidance of Failure for Husband/Evidence of Wife's Loyalty to Her Biological Children	Decreased Father/ Step-daughter Conflict and Greater Participation of Husband In Parenting	Structured Separateness In Father/Child Subsystem ------- Structured Disengagement In Marital and Stepfather-Stepchild Subsystems

REFERENCES

Kerr, M. (1981). Family systems theory and therapy. In A. Gurman and D. Kniskern (Eds.), *Handbook of family therapy*. New York: Brunner/Mazel.

Minuchin, S., Rossman, B. L., & Baker, L. (1978). *Psychosomatic families: Anorexia nervosa in context*. Cambridge: Harvard University Press.

Olson, D. H., Russell, C. S., & Sprenkle, D. H. (1983). Circumplex Model VI: Theoretical update. *Family Process, 22*, 69-83.

Stanton, M. D. (1977). The addict as savior: Heroin, death and the family. *Family Process, 16*, 153-160.

Whitaker, C. (1982). Psychotherapy of married couples. In J. R. Neill and D. P. Kniskern (Eds.), *From psyche to system: The evolving therapy of Carl Whitaker*. New York: Guilford.

The Clinical Use of the Circumplex Model in the Assessment and Treatment of Intrafamily Child Sexual Abuse

Terry S. Trepper
Douglas H. Sprenkle

SUMMARY. This paper demonstrates how the theory and research related to the Circumplex Model have guided the development and operation of a treatment program targeted at intrafamily child sexual abuse. The authors demonstrate how the Circumplex Model fits into a larger assessment framework. Suggestions for utilizing FACES III with this population are offered along with typical patterns evidenced by incest families. A case illustration shows how the approach is useful in treatment planning and in guiding therapeutic interventions.

FACES III and the Clinical Rating Scales, both based on the Circumplex Model, were developed for both research purposes and clinical use. While there has been an increasing amount of research on the psychometrics of these instruments (Olson, 1986), especially FACES III, comparatively little has been written about the clinical utility of the Circumplex Model. This is unfortunate since the developers of the model believe strongly that theory and research should not be divorced from practice, but rather should be related synergistically (Olson, Russell, and Sprenkle, 1980; Olson, 1976; Sprenkle, 1976). In this paper we offer a concrete illustration of

Terry S. Trepper, PhD, is Director of Family Studies Center, Behavioral Sciences, Purdue Calumet Campus, Hammond, IN 46323.

Douglas H. Sprenkle, PhD, is Professor and Director, the Marriage and Family Therapy Program in the Department of Child Development and Family Studies, MFT Building, 523 Russell Street, West Lafayette, IN 49706.

how the theory and research related to the Model have guided the development and day-to-day operation of a treatment program targeted at one of family therapy's most difficult and challenging clinical populations.

We have used FACES III and the Clinical Rating Scales for the last few years in a large-scale treatment program for intrafamily child sexual abuse (Trepper and Barrett, 1986a). We have found the instruments, and the Circumplex Model upon which they are based, quite useful in both assessment and treatment planning. It is the purpose of this paper to describe how the Circumplex has been used as an effective adjunct to family therapy for child sexual abuse.

OVERVIEW OF THE TREATMENT PROGRAM

The program has been described in detail elsewhere (Trepper and Barrett, 1986a; Barrett, Sykes, and Barnes, 1986). However, a brief description of the underlying framework and the program model may be useful before discussing how the Circumplex is used in assessment and treatment planning.

The program is based on the Multiple Systems Perspective for the treatment of intrafamily child sexual abuse (Trepper and Barrett, 1986a). This perspective is an ecosystemic model, which views incest[1] as resulting from a number of factors from a variety of systems. Treatment, therefore, needs to address each of these factors. While it is tempting to see incest as resulting solely from the psychopathology of the perpetrator, research and clinical experience suggest the etiology is far more complex and includes sociocultural, family, individual personality, and family of origin factors (Trepper and Barrett, 1986b).[2] Once the family is assessed for the presence of these factors, a treatment plan is developed and instituted to reduce its vulnerability to incest and thus decrease the likelihood of further abuse.

Therapy is divided into three distinct stages. During each of these stages, a variety of clinical modalities is used, including entire family sessions, individual and subsystem sessions, and sessions with the parents' families of origin. Although a number of intervention models are used, the program orientation could best be described as a combination of structural, strategic, and systemic family therapies. The family usually has two contacts with the program per week. Although family sessions are most often conducted by one therapist, co-therapy is often used with more difficult families. The entire therapy lasts two years, with two years or more of follow-up.

The goals of Stage One are to: (1) enlist the support of outside agencies involved with the case; (2) reduce the family's resistance to change; (3) conduct formal assessment of the family's vulnerability to incest; and (4) help the family understand what contributed to their vulnerability to sexual abuse. These goals are accomplished through a set of structured activities, both in and out of session. If there is denial on the part of either parents or children, the therapist will work directly for its end before proceeding to Stage Two.

The major goal of Stage Two is to change the family structure so that the sexual abuse cannot again occur, and to help the family achieve other therapeutic goals that they may have. While Stage One created the context for the family's change, Stage Two directs that change. The factors assessed to be contributing to a family's vulnerability to incest are directly confronted therapeutically to reduce or eliminate them. Families during this stage are encouraged by their therapist to try alternative behavioral patterns and communication styles.

The goal of Stage Three is to consolidate the family's changes by allowing the family members to take on more responsibility for their lives and future functioning. The therapist becomes increasingly less involved and instead supports the family's independence. During this stage, therapy sessions become less frequent, until a family may only be seen once every few months.

USE OF THE CIRCUMPLEX IN ASSESSMENT

The Circumplex Model is an important framework for better understanding the family structure on the dimensions of adaptability and cohesion. These are not the only areas assessed, however. During the assessment period within Stage One, the program formally assesses individuals and the family unit using a variety of objective, projective, and interview methods.

Overall Assessment Scheme

The major factors that we evaluate include the following: (1) *socioenvironmental factors*, which includes chronic stress, social isolation, and membership in a subcultural group that is tolerant to abuse against children and women; (2) *family factors*, such as adaptability and cohesion as measured by the Circumplex (see below), family sexual style (which would include affection-seeking, pansexual, hostile intent, or violent rape [see Trepper and Barrett, 1986a]), and family communication; (3) *individual personality factors*, such as sociopathy, obsessive-compulsive sexual behavior, locus of control, and the presence of psychosis or other severe psychopathology of the offending parent; and (4) *family of origin factors*, such as the occurrence of abuse in the childhood of the offending or the nonoffending parent. Also assessed are precipitating events that may have directly preceded the incestuous episodes and the family's coping mechanisms.

The Circumplex

A dysfunctional family structure has been theorized by many to be a contributing factor to the development of intrafamily child sexual abuse (Straus, 1973; Rist, 1979; Renvoize, 1982; Trepper and Traicoff, 1985). Although there is some disagreement as to what operationally defines structure, the authors have found the Circumplex Model to be exceptionally useful as both an organizing framework and as a way of measuring structural changes as a result of therapy.

Olson, Russell, and Sprenkle (1983) hypothesized that dysfunctional families should fall in the balanced (and possibly midrange) portions. The incestuous families referred to this program clearly present as dysfunctional by lacking important skills usually found in "healthy" families, such as open communication, trust, and ability to problem solve and resolve conflict. On the Circumplex, most of the families typically fall in the extreme range as predicted. When therapy is complete, most fall within the balanced or midrange level.

Administration and Scoring

Families are assessed on the Circumplex using the Clinical Rating Scale and FACES III. The Clinical Rating Scale is completed by the therapist after he or she has seen the family interact a number of times, usually after the third or fourth family session. Sometimes we find it useful to encourage an "enactment," where the family engages in a behavioral sequence common to them outside of treatment. The therapist rates the family *globally* using the criteria specified on the Clinical Rating Scale. The therapist attempts to rate the family system as a whole, noting individual or subsystem differences separately.

FACES III is completed by the parents and adolescents under the supervision of the therapist to prevent any family member from influencing another's responses. We obtain a number of scores which provide us with a picture of the richness and complexity of the family structure.

We first calculate individual scores on adaptability and cohesion for both the "perceived" (how the respondent feels the family is now) and "ideal" (how the respondent would like the family to be) perceptions. These scores provide us with individual placements on the Circumplex which we then plot to obtain a graphic picture of the family. We then calculate the couple and family mean scores. This provides us with a representation of subsystem and system placement on the Circumplex.

When there is disagreement among family members as to placement (a not uncommon occurrence), the mean scores alone will be of less use. We, therefore, also calculate the discrepancy scores, which tell us how much disparity there is among the family members. This is a useful and interesting score in and of itself, but used in conjunction with the couple and family means, it can tell us if the mean placement is an accurate portrayal of the family or a statistical artifact. In general, the higher the discrepancy score, the less valid the family mean placement.

Finally, we also calculate the distance from center score for individuals, couple, and family. This is ostensibly a measure of the magnitude of the family's dysfunction, since it measures the average distance from the theoretical "balanced" point. The higher the score, the more dysfunctional the family is thought to be.

As can be seen, the accurate and specific placement of the entire family on the Circumplex with FACES III (for example, as chaotic-disengaged) is neither fully possible nor necessary for clinical evaluation. Rather, the richness and complexities of the family structure are better understood by examining the record of scores as a whole.

Diagnostic Considerations

A family therapist may use the information derived from the Circumplex in a variety of ways. As an example, we will present some common "extreme" quadrant patterns the incestuous families in our program display and how we interpret these patterns. This is presented as an example of how a clinician might use the Circumplex in analyzing assessment information. It should be noted that the categories represent the overall clinical impression rather than discrete scores on FACES III.

Family Enmeshed. Enmeshment on the cohesion dimension is a very common pattern among incestuous families. Overinvolvement with each other's emotional and personal life is typically present, with a desire for privacy equated with lack of love. As a function of the enmeshment, these families are often socially isolated and thus lack the scrutiny of others outside the family, making both the opportunity for incest possible and its detection more difficult. Families scoring enmeshed are seen as affection seeking and nonhostile in their sexual patterns. The child victim in these families usually says she loves her father and does not wish to see him removed from the family. She may even have interpreted the abuse to have occurred within a "love and affection" framework. The mothers and victims of enmeshed families often deny either the fact or impact as a way to keep the family together; when discovered, the fathers rarely deny.

Individual Enmeshed. If the father scores enmeshed while the rest of the family scores toward the balanced or disengaged, this may indicate a certain emotional neediness that is not present in the others. This is common in families where the child victim would likely view the abuse as hostile. If the victim scores enmeshed while others do not, she is more likely to deny either the fact or the impact, and may even recant previous accusations.

Family Disengaged. This is fairly uncommon among incest families, but may be seen most frequently in reconstituted families. If the family scores disengaged, they likely have not made familial attachments, and the incest may appear more aggressive. Sibling sexual abuse is possible in these families. The father may have a more generalized pedophile sexual orientation, and the father should be further tested for more serious psychopathology. In the few cases where a child falsely accuses her stepfather, the family often scores disengaged.

Individuals Disengaged. When one member scores disengaged while others do not, this may indicate an individual who feels isolated from the rest of a basically cohesive family unit. If this occurs for the father, his vulnerability to incest may be tied to his lack of "fatherly" feelings for his daughter, allowing for a denial of impact ("Well, she isn't really my daughter anyway"). A mother scoring disengaged while the rest of the family does not may signal an indifference to her family, and an inability to protect her daughter from further abuse.

Family Rigid. Incest families typically score in the rigid range on the adaptability dimension. These families typically adhere to an overstrict and even irrational set of rules. A variant of "Do what Daddy says at all times" is usually present, making many abuse victims (particularly the younger ones) unaware that they are doing anything wrong. The child will often not tell her mother for years because she was told not to. Families scoring rigid, not surprisingly, are often the most resistant to outside intervention.

Individuals Rigid. Although it is uncommon for only one family member to score rigid while the others do not, occasionally the father scores in that direction. This usually indicates a father who feels overly responsible for the workings of the family, may feel highly stressed, and may abuse his child during times of high frustration, or even to "punish" her for not following his directions.

Family Chaotic. In these families, rules for daily activities and behavior are either extremely inconsistent and fluctuate, or are nonexistent. Intergenerational boundaries are often crossed by family members, so fathers appear clinically to "be one of the kids," or one of the children periodically takes on the role of parent. Incestuous activities between fathers and daughters in chaotic families almost appear like childhood sex-play. These families are particularly vulnerable to abuse by extended family members, such as cousins and uncles. Parents in these families lack basic parenting skills, often seem overinvolved with commonly occurring crises, and the mother appears unable or unwilling to protect the children from abuse even when she is clearly aware of it.

Rigidly Enmeshed. This is the most common two-dimensional pattern among incestuous families. They are usually seen as affection-seeking and nonhostile when the abuse occurs. The combination of an overstrict adherence to rules and the secretiveness which follows, plus the personal overinvolvement with each other's emotional lives and concomitant social isolation, make families with this pattern particularly vulnerable to incest.

High Distance from Center (DFC) Scores. The DFC score generally indicates the amount of dysfunction present in a family system, and not surprisingly, incest families at the beginning of treatment tend to have high DFC scores. This is a particularly important score, since many incest families have members scoring in the extreme quadrants, but not necessarily in the same ones (e.g., child rigidly disengaged, mother chaotically enmeshed, father rigidly enmeshed).

High Discrepancy Scores. An analysis of these scores provides important diagnostic information with regard to coalitions and alliances among members. One group of incest families (typically scoring rigidly enmeshed) show very low discrepancy scores among each other, reinforcing the assessment of strong family cohesion, and a view that maintaining the family unit is more critical than the sexual abuse. Another common pattern is for father and daughter to have a low discrepancy score between each other, but for father and mother, and mother and daughter to have high discrepancy scores. This may indicate an "unholy" alliance between father and daughter, and problematic relationships between the parents and between mother and daughter.

Problems with the Circumplex in Assessment of Incest Families

As can be seen, the Circumplex provides some extremely useful information for the assessment of intrafamily child sexual abuse. At the same time, two problems exist that need to be noted by clinicians.

First, self-report scales have a potential for unreliability, particularly when individuals have a reason to "look good." Many incestuous families are in some form of litigation, either civil or criminal, or have someone removed from the home that the family would like back. If a family does have a vested interest in a particular assessment outcome, the Clinical Rating Scale should definitely be used, and if possible, corroborated by another clinician who has viewed the family, either live or on tape.

Second, FACES III, though compiling an impressive record in validity studies (cf. Olson, 1986), is just beginning to be normed with clinical populations. While the ability to differentiate clinical populations is still in question, we use FACES III and the Clinical Rating Scale to generate clinical hypotheses that can be further tested throughout the course of therapy.

THE CIRCUMPLEX AND TREATMENT PLANNING

It should be emphasized again that family structure is only one factor that is addressed in the Multiple Systems Model for treating intrafamily child sexual abuse. However, because of its pervasive influence, family structure assessment as conceptualized by the Circumplex, is an extremely important part of our assessment, and much of our treatment, particularly during Stage Two, is directed to reduce structural dysfunction.

The general treatment goal is to bring the extreme scoring families into the midrange and perhaps eventually the balanced scoring regions.

More important than the scores themselves, of course, is the ability to modify behavioral patterns associated with them. For example, the rigidly enmeshed family may display a pattern of strict adherence to a patriarchal set of rules ("Dad is always right, do what he says"), and an intolerance to outside relationships ("We do everything as a family; we don't need outside friends").

Through therapeutic interventions the family would be encouraged to try alternative behaviors. These interventions can be in the form of homework assignments ("This week let's give Dad a vacation from disciplining the children . . . Mom, we'd like you to be in charge of the family rules"); enactments ("Dad, you try asking Mom for help with that decision, and Tommy, you watch to see how they do"); insight-oriented questions ("Mary, how does it feel not to be allowed to visit friends from school?"); or any other intervention the clinician uses to effect change.

As Olson et al. (1983) suggest, we do not attempt to "move" a family too quickly to balanced functioning, nor do we work on both adaptability and cohesion behaviors at the same time. An incestuous family's pattern of behaviors is particular resilient, and even when the family has successfully completed Stage One of our program, we have found it more useful to intervene on one dimension at a time.

We have found the Circumplex especially useful in ongoing assessment of a family's progress through therapy, using either FACES III, the Clinical Rating Scale, or both. Changes on objective measures support the therapist's work and provide important information on which area should be focused on next. For example, once a family's rigidity is decreased, the therapist may then want to focus on the problematic relationship between mother and daughter, and on breaking up the father's alliance with daughter.

The Circumplex becomes critical for therapists in deciding when Stage Three is ready to begin. This consolidation stage implies the family can live all together again, and the therapist need have only a "consulting" relationship. A clinician should be cautious about moving a family in that direction who still is in any extreme quadrant, or has an isolated member who is (for example, the daughter who still feels disengaged from her family, possibly because she still feels afraid or hesitant to be alone with her father). Of course, the Circumplex is also used in follow-up assessment to note any continued progress or "regression" a family may experience.

The following case example demonstrates how the Circumplex was used in assessing family structure, in formulating a treatment plan, and in guiding therapeutic interventions.

THE SMITH FAMILY

The Smith family consists of Joe, 38, who works in a local steel mill as an administrative supervisor; Alice, 35, who is a housewife; Mary, 12, who is in seventh grade; and Joey, 8, who is in the third grade. The family was referred for therapy by Protective Services after Joe admitted to having had sexual contact with Mary for the past two years. This contact included kissing, fondling, and eventually intercourse. Mary had admitted to a school friend (actually "showed off" by her account), who told her mother, who reported it to Protective Services. Joe was ordered out of the home and the family referred to the program for therapy by a hearing officer.

The family was cooperative during the first few sessions, although all were somewhat angry at Mary for telling her friend. Alice was angry at Joe, but was insistent that she did not want a divorce. Both Joe and Alice reported an excellent relationship, which confused Alice: "Why would he want to have sex with our daughter when our sex life was so good?" Joey acted as the family "mascot," always bringing a laugh to the family during the sessions, particularly during conflict.

The sexual abuse began when Alice was in the hospital for minor surgery, and Mary had asked Joe a question about sex, specifically, "What is fellatio?" Instead of answering her, he showed her. He then would periodically sneak into her room during the night or when Alice was gone, to fondle, have oral sex, and eventually have intercourse with her. Mary admitted to the therapist in individual sessions that although she didn't like the sex part, she occasionally would ask Joe if he wanted to "play."

Although the entire family admitted to the fact, Joe denied impact ("She seemed to like it; besides we only had intercourse a few times"), and Mary denied appropriate responsibility, i.e., she blamed herself ("None of this would have happened if I hadn't asked that question"). Alice denied awareness, even though she, herself, was an incest daughter as a child, and stated that she "wondered if this was ever going to happen to her daughter."

The family system and the individual members were formally evaluated by the therapist and consulting psychologist. We will focus here on the Circumplex results and how they were used in therapy; however, a brief summary of the other findings will be given.

None of the individuals showed signs of significant psychological problems. Mary was somewhat depressed, as was Alice, and Joe exhibited anxiety symptoms, although these were diagnosed as situational. The family was under much stress during the past two years, due to the constant threat of layoffs at Joe's plant, and two moves during this period as cost-saving measures. The family, because of the moves and their somewhat rural location, were socially isolated; they had no extended family living nearby. They were assessed as an "affection-seeking" incest family type (Larson and Maddock, 1984), as opposed to "pansexual," "hostile intent," or "violent rape" types. Both parents were sexually abused as children by their respective fathers, with Joe's father being physically abusive at the same time.

Clinical Rating Scale

The family was rated by the therapist as being Enmeshed and Rigid on the Clinical Rating Scale as shown in Figure 1. The following contributed to these ratings.

Contributors to Enmeshment. The Smith family demanded loyalty to one another; in fact, Alice acted in a fairly deviant fashion by going to their minister, which led to the others in the family being quite angry at her. The family demonstrated much interdependence upon one another, and had confused intergenerational boundaries as evidence by Mary's intense, adult-like emotional relationship with Joe irrespective of sex. Privacy in the family was not tolerated; in fact, bathroom doors were never shut when a family member was inside, and even the parents' room door was never shut. The family members had few outside friends; unfortunately, Mary's one outside the family friend was the girl she confided in about the sexual abuse, and the results of this were interpreted by the family as evidence of what happens when one has "too close a friend."

Figure 1: Therapist Rating of Smith Family on the Circumplex Clinical Rating Scale - Before and After Therapy

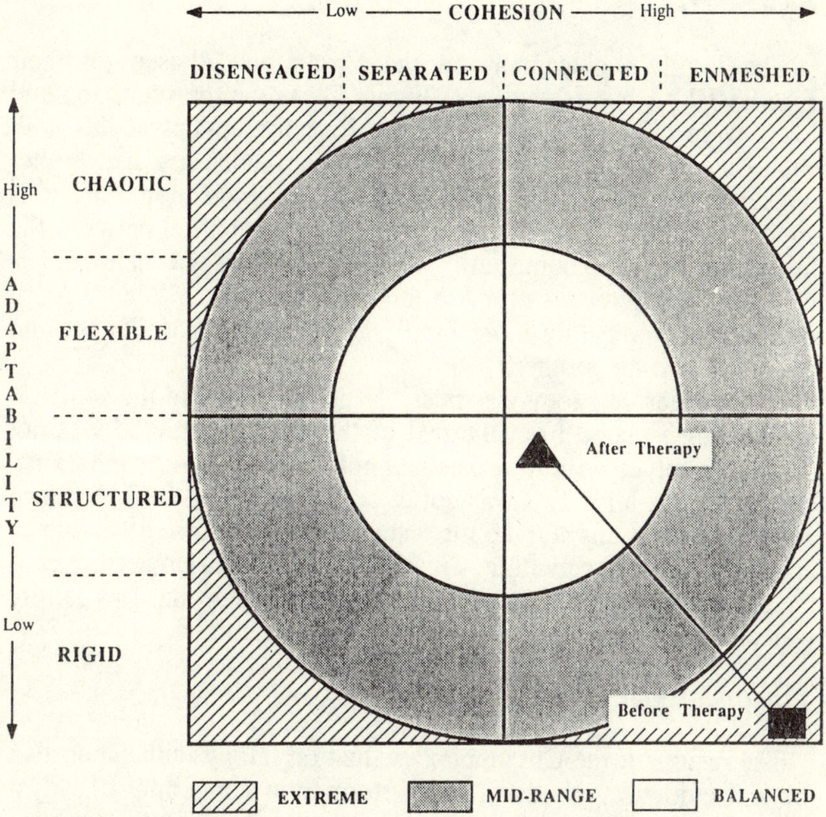

Contributors to Rigidity. The Smiths were clearly a patriarchal family, with Joe the authoritarian leader. Although it was experienced by the family as within a loving context, all agreed that "Dad is in charge." One of the reasons Mary did not consider telling Alice about the sexual abuse was that Joe told her not to, and one simply obeyed Dad when an order was given. Alice continually deferred to Joe, and Joe admitted part of his personal stress came from having to always be the responsible one. His rule was basically autocratic, and changing a rule in the family was difficult, particularly if Joe felt it right. Family roles were clearly defined, and were highly sex-role stereotyped.

FACES III

The family's placement on the Circumplex, based on their FACES III scores, is shown in Figure 2. As can be seen, Joe and Mary were closely aligned (i.e., had low discrepancy scores with each other), but Joe and Alice, and Alice and Mary had higher discrepancy scores. This was interpreted as an indication of the alliance between the father/daughter and possible conflict between the husband/wife. Also contributing to this hypothesis was that the perceived/ideal discrepancy for Joe and Mary was low, while for Alice it was high, indicating more family satisfaction for the father and daughter than the mother.

It was clear that Joey was possibly getting "lost in the shuffle" and feeling isolated from the rest of the family, since he was not directly involved with the crisis and his parents had little emotional energy left for him. This was not directly seen on FACES III, since Joey was too young to take the test, but inferred from other scores and from direct observation. Finally, the family distance from center score was high, supporting the clinical hunch that this family was clinically more dysfunctional than most families.

Treatment Planning

The results of the Circumplex evaluation, along with supportive clinical evidence, yielded much information concerning the dysfunctional family structure that may have contributed to this family's vulnerability to incest. Based on this information, the following long-term family structural goals were incorporated into the treatment plan:

1. *Decrease enmeshment* by: (a) helping the family put loyalty in perspective; (b) reducing interdependence by encouraging individual achievement; (c) strengthening both the spousal and the parenting subsystems for Joe and Alice so as to clarify

Figure 2: Smith Family's Placement on the Circumplex with FACES III Prior to Therapy

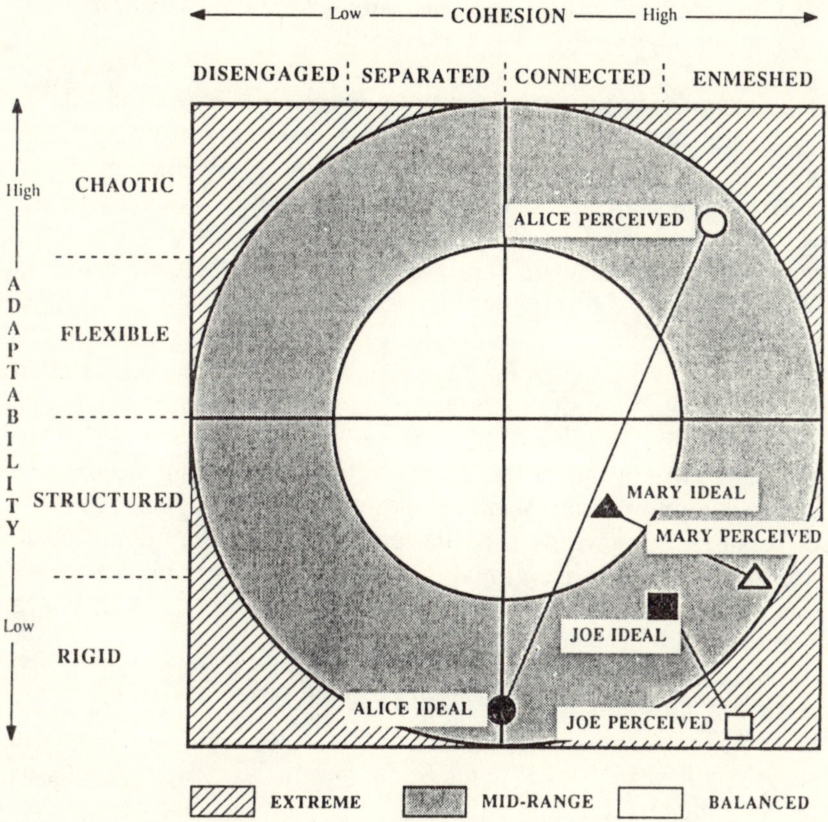

generational boundaries; and (d) encouraging outside relationships for all family members.

2. *Decrease rigidity* by: (a) reducing Joe's patriarchal reign on the family; (b) increasing Alice's leadership role in the family; (c) encouraging more flexible family rules and discipline; and (d) working to change the strict sex-linked roles to a more androgynous behavior.

3. *Other treatment goals* included: (a) ending the strong alliance between Joe and Mary; (b) reopening the lines of communication between Joe and Alice; (c) improving the relationship between Alice and Mary; and (d) bringing Joey "back into the family" and encouraging his parents to remain sensitive to his needs.

The family was seen for two years in therapy. Each of the above goals was met through intensive direct intervention during Stage Two of the treatment program. An example of an intervention to reduce enmeshment was to encourage all family members to develop outside activities. Joe joined a bowling league, Alice got a part-time job in a music store, and the children became active in YMCA and YWCA activities and developed many new friendships. To reduce rigidity, the family engaged in enactments where problem solving was expanded from a "Daddy makes the rules" format to one where all family members participated in solving problems. Alice and Mary's relationship was strengthened by a series of assignments to engage in fun activities together, during which time they talked more and began to "know" each other again. A couple of sessions designed as "marital enrichment" were conducted to improve Joe and Alice's relationship. The family's placement on the Circumplex after treatment, based on FACES III, is shown in Figure 3.

These family structural interventions were only part of the larger treatment program for intrafamily sexual abuse. These changes, however, based upon Circumplex analysis, were critical not only in stopping the sexual abuse in the Smith family, but also in making its reoccurrence next to impossible.

CONCLUSION

This paper has emphasized the clinical utility of the Circumplex Model in treating a difficult client population. Both the Clinical Rating Scale and FACES III were shown to be useful both in assessment and treatment planning for intrafamily child sexual abuse. As the case example illustrated, both diagnosis and intervention were

Figure 3: Smith Family's Placement on the Circumplex with FACES III After Therapy

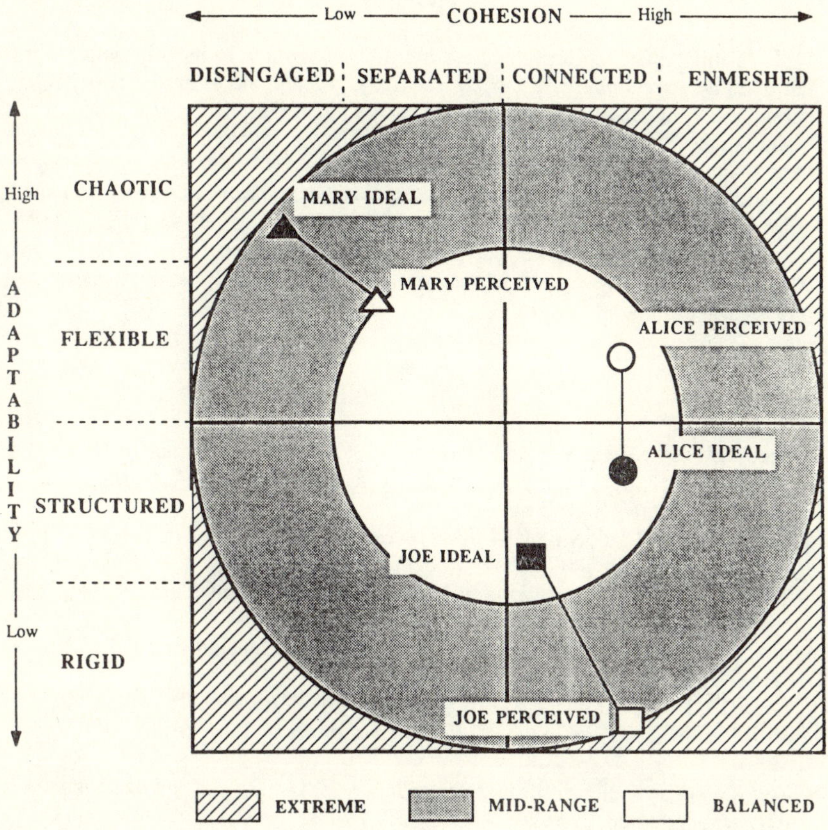

clearly grounded in the theory underlying the Circumplex Model. Hopefully, this report will stimulate the reader to experiment in using the model in his/her own assessment and treatment planning. It is our belief that many of the same principles described here could be adapted to other client populations. Since family structure is at the heart of the dysfunctional-functional continuum (regardless of presenting problem), intrafamily child sexual abuse should be only one of many problems to which the Circumplex Model is clinically relevant.

NOTES

1. In this paper, the term "incest" will be used interchangeably with "intra-family child sexual abuse." Also, we will use "father" to indicate the offending parent, since fathers/stepfathers are by far the most likely to present clinically as perpetrators. We understand there may be different dynamics present between fathers and stepfathers, and that mothers, grandfathers, uncles, etc. may also be perpetrators; we merely wish to reduce the semantic clutter of having to list all options each time we refer to a perpetrator.

2. A distinction is made in our program between *responsibility* for the incest, which we see as always that of the offending parent, and *etiology*, which can include a multitude of factors.

REFERENCES

Barrett, M. J., Sykes, C., and Barnes, W. (1986). A systemic model for the treatment of intrafamily child sexual abuse. *Journal of Psychotherapy and the Family, 2*(2), 67-82.

Larson, N., and Maddock, J. (1984). Incest management and treatment: Family systems vs. victim advocacy approaches. Paper presented at the Annual Meeting of the American Association for Marriage and Family Therapy, San Francisco, October, 1984.

Olson, D. H. (1986). Circumplex Model VII: Validation studies and FACES III. *Family Process, 25*, 337-353.

Olson, D. (1976). Bridging research, theory and application: The triple threat in science. In D. Olson (Ed.), *Treating relationships*. Lake Mills, IA: Graphic Press.

Olson, D. H., Russell, C. S., and Sprenkle, D. H. (1983). Circumplex Model VI: Theoretical update. *Family Process, 22*, 69-83.

Olson, D., Russell, C., and Sprenkle, D. (1980). Marital and family therapy: A decade review. *Journal of Marriage and the Family, 42*, 973-993.

Renvoize, J. (1982). *Incest: A family pattern*. London: Routledge and Kegan Paul.

Rist, K. (1979). Incest: Theoretical and clinical views. *American Journal of Orthopsychiatry, 49*, 630-631.

Sprenkle, D. (1976). The need for integration among theory, research, and practice in the family field. *Family Coordinator, 24*, 261-263.

Straus, M. (1973). A general systems theory approach to a theory of violence between family members. *Social Science Information, 12*, 105-125.

Trepper, T. S., and Barrett, M. J. (1986a). Vulnerability to incest: A framework for assessment. *Journal of Psychotherapy and the Family, 2*(2), 13-26.

Trepper, T. S., and Barrett, M. J. (1986b). Introduction to the multiple systems perspective for the treatment of intrafamily child sexual abuse. *Journal of Psychotherapy and the Family, 2*(2), 5-12.

Trepper, T. S., and Traicoff, E. M. (1985). Treatment of incest: Conceptual rationale and model for family therapy. *Journal of Sex Education and Therapy, 11*, 18-23.

Sexually Addicted Families: Clinical Use of the Circumplex Model

Patrick J. Carnes

SUMMARY. The Circumplex Model adapts easily to help families understand their own dysfunction. The model can serve as a structure to organize a therapeutic curriculum for families who participate in a treatment program together. It supplies a vocabulary for family members to talk about issues and a concrete way of understanding similarities and differences. This article describes the use of the Circumplex as the organizing structure of the Family Week at the Sexual Dependency Unit at Golden Valley Health Center in Minneapolis. The objective is to supply a working model of the Circumplex as an applied concept versus theoretical or research tool.

SEXUAL ADDICTION: A FAMILY ILLNESS

Sex addicts have lost control over their sexual behavior. In the book *Out of the Shadows: Understanding Sexual Addiction*, I have defined it as a "pathological relationship" with a mood altering experience. Parallel to the alcoholic, the compulsive gambler, or the compulsive overeater, the sex addict will sacrifice family, friends, work, health, and values in order to maintain that relationship with the sexual behavior. Sex becomes the primary source of nurturing and care – no matter what the cost. We have learned much about sex addicts, including:

Patrick J. Carnes, PhD, is a consultant to the Sexual Dependency Unit, Golden Valley Health Center, Golden Valley, MN. Those interested in further information regarding the subject of this article may contact the Sexual Dependency Unit, Golden Valley Health Center, 4101 Golden Valley Road, Golden Valley, MN 55422.

Portions of this article were adapted from Patrick J. Carnes' *Contrary to Love: Helping the Sexual Addict*, CompCare Publications, Minneapolis, MN (in press).

– that estimates range that it affects between three to six percent of the population;
– that it affects women as well as men;
– that it can involve the entire spectrum of sexual behavior;
– that it often is found concurrently with other addictions such as chemical dependency or eating disorders; and
– that it is dangerous with complications including suicide, life threatening violence, and AIDS.

We also have learned that it very much is a family illness. We know that a high probability exists that sexual addiction or another type of addiction was present in the previous generation. Repeatedly cases emerge in which the same out-of-control sexual behavior patterns are recycled over a number of generations. Sixty-five percent of women addicts and 45% of men addicts report being abused sexually as children. Other family based factors in the etiology of the illness include:

– extreme and mid-range family behavior as defined by the Circumplex Model;
– extremely chaotic or rigid rule systems around sexuality;
– early childhood sexual experiences;
– other types of child abuse (physical and emotional);
– family participation in subcultures with extreme rule systems about sexuality; and
– anti-sexual beliefs in the family.

Further, we have documented clinically how family members participate in the illness through such mechanisms as denial, enabling, or controlling behavior parallel to the alcoholic's family. Unlike alcoholism, in which a spouse can detach when the alcoholic chooses alcohol over the family, the spouse of the sex addict must cope with possible sexual involvements with others – maybe even large numbers of others. The result is a much more intensive and explosive situation.

Family members share in the illness of the addict through obsessing about the addict's behavior. Hence, the term that is used to describe their participation in the illness is "co-addiction" or "codependency." Their behavior is characterized by compulsive, self-destructive cycles around the addict's acting out. As so often happens in systemic functioning, the co-addict's efforts to change or control the situation simply serve to intensify the addictive cycle of the addict.

The Circumplex Model emerges as a helpful tool to entangle the layers of addictive systemic functioning in the family. Before exploring clinical options using the Circumplex Model, professionals must understand how the concepts help clarify the role of addictive illness in the family system.

THE CIRCUMPLEX MODEL AND ADDICTION

There are two dimensions to the Circumplex Model. One is adaptability – the capacity for a family to organize itself, especially as the family grows and changes. Each of the four levels of adaptability: rigid, structured, flexible, and chaotic, represents a range of behavior options for the family:

– *Rigid* – Families use extremely autocratic decision-making styles in which there is limited negotiation and strictly defined roles and rules.
– *Structured* – Families mix authoritarian with some equalitarian leadership resulting in very stable roles and rules.
– *Flexible* – Flexible families use equalitarian leadership seeking negotiated agreements making for easily changed rules and roles.
– *Chaotic* – Chaotic families have erratic and ineffective leadership which results in impulsive decisions, inconsistent rules, and role reversals.

Table 1 provides an overview of various components of adaptability. Note that the middle range is the optimum for family growth. For example, a family with three children under the age of five would thrive with a structured format given the need for consistency and direction of small children. The same family when the children are between the ages of fifteen and twenty will shift to a more flexible mode.

Every family will have its chaotic and rigid moments. Families

Table 1: Clinical Rating Scale - Family Adaptability

	COUPLE OR FAMILY SCORE	RIGID (Very Low) 1 2	STRUCTURED (Low to Moderate) 3 4	FLEXIBLE (Moderate to High) 5 6	CHAOTIC (Very High) 7 8
LEADERSHIP (Control)		Authoritarian leadership. Parent(s) highly controlling.	Primarily authoritarian but some equalitarian leadership	Equalitarian leadership with fluid changes.	Limited and/or erratic leadership. Parental control unsuccessful, rebuffed.
DISCIPLINE (For Families Only)		Autocratic, "law & order". Strict, rigid consequences. Not lenient.	Somewhat democratic. Predictable consequences. Seldom lenient.	Usually democratic. Negotiated consequences. Somwhat lenient.	Laissez-faire and ineffective. Inconsistent consequences. Very lenient.
NEGOTIATION		Limited negotiations. Decisions imposed by parents.	Structured negotiations. Decisions mainly made by parents.	Flexible negotiations. Agreed upon decisions.	Endless negotiations. Impulsive decisions.
ROLES		Limited repertoire; strictly defined roles.	Roles stable, but may be shared.	Role sharing and making. Fluid changes of roles.	Lack of role clarity, role shifts and role reversals.
RULES		Unchanging rules. Rules strictly enforced	Few rule changes. Rules firmly enforced	Some rule changes. Rules flexibly enforced.	Frequent rule changes. Rules inconsistently enforced.
GLOBAL ADAPTABILITY RATING (1-8)					

which remain in the extremes, however, damage their members. For example, children who live in rigid families end up with life-long struggles around rules and authority because of the unreachable expectations of their parents. Chaotic families produce children who have difficulty incorporating a consistent set of standards into their own conscience because no one ever demanded it of them. An intriguing aspect of systems is that opposite extremes have similar ends. Rigidity and chaos both affect conscience formation.

For the focus of this article, adaptability becomes extremely important because of the close connection between dependency and addiction. Who and what one depends upon are central questions in personal development. To illustrate, in rigid families a child who asks for help may receive assistance but with a heavy price in the form of lectures, high expectations, and moralizing about failure. Under those conditions, a child learns quickly not to ask. In a chaotic family, when a child asks for help, the assistance is inconsistent or does not come. Rather than embarrass the parents again, the child simply does not ask.

Children need to be able to count on—depend upon—the structure of their families. If not, they look for what they can depend upon—and they find it. Drugs, alcohol, food, and sex—they always do what they say they will. If children grow into addicts, these pleasurable experiences will become the "primary relationship" upon which the addict relies.

COHESION

Besides dependency, the other crucial variables in addiction are self-esteem and the capacity to have intimacy with others. These variables bring us to the other major family dimension in the Circumplex Model, cohesion. Simply defined, cohesion is how close a family sticks together. The emotional bonding and support available in a family are vital to self-concept. Reciprocally, a person's self-perception determines the ability to have relationships.

As in adaptability, cohesion has four levels: disengaged, separated, connected, and enmeshed. Each offers a combination of options in terms of the degree of closeness the family environment will support:

- *—Disengaged*—Disengaged family members distance themselves from one another maintaining extreme separateness and little family loyalty.
- *—Separated*—Separated families mix emotional independence with some involvement and joint effort and occasional family loyalty.
- *—Connected*—Connected families emphasize emotional closeness, family loyalty, and joint efforts while allowing for some individuality.
- *—Enmeshed*—Enmeshed families demand extreme family closeness and family loyalty and allow for little individuality.

Table 2 provides an overview of these levels of family cohesion.

Everyone experiences moments of being too close or too far from their family. Families who remain locked into a specific extreme mode, however, characteristically develop unstable relationships and low self-esteem. In disengaged families, for example, children learn that support is conditional. If children do something wrong, they lose the relationship. Pulling away from a child is a potent weapon for parents to use against their children because of their fear of abandonment. And abandonment is a critical part of the formation of the addictive system (again looking for what you can depend upon). In healthy families, the behavior is criticized, but the relationship remains strong. Children in disengaged families end up feeling like they have to be perfect in order to be accepted. Since they know they cannot, and they do not want to be rejected, they simply avoid being close.

In enmeshed families, children have little opportunity to develop personally because of the relationship demands of the family. Parents, for example, view child misbehavior as a direct reflection on them. They then shame and guilt the child heavily for what they have done to the family. Sometimes they will cover up for the child in order to protect the family name. The child does not learn to accept responsibility for his own behavior.

Adults who were raised in an enmeshed family environment struggle with intimacy issues. If they do not want to replicate what their parents did, they might go to the opposite extreme rejecting any form of dependency out of the fear of being swallowed up again. Whichever option they select, intimacy will remain elusive. Like the adaptability dimension, the extremes of cohesion have similar results: low self-worth and low trust of others. A poor sense of self and a fear of intimacy add crucial energy to the addictive system.

COMBINING ADAPTABILITY AND COHESION

When the dimensions of adaptability and cohesion are combined, a map of possible family behaviors emerges. Figure 1 displays the parameters of the Circumplex Model. Note that sixteen possible combinations of adaptability and cohesion exist. Graphically, they are divided into three ranges: balanced, mid-range, and extreme.

Most healthy families fall into the balanced range. A helpful metaphor to understand the Circumplex is to think of it as a hill with most families at the center and fewer and fewer families as you move away from the center. Being in the center allows families more options.

Not all families are able to change as easily. Families in the mid-range maintain one extreme level on one dimension. Thus, a family might be both connected and rigid. Some very wounded families reach an extreme on both dimensions. To be both rigid and enmeshed would place a family in the "extreme" range of the Circumplex. Olson and his colleagues (1983) suggest that "to deal with situational stress and developmental changes across the family life cycle, balanced families will change their cohesion and adaptability, whereas extreme families will resist change over time."

To illustrate the impact of the extreme family ranges, let us use an example. The following excerpts come from the autobiography of a client named Fred who describes his early years in which abuse and alcohol added to the turmoil of the family. Much of his early years were spent with his mother and siblings trying to escape his father:

> I remember one time when Dad came home intoxicated, he threw the family out of the house. On that occasion my mother carried me in her arms in the dead of winter to a hotel. However, after we arrived at the hotel there were no rooms avail-

Table 2: Clinical Rating Scale - Family Cohesion

	COUPLE/ FAMILY SCORE	DISENGAGED (Very Low) 1 2	SEPARATED (Low to Moderate) 3 4	CONNECTED (Moderate to High) 5 6	ENMESHED (Very High) 7 8
EMOTIONAL BONDING		Extreme emotional separateness. Lack of family loyalty.	Emotional separateness. Occasional family loyalty.	Emotional closeness. Loyalty to family expected.	Extreme emotional closeness. Loyalty to family is demanded.
FAMILY INVOLVEMENT		Very low involvement or interaction between members. Infrequent affective responsiveness between members.	Involvement acceptable but personal distance preferred. Some affective responsiveness is demonstrated.	Involvement emphasized but personal distance allowed. Affective interactions encouraged and preferred.	Very high symbiotic involvement, members very dependent on each other. Affective dependency is demonstrated.
MARITAL RELATIONSHIP		Extreme emotional separateness.	Emotional separateness.	Emotional closeness.	Extreme emotional reactivity.
PARENT-CHILD COALITIONS		Lack of parent-child closeness.	Clear sub-system boundaries some p/c closeness.	Clear sub-system boundaries with parent-child closeness.	Parent-child coalition. Lack of generational boundaries.

	COUPLE/ FAMILY SCORE	DISENGAGED (Very Low) 1 2	SEPARATED (Low to Moderate) 3 4	CONNECTED (Moderate to High) 5 6	ENMESHED (Very High) 7 8
INTERNAL BOUNDARIES		Personal separateness predominant.	Some personal separateness encouraged.	Need for separateness respected but less valued.	Lack of personal separateness.
TIME (physical & emotional)		Time apart from family maximized. Rarely time together.	Time alone important. Some time together.	Time together important. Time alone permitted.	Time together maximized. Little time alone permitted.
SPACE (physical & emotional)		Separate space needed and preferred.	Separate space preferred; sharing of family space.	Sharing family space. Private space respected.	Little private space permitted.
DECISION MAKING		Independent decision making.	Individual decision making but joint possible.	Joint decisions preferred but not necessary.	Decisions subject to wishes of entire group.
EXTERNAL BOUNDARIES		Mainly focused outside the family.	More focused outside than inside family.	More focused inside than outside family.	Mainly focused inside the family.
FRIENDS		Individual friends seen alone.	Individual friendships seldom shared with family.	Individual friendships shared with family.	Family friends preferred with limited individual friends.
INTERESTS		Disparate interests.	Separate interests.	Joint interests preferred.	Joint interests mandated.
RECREATION		Mainly separate recreation.	More separate than shared. recreation.	More shared than individual recreation.	
GLOBAL COHESION RATING (1-8)					

FIGURE 1. CIRCUMPLEX MODEL: SIXTEEN TYPES OF MARITAL AND FAMILY SYSTEMS

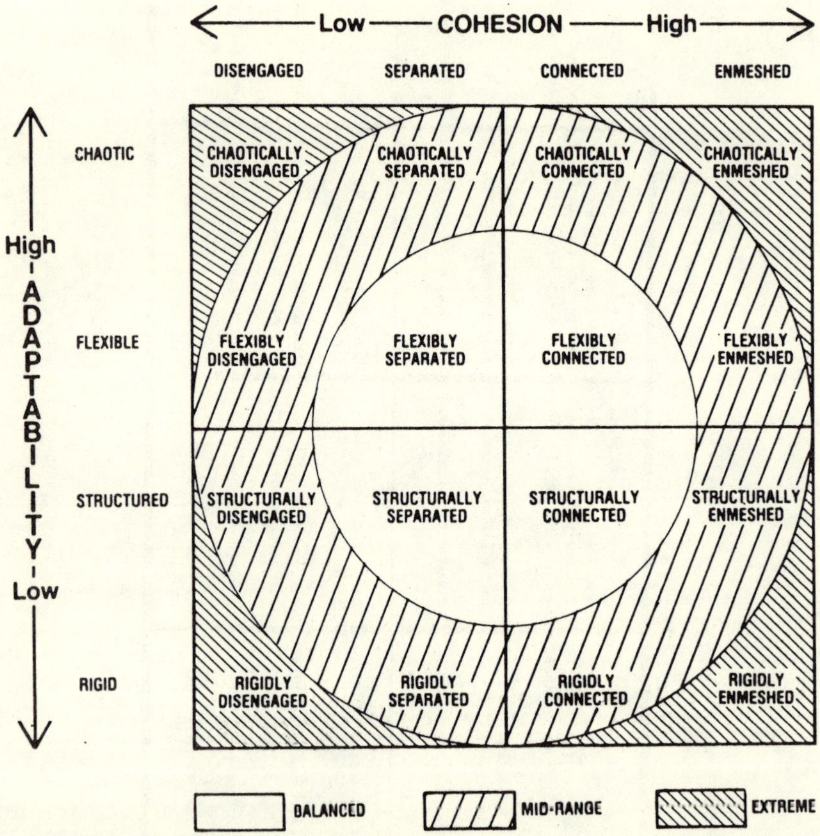

able so the other kids and myself spent the night with Mother in a restroom, with Mother sitting on the toilet seat and cradling me in her arms. . . .

I remember as if it were yesterday how I watched as he beat my mother to the floor and how he kicked her in the face and stomach with his boots as she lay helpless on the floor. My brothers and sisters tried to stop him but they couldn't. . . .

When I saw my father, I started crying and coughing at the same time. I will remember 'til the day I die how he came over

> to me and said, "You little bastard, shut up or I'll kill you." He then got a butcher knife and grabbed me by the hair and said that he was going to cut my throat. My other brother grabbed a skillet and hit him from behind and when Dad let go of me one of my sisters picked me up and ran out the door with me. We left Dad in the room and all of us ran down an alley and hid behind some trash. . . .

Although brief, these excerpts show how a child could end up feeling precarious in what was clearly a chaotic family. In the efforts to escape the father, Fred's family was constantly moving. He writes, "Every time that I would get settled in a new school, I'd have to start in another one." Under the circumstances, it was hard to know what to count on. While many ways exist in which a family can be chaotic, alcohol and abuse damage with an intense power.

Fred's family went to extremes in terms of cohesion as well. He wrote about his brothers:

> They would come home and fight each other with knives or beer bottles. I watched as they cut each other, then one of them would have to go to the hospital to get stitched up. What I never understood is the fact they were always saying that we were family and it was alright to fight amongst ourselves, but if anyone outside of the family gave us any trouble then they had the whole family to fight. . . .
>
> There were times when they came home that Mother was gone to work and they would grab me and try to force me to drink alcohol and when I refused, they would slap me around and tell me I was Mother's little boy and that I was acting like a baby. I was a Smith [not real name] and I should act like a man. Sometimes they would take turns holding me by the arms while the other hit me in the stomach and they would keep saying that it would make a man out of me. I was also told that a Smith is not afraid of anything or anyone and since one of my brothers was real good with knives and ice picks, I would be placed against the door and he would throw ice picks at me and stick them in the door around my body. If I moved, it meant a good beating because that showed that I was afraid

and, like I said, Smiths were not supposed to be afraid of anything or anyone.

A family united against the world demanding high prices for being a member demonstrates classic features of an enmeshed family. The Smiths were a chaotic enmeshed family in which both the adaptability and cohesion extremes supported violence and alcoholism. For the purposes of comparison, let us use an example of the opposite extremes of a rigid disengaged family. The following excerpt comes from the autobiography of Sam who describes his growing up with his sexually addicted and alcoholic father and his co-addictive mother:

> It seemed like our parents were always gone. And when they were around they were always fighting or snapping at us or uncomfortably silent. My parents always had a lot of problems which I never understood then and didn't much care. The main problem it seemed was how much my father was gone and how much he drank. They were always talking about divorce and asking us to decide between them. What really hurt was that neither one of them wanted custody. We made up our minds not to go with either of them. I felt really unloved and neglected. . . .
>
> I really liked it when they were gone, too. I could do anything I wanted and the relief of tension was welcome. The feeling when they were around was like there was a live bomb and any wrong movement, word, or gesture could set it off.

In the rigid disengaged family, "every person for him/herself" becomes a way of life along with fear of being caught out of line. Sam's family has a very different quality from Fred's, but it is easy to see how a child would feel in jeopardy as well as have low self-worth in both.

Note that both families struggled with alcoholism. Traditional alcoholism theory suggests that as a unitary and progressive illness everyone's experience including the family members' is the same. They may end up in the same situation with the same illness, but how they got there in terms of the family dynamics can be radically different. Much has been done to establish the importance of "differential diagnosis'' of families in the field of chemical dependency. The same need exists for the treatment of sexual addiction. Clients need to understand the differing processes that sustain their commonly shared behavior. Towards that end, the Circumplex Model serves as a helpful diagnostic, clinical, and teaching tool.

FAMILY OF ORIGIN AND CLINICAL DIRECTION

To demonstrate the utility of a model like the Circumplex in treatment, 35 sex offenders who were in rehabilitation programs in state correctional facilities in Georgia and Minnesota were asked to assess their families of origin. Each inmate was asked to complete FACES II, a family assessment profile based on the Circumplex Model (see Olson, Portner, and Laves, 1983). First, they were asked to rate their families' life when they were adolescents. Given that the results are retrospective and represent only one family member's perception, few conclusions can be made. Interesting contrasts occur, however, when the offenders' memories are compared with a normal sample of 416 adolescents. Divided into balanced, mid-range, and extreme, the comparisons are as follows:

	Normal	Sex Offender
Balanced	47%	11%
Mid-Range	34%	40%
Extreme	19%	49%
	100%	100%

Sex offenders remember their families as more extreme than most adolescents perceive their families. In fact, 77% of the offenders saw their families as rigid and 57% perceived their families as disengaged. When a specific clinical population has that much commonality, critical factors emerge for program development in specific institutions and probably corrections in general. Individual treatment plans must reflect this type of data. Much research must be done in this area for all levels of addiction. The social policy implications alone are of grave significance.

Some research has been done on the current families of sex offenders. Usually, these efforts represent very small sample sizes ranging from three to thirty offenders. Almost always psychometric, as opposed to family assessment procedures, are used when anything beyond case histories are reported. Again, for purposes of illustration, we asked thirty-two of the offenders who were married to complete FACES II on their current families. Comparing their current families with retrospective assessments of their adolescent family life produced the following contrasts:

	Adolescent	Current
Balanced	11%	19%
Mid-Range	40%	15%
Extreme	49%	66%
	100%	100%

While a few families became more balanced, many more became extreme. The largest increase being in cohesion with 72% of the families being disengaged, which might reflect the inmates' current prison status. The point remains that this very preliminary data supports the clinical observations that unhealthy family systems are perpetuated in the current family of these offenders as they perceive it (see Figure 2).

But how does the current family perpetuate the themes of the family of origin? In what ways do the spouse and children participate in the addictive system? To appreciate the roles of the family members, we must explore co-addiction—that is, the illness that those close to an active addict have.

CO-ADDICT EXTREMES AND THE CIRCUMPLEX

As in the addict's family of origin, the Circumplex can serve as a guide to the extreme behavior in the addict's current family. Figure 3 categorizes typical (but by no means all) co-addictive behaviors into dependency and intimacy issues. Co-addicts who look at this chart often remark, "I've done all of those." While that can be very true, usually there is a pattern or collection of behaviors which favor one set of extremes. Taken together, this behavioral constella-

Figure 2: Sex Offenders

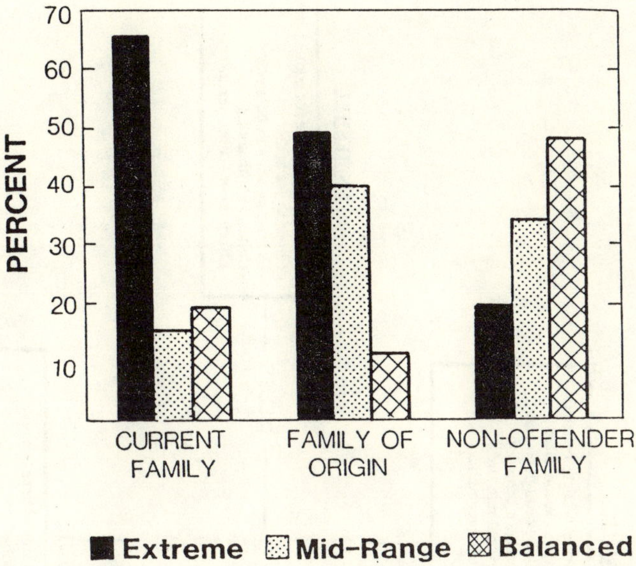

tion—as opposed to helping the situation—works only to support and to intensify the addictive system of the addict. The paradox is, of course, that the co-addict intends for them to stop or limit the addiction.

One way that co-addicts cope is to remove themselves from the situation. The act of detachment protects the family member from being hurt yet again. With detachment, a self-righteous disdain exists for the addict which pressures the addict to change. The co-addict remains emotionally unavailable, and safe, to punish the addict. But the most threatening is the withdrawal of sex as a way to control the addict's behavior. Many co-addicts report that sexuality goes "cold" for them in response to discoveries. Given what sex signifies for the co-addict, it is one of the most important messages co-addicts try to send addicts about the level of their pain. For co-addicts to admit their physical and sexual attraction for the addict becomes too great a risk. First, to tell the addict they are attractive is an invitation to intimacy—and more rejection. Second, co-ad-

Figure 3: Co-Addict Behavior Extremes

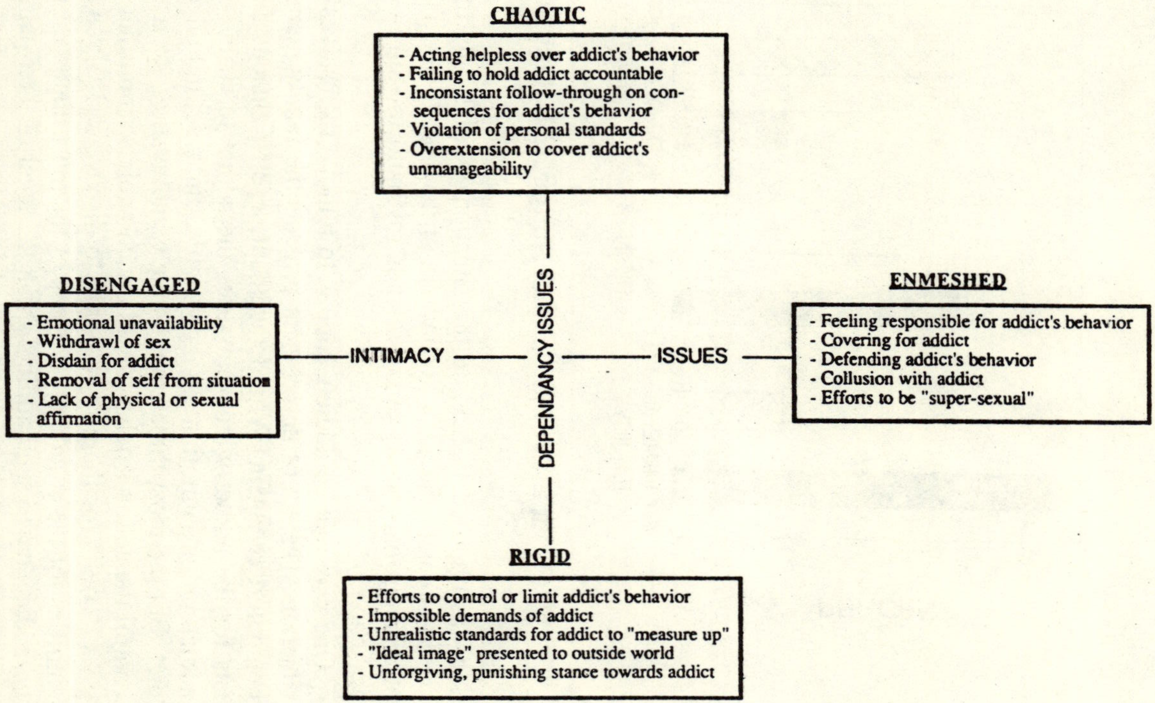

dicts fear that to tell the addict they are physically or sexually attractive will simply foster more sexual acting out by the addict.

Unfortunately, addicts totally miss the message of the co-addict's pain. They experience the co-addict as punishing and unresponsive. The posture of the co-addict validates all the addict's beliefs about unworthiness, unlovability, and the undependability of others. The withdrawal of sex when it is the addict's "most important" need adds a most fundamental panic to the interior life of the addict. The addict's impaired thinking engages full force blaming the co-addict for the behavior: "I need to do this because she(he) will not meet my needs." The "disengaged" behavior of the co-addict works to bring about everything that was to be avoided.

Other co-addicts go to the opposite extreme of actually involving themselves in the addictive behavior of the addict. Rather than fighting, they try to join. For some, involving themselves in the addict's behavior simply continued the enmeshment of their own family of origin. For others it was simply a matter of not wanting to be left out.

Sarah, for example, was told by her husband that making a threesome would add "zest" to their marriage. Since the first threesome would be the adding of another man, she would be the one to benefit. So she said "yes." Soon they had a pattern in which her husband, George, would recruit someone to join them. While that person would have intercourse with Sarah, George would masturbate and watch.

From the beginning of their marriage, Sarah had tried to be "super sexual" because of George's intense interest in sex. She would go along with things simply because she felt she had to in order to keep him. Some of it she felt terrible about but never told him. The worst was when he had her pose nude with her legs spread for a picture which he submitted to a porno magazine to be printed in a section for nude pictures of readers' girlfriends. At night she could not sleep for fear that people she knew would see her. Nor did she like the threesomes but acted enthusiastic for fear of being judged inadequate and being left by George.

Many co-addicts cover for the addict or even defend the addict's behavior because they feel responsible for the addict's behavior. For some, it is because of what they perceive to be their own inadequate sexual performance: "He does this because I am not good enough." In Sarah's case, she felt responsible because she participated in it. George, for example, became sexually involved with a neighborhood teenage girl. Sarah knew about it but felt she could not complain because of the threesomes. When confronted with angry parents Sarah found herself not only lying, but attacking the parents for allowing their daughter to dress and act in a seductive manner. Her message was that if something happened to their daughter it was not from her husband and whomever did it, the daughter was asking for it. Sarah felt just awful about herself for defending George's behavior.

Some co-addicts take enmeshment a step further and become sexual addicts as well. Many women addicts report that they started in a co-addictive posture seeking love and nurturing and changing focus to sex as the primary obsession. The transition is from a core belief in which sex is the significant sign to one in which sex is the end goal.

Enmeshment on whatever level fuels the addictive system. The addict is actively aided or at the minimum protected. No one feels any better about what is happening in the family. It just happens differently than in a disengaged family.

Sarah's life with George progressively became more chaotic. The threesome scenarios started to be so violent that Sarah would be injured and would have to fabricate elaborate stories to explain how she received her injuries. Frequent vaginal infections, including gonorrhea, added to the unmanageability. When George started taping the sessions with video tape recorder she could not handle it any more. She told him that she would never do another threesome. Yet, George talked her into it again and again.

George had now become involved with a number of other women whom he talked into having threesomes. When Sarah objected, George pointed to the many times she had sex while he watched, and asked how she could object to his being sexual with someone else when she did not even have to watch. Because of his involvements, George was spending less time at his work, as a result earning less, and spending more. Sarah had to borrow extensively on her own name to keep the household going. Her financial overextension presented a problem every time she considered moving out.

She felt totally helpless with her life out of control. Her only certitude was that somehow the man she had married had been replaced by someone awful and she desperately wished to return to the way it was.

Not all co-addicts respond in the same helpless fashion as Sarah. Some declare a "holy war" against the addict, the addiction, and in fact, anything sexual. These co-addicts will go to any lengths to control or limit the addict's behavior. Impossible demands of the addict are coupled with the co-addict's unrealistic standards to "measure up." The co-addict starts with the assumption the addict is not going to meet the standards and in effect sets into motion the self-fulfilling prophecy that the addict will fail. Convinced of the righteousness of his or her own position, the co-addict maintains a punishing, unforgiving stance towards the addict. It is a siege mentality which dares the addict to get out of line. Threats are immediately carried out except one—the co-addict does not leave. More than anything, the co-addict tries to maintain appearances that everything is under control—that their family is but a "Better Homes and Garden" family presenting a united front to the world. To leave would break the image and acknowledge to the world the weakness of the structure, that the effort was not "strong enough." In a rigid family, failure is having not tried hard enough.

The unyielding pressure of the rigid system unwittingly adds great power to the addictive system. The control demeans the addict, keeps the addict one down, and invites defiance of a spouse who, in effect, is acting like a parent. The rigid system—like the chaotic, enmeshed, and disengaged systems—only adds energy to the addictive system.

CO-ADDICT COMMONALITIES

Despite the differing extremes co-addicts reach, they all make the same three mistakes. Taken together, these mistakes become almost propositions for action or "behavioral corollaries" flowing out of the core beliefs. First, they mistake intensity for intimacy. Life in the addict's family is seldom boring. Crisis, unmanageability, struggle, and pain become a steady emotional diet. Ironically, the disengaged are often the most intense, for it takes a great deal of energy to maintain the obsession from a distance. Because the emotions are so immediate, intensity feels like intimacy—but there is no closeness. And it fills up one's life but leaves needs unmet.

Angry tirades get the adrenalin running and in the short term feel good. At least something is happening. What co-addicts invariably leave out are their own feelings. They do not share their own interior life with its sadness, fear of failure, pain, and loneliness. The addict only hears fear of the addict's failure, anger at the addict, and disappointment in the addict. To share the personal feelings would be an invitation to intimacy and too great a risk for the co-addict. So the siege continues. The addict never hears the one message that might break through the denial about the impact of the addiction.

And the co-addict keeps coping with different options such as being understanding one moment, rageful the next. And the reason the options fail, so the co-addict believes, is that he or she has not pushed hard enough. The co-addict's impaired thinking leads to being even more rageful, even more understanding, even more sexual and so the list goes on. And the intensity. And the extremes in the family. But the co-addict continues to focus all feeling life on the addict.

Which brings us to the second common mistake the co-addict makes: co-addicts mistake obsession for care. Like care, obsession focuses on the other, but makes the other into an object. Obsession originates in terror of being left alone, care trusts in the other's ongoing availability. Obsession fosters manipulation, care creates respect for self and the other. Obsession with the other obliterates knowledge of self, care assumes that fidelity to the other starts with faithfulness to oneself.

At its worst, obsession takes over the life of the co-addict. Like the addict, co-addicts who obsess about addicts lose a sense of their own lives. Preoccupation becomes a way that personal life issues can be ignored. Pain, boredom, lack of direction disappear as obsession gives new meaning and even excitement to life. Many co-addicts talk of how they have changed. They do not like the person they have become. Frequently, phrases like "losing myself" are used by co-addicts to describe a personality shift that almost parallels the Jekyll-Hyde scenario of the addict. But obsession does have payoffs. One payoff is that obsession guarantees a connection with the addict – even when the addict is not there. Obsession helps prevent feelings of abandonment. For example, Herb's obsession with Emily for years after he had left her was a way to keep her present in his life. His preoccupation helped stave off the grief of losing her to the addiction.

Another illustrative payoff for obsession is that co-addicts do not have to make choices for themselves or deal with their own issues and pain. The obsession with the addict becomes the organizing principle of their lives. Co-addicts are often filled with self-righteous impaired thinking and rage about how much they have invested in the relationship. They need to gain clarity about the rule of obsession over their lives, and to feel sadness over their loss of identity.

The third mistake that co-addicts make is: co-addicts mistake control for security. In all relationships, there is a risk that the other might leave. In healthy relationships, commitment and history transform risk into a loving confidence that one can be oneself and intimate without fear. Because of the core beliefs, the co-addict feels compelled to guarantee there will be no abandonment. Co-addicts view the world through "if only" lenses in which the relationship would survive if only the addict would change. So changing the addict becomes the task. An additional benefit is that by being "in charge" the co-addict's inadequacies are never exposed. Gone is the chance for mutuality.

Helping professionals who are using the Circumplex Model to assist co-addicts like Sarah must recognize first how co-addicts can be remarkably different and then identify what they have in common. Both the extreme differences and the common behavioral "corollaries" are equally important in treatment.

SEXUAL ADDICTION AND FAMILY TREATMENT

Treatment for sex addicts and their families is available in a number of hospital facilities throughout the United States. Self-help programs based on the twelve steps of Alcoholics Anonymous exist also across the country. They have different titles such as Sexual Addicts Anonymous or Sexaholics Anonymous. They also have self-help programs for spouses such as S-Anon or Co-Addicts to the

Sexual Addict (CO-S.A.). Treatment facilities often rely on the local Twelve Step programs for both referrals and for ongoing support for patient's post-treatment.

Golden Valley Health Center is a 350-bed psychiatric and chemical dependency facility located in suburban Minneapolis. The hospital's Sexual Dependency Unit is a twenty-bed inpatient program designed for sex addicts and their families. Opened in January of 1985, the unit specializes in patients whose obsessive behavior does not include major sex offenses. Preliminary surveys of addict populations indicate that less than ten percent of sex addicts do anything illegal. The unit is designed, therefore, for the much larger nonoffending sex addict population.

Admissions to the six-week inpatient sexual co-addiction program, or sexual dependency program stem from a long list of life compromising factors including suicidal ideation, disease, malnutrition, insomnia, and treatment failure on an outpatient basis. Thirty-eight percent of the admissions are chemically dependent: another 38% are eating disordered. Over 70% suffer a concurrent addiction of some type. An early follow-up survey found that 86% of the patients reported being able to maintain appropriate sexual behavior. Of those who recividated only one factor was common to all: their family failed to participate in Family Week.

FAMILY WEEK PROGRAM

Family Week is offered once every five weeks with the goal of including significant others and family members in the treatment process. Over six days family members participate in the following program components:

- an orientation to the program,
- a series of psychoeducational labs combining both lecture and group exercises,
- family groups or couples groups,
- lectures,
- individual or family counseling sessions,
- twelve step group work,
- post-treatment planning workshop.

By participating patients receive the following:

- an orientation to sexual addiction as a family illness,
- an appreciation of their own role in the illness,
- strategies for building their own recovery programs,
- initial therapy around the primary relationship with the addict,
- an assessment of family dysfunction currently, and
- an assessment of dysfunction, including other addictions, in the families of origin of both addict and co-addict.

From the beginning, the Circumplex Model is central to the learning process. Starting with the initial orientation, patients and family members learn about the Circumplex as a way to understand family behavior. In order to make the concepts more concrete, participants went through exercises designed to illustrate the concepts of adaptability and cohesion. In one such exercise families were instructed to build a house using construction paper and other materials. An observer family watched the nonverbal interaction and gave the housebuilders feedback on their adaptability. Then they switched their observer/builder roles. This exercise and the others used are taken from elements of a program called *Understanding Us*. Designed by the author of this article, the four-session program supplies planned experiences and support materials as a prevention experience for healthy families. It is built on the Circumplex Model, so is readily available for treatment applications as well.

To make the Circumplex Model real in terms of sexual addiction, Family Week participants are asked to complete a checklist on their family of origin (see Figure 4). The checklist contains a number of descriptors that characterize extreme behaviors found in the types of families that addicts and co-addicts grow up in. After checking those that are appropriate, they receive another handout which organizes the same descriptors into the Circumplex Model (see Figure 5). By transferring their checks to the new sheet, the participants then can see patterns emerge about the behavior. Staff persons then explain that as a self-assessment tool the goal is not to obsess about whether they did the exercise right or its accuracy. Rather, their main task is to use the occasion to reflect about their families and the impact on the development of this illness.

Figure 4: Family of Origin Checklist

Review this list of family behaviors and check the one which apply to your own family of origin. Then proceed to the next page.

	Behavior
____	Lack of sexual boundaries (enmeshed)*
____	Unreachable expectations about sexuality (rigid)
____	Sex as matter of "find out by self" (chaotic)
____	No accountability for sexual behavior (disengaged)
____	Anxiety about sexual behavior reflecting on family (enmeshed)
____	Moralistic black and white standards (rigid)
____	Emotional abandonment (disengaged)
____	Discrepancies between values and behavior (chaotic)
____	Secrecy preserved by no talk with outsiders (enmeshed)
____	Extreme efforts to control child sexual behavior (rigid)
____	Tension and distance around sexual behavior (disengaged)
____	Parental sexual unmanageability (chaotic)
____	Sexual abuse, covert and overt (enmeshed)
____	Severe punishment of sexual behavior (rigid)
____	Lack of physical of sexual affirmation (disengaged)
____	Inconsistent standards and consequences (chaotic)
____	Limited sexual privacy (enmeshed)
____	Unrealistic "models" of appropriate sexual behavior (rigid)
____	Evasion of sexual issues (disengaged)
____	Role reversals around sexual behavior (chaotic)

* Delete these codes when giving to individuals

This self-assessment procedure is then combined with other exercises such as completing a genogram on the family about addictions in the previous generation and extended family. An important aspect of treatment of any addiction is for the patients to have a keen sense of their powerlessness over their illness. This realization generates a powerful commitment to a recovery program. The family of origin is part of what was beyond the patient's control. Understanding that also lays groundwork for significant therapeutic tasks such

Figure 5: Typical Behaviors in Addict's Family of Origin

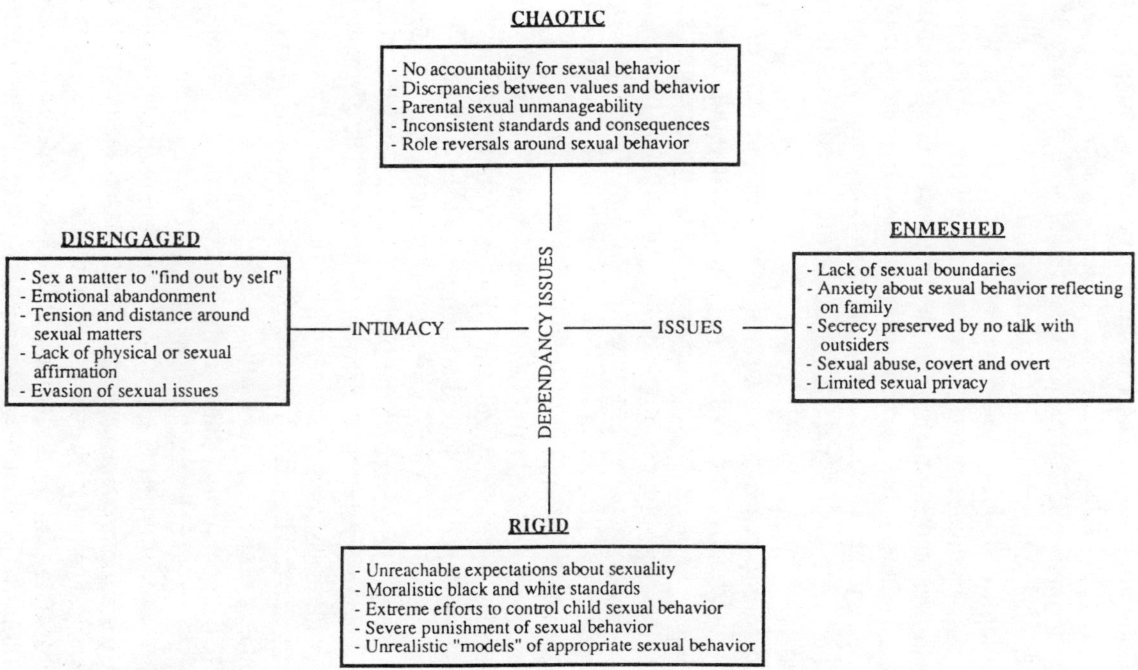

Enter checks from previous page. Are there any patterns which emerge?

as changing responses to family rules, unrealistic beliefs, and inappropriate boundaries. The Circumplex provides a map to help organize their understanding.

Participants follow this self-assessment with a brainstorming exercise on how their families of origin created sexual shame. The Circumplex Model becomes a way to think about shameful memories. For example, when a participant describes extreme physical punishment and humiliation as the response to boyhood masturbation, he can see his parents' behavior as an extension of overall family rigidity. The concept then becomes a shame reducing tool on the part of the staff because it helps the patient community gain perspective on their past.

Co-addicts repeat a similar self-assessment process on their current co-addictive behavior. They complete both a randomized checklist and then the Circumplex version of the same behaviors. Repeating the process impacts the participants in several ways. First, they become even more comfortable with the Circumplex language. Second, they can identify patterns in their current behavior which had precedents in the previous generation.

Another impact is to reduce blame. One of the most destructive dynamics in these very volatile families is blame. Given that addiction – and especially sexual addiction is a shame-based illness – it is not surprising the lengths addicts and co-addicts go to identify who is at fault. The design of the Family Week calls for participants to take responsibility for their own behavior. The Circumplex self-assessment assists this ownership process. Family members then complete exercises in which they identify specific behaviors hurtful to other members in the family.

To deepen further the family understanding of their problem, they receive back sets of *FACES III* (Olson, Portner, & Lavee, 1985) which they had completed at the beginning of Family Week. FACES III serves as a source of data-based learning for the families. First, a staff presentation contains a summary of how the group scored in aggregate and a discussion of the implications of the results. The clinical advantage to presenting a group-only set of data is that groups will shift from week to week. Comments can then be directed to the areas that particular group of family participants is working on.

In one week, for example, 23 out of 25 participants (92%) placed their family of origin in the "rigidly disengaged" or "structured disengaged" category. In their current families, only 56% remained in those categories. All the change was on the adaptability dimension, since 88% continued to be in the disengaged category. Staff could then focus on the role of isolation and alienation in addictive families.

Eventually the staff intends to be able to present a baseline of treatment families with which each group can compare scores. Participants receive their individual scores and can discuss them in light of their group scores—and eventually of all Family Week participant scores.

The process impacts the families with layers of feedback using the Circumplex as a way to structure their learning:

- feedback from other participants and family members through group exercises;
- feedback from self-assessments of their own behavior;
- feedback from both individual and group scores on their FACES III instruments; and
- feedback from staff on all of the above.

With this information, residents and Family Week participants can focus on the two primary areas of recovery, intimacy and dependency. The cohesion dimension becomes a context for appreciating that addiction and co-addiction are partly an anxiety reaction to the loss of intimacy and fundamental abandonment issues. The adaptability dimension provides a way to grasp the role of dependency—"what you can count on"—as part of the genesis of the addiction.

The Circumplex Model adds to the therapeutic community by creating a language lay people can understand and use. It serves as a concrete way to convey the message that everyone is involved. Further, shame and blame reduction occur since participants can see that it no longer is an issue of right and wrong. Rather, the Circumplex provides a model of health as something to work towards together. For many of these families in which dysfunction has generations of history, the concept of a healthy family is revolutionary and hopeful.

REFERENCES

Olson, D. H., Portner, J., and Lavee, Y. (1985). *FACES III Manual*. St. Paul, MN: Family Social Science, University of Minnesota.

Olson, D., McCubbin, H., and Associates (1983). *Families: What Makes Them Work*. Beverly Hills, CA: Sage Publications.

Carnes, P. J. (1983). *Out of the Shadows: Understanding Sexual Addiction*. Minneapolis, MN: CompCare Publications.

Carnes, P. J. (in press). *Contrary to Love: Helping the Sexual Addict*. Minneapolis, MN: CompCare Publications.

Integrating Milan Therapy and the Circumplex Model: Ecosystemic Consultation with Families and Their Helpers

James W. Maddock
Carol G. Lange

SUMMARY. Some families who come to therapists for help are already heavily involved with a variety of social services, and perhaps also with legal and/or criminal justice systems, e.g., divorcing couples with custody disputes, incest families, or families in which some members have been court-ordered for treatment. This article describes a clinical intervention process based upon an ecosystemic perspective, utilizing the Circumplex Model with a consultation team to counterbalance those aspects of the multi-helping situation which sometimes hamper family improvement. Thus therapeutic change in the family is facilitated by creating an overall balance in the larger social services ecosystem.

INTRODUCTION

The clinical program described here is organized within an ecosystemic, or ecological, framework (see e.g., Auerswald, 1968; Bateson, 1972; *Family Process*, 1982). From this perspective, the interaction between two or more systems is just as important as what goes on "inside" a given system. Every system has a context

---

James W. Maddock, PhD, is Associate Professor in the Department of Family Social Science at the University of Minnesota and practices marriage and family therapy at Meta Resources in St. Paul, MN.

Carol G. Lange, MA, is a licensed psychologist and a marriage and family therapist at Meta Resources.

which is composed of other systems and is at the same time part of the context of other systems (Bateson, 1972; Selvini-Palazzoli et al., 1980). Thus every system both has and is an ecosystem (Maddock, 1987). The autonomy/identity of a given system is determined by its own particular organization, i.e., its boundaries determine what will and what will not be included in the system. However, through its transactions with its ecosystem, a system undergoes continuous transformation of its internal structures, i.e., the relationship between its parts as they actually exist at any given point in time (Dell, 1985; Maturana, 1985; Tomm, 1986).

Because organizational boundaries define systems, they also define the nature of the interaction between systems. Since every system has an ecosystemic context (composed of other systems), its organizational identity is, in turn, a structural element of this larger ecosystem. Thus the identities of systems are interdependent subsystems within a larger ecosystem. At the same time, the configuration of these subsystems constitutes the organizational identity of the larger ecosystem (Maddock, 1987).

The concept of change implied in the ecosystemic paradigm is also contextual and dialectical. On the one hand, systems operate to stabilize themselves within their ecosystems. However, they can do this only by constantly transforming themselves via their interaction with other systems in their ecosystem (Keeney, 1983). Thus ecosystemic approaches to therapy recognize that change is ultimately a "co-evolutionary" process, a creation of the mutual efforts of therapist and client(s) within a larger ecosystem called "therapy" – something that neither can accomplish without the other (Hoffman, 1981).

The Consultation Team as an Ecosystem

Consultation has a rich history in the medical tradition, but has only recently achieved some prominence among nonmedical professionals, including family therapists (e.g., Wynne, McDaniel, & Weber, 1986). The use of a consultation team is, in part, an outgrowth of supervision and training modalities. However, in the past five years, live consultation has been extensively used in the process of therapy itself, particularly by therapists using an ecosystemic approach (cf. Bernstein, Brown, & Ferrier, 1984; Campbell & Draper, 1985; DeShazer, 1982; Hoffman, 1981; Keeney & Ross, 1985; Selvini-Palazzoli et al., 1980; Tomm, 1984a, 1984b).

The focus of consultation is upon the interaction of two or more systems and always includes a strong emphasis on the "fit" between the activities of the therapist and those of the client(s), i.e., on the nature of the therapeutic system that is co-evolving. Key to conceptualizing the operations of a team is the recognition that therapeutic interventions create a context for the clients by working at a different system level, thus providing an additional dimension of "depth" in the therapeutic endeavor (DeShazer, 1982; Keeney, 1983). In Maturana's terms, it could be said that the use of a consultation team increases the richness of opportunity for structural couplings to occur within the therapeutic system, adding new possibilities for creative transformations (Maturana, 1985; Tomm, 1986).

The Circumplex Model of Systems and Ecosystems

Within the context of an ecosystemic paradigm, the Circumplex Model serves as a useful organizing framework and heuristic device. As a bridge between theory and clinical application (Olson, 1986; Olson, Russell, & Sprenkle, 1983; Olson, Sprenkle, & Russell, 1979), the model facilitates (a) conceptualizing structural linkages (isomorphism) between the client system and systems in the helping environment, i.e., between system and ecosystem; (b) interpreting various forms of the stability/change dialectic in the client system; (c) organizing interventions from an ecosystemic perspective around the notion of "balance"; and (d) analyzing the operations of the consultation team itself in the process of formulating and implementing interventions.

We understand and apply the Circumplex Model within an ecosystemic paradigm. In our view, the cohesion dimension reflects the capacity of a system to retain its overall organizational identity as a particular system even while undergoing the transformations required to maintain itself within the context of its ecosystem. Cohesion, then, refers to those characteristics that make a particular system what it is, distinguishing it more or less clearly from other systems. Descriptions of family cohesion indicate how the family goes about maintaining its identity as a system. If "enmeshed," its structures are highly distinct from those surrounding it. Thus its boundary characteristics do not permit much interaction with other systems in its ecosystem; its stability in this ecosystem is primarily dependent upon its own structural characteristics. In contrast, if the family is "disengaged," it risks complete disintegration as a system via its ready availability for interaction with systems outside of itself. Stable structural couplings within the system are minimal, while parts of the system interlock more readily with other systems they encounter in their ecosystem. Internal boundaries and structural characteristics of the system are primarily determined externally and thus are highly vulnerable to changing conditions in the environment. "Mid-range" families are those who succeed in balancing the centripetal and centrifugal patterns of interaction to maintain organizational identity.

In our work, the adaptability dimension (represented at the extremes by absolute rigidity and chaotic randomness) reflects the relative capacity of a system to alter itself in response to transactions with other systems that are a part of this ecosystem. Descriptions of family adaptability indicate how the family goes about remaining a viable part of its ecosystem. "Rigid" systems are those that change so minimally that they cannot accommodate themselves to the full range of complex changes in their environments. At this extreme, such systems attempt to overstabilize by reacting against the changes occurring in their ecosystems. At the other extreme are "chaotic" systems that destabilize themselves by "going with" each and every ecosystemic alteration. These systems have no rules for change and thus overreact with maximal alterations in structure, even to the point of organizational disintegration as a system. For "flexibly structured" systems which fall toward the center of the Model, changes are understood as actions to preserve the overall system within its ecosystem. Thus each change by the system is balancing some other aspect of the larger ecosystem that is remaining unchanged.

The concept of balance in the Circumplex Model is considered to be both a key theoretical construct and the primary goal of our clinical work. The term "balance" is used as a highly dialectical concept, a dialectic that is implicit in both ecosystemic theory and in the Circumplex Model. It refers not simply to the tension between polar opposites, such as disengaged/enmeshed or chaotic/rigid, although it includes these. However, it also refers to the relationship between the Model's dimensions themselves. The dimensions point to the dialectical relationship of stability and change in systems (Keeney, 1983). And, most fundamentally, there is a dialectical relationship between the stability/change patterns of any given system and the stability/change patterns of other systems in its environment, i.e., its ecosystem.

In order to fully appreciate the concepts of cohesion or adaptability from an ecosystemic perspective, we must remind ourselves that every given system both has an ecosystem and is an ecosystem to other systems. Therefore the balance within a system (cohesion) and the balance of a system within its ecosystem (adaptability), as well as the balance between cohesion and adaptability, will assure the survival of the system and will determine its life course (Maddock, 1987).

In our view, the communication (facilitating) dimension of the Circumplex Model reflects a dialectical process of structural transformation that systems undergo as they adapt themselves to their changing environmental circumstances without losing the stable cohesiveness which is their organizational identity. Communication encompasses the multiple variables among which a system must strike a balance in order to insure its survival in an ever-changing ecosystem. Thus the key variable in communication patterns (both in family systems and in therapy systems) is the balancing that connects a system with its ecosystem in such a way as to contribute to the survival of both, for "if [a]creature destroys its environment, it destroys itself" (Bateson, 1972, p. 332).

Some systems mutually enhance one another through cooperation and balance takes the form of positive intersystem mutuality. For example, parents can work together to handle a childrearing problem in such a way that the child becomes appropriately cooperative with the rules of the older generation. However, sometimes the dysfunctional aspects of the family and/or the helping systems act together to produce a situation in which one system changes at the expense of another. A common example is a divorce and custody battle which leaves so much alienation that one parent may completely withdraw from meaningful contact with his/her children. Thus one system—the children's relationship with the custodial parent—may endure at the expense of another—a parental bond with the noncustodial parent.

TREATMENT GOALS

The Circumplex Model posits that there is a positive relationship between healthy family functioning and balance on the various dimensions (Olson, 1986; Olson, Russell, & Sprenkle, 1983; Olson, Sprenkle, & Russell, 1979). We have extended this principle isomorphically to include both the therapeutic system (i.e., the relationship between therapist and family) and the larger social ecosystem of the family that involves not only the therapist but other helping professionals, social agencies, and community representatives. Most important, we assume the role of the consultation team to be one of balancing—between all parts of the systems/ecosystems named above. This orientation requires that we conceptualize the efforts of the team as being "meta" to the interactions of the other systems/ecosystems. We recognize that the team, too, is only one component of a yet broader ecosystem which involves balancing operations of its own. Complex, and sometimes difficult, choices must be made. As in all ecological analysis and action, "relevant survival units" must be selected and prioritized from among the potential systems/ecosystems. Certain principles guide us in this endeavor.

Under the terms of our understanding with a staff therapist who requests work with a consultation team, top priority is typically given to the maintenance and enhancement of an effectively operating therapeutic system. Closely correlated with this is the "survival" of the two major subsystems that compose the therapeutic system—the family that entered treatment and the therapist (who is operating both as a person and in a professional role). Further down the priority list, the standing of various systems becomes more ambiguous, and systems begin to compete for the scarcer resources of the team. Biases that families ought to remain intact as families may be in tension with beliefs about the differentially perceived welfare of individual family members (cf. e.g., Hare-Mustin, 1987). Similarly, the goals and activities of various helping systems may conflict with one another (Imber-Black, 1986).

Guiding our efforts is a commitment to stretching the boundaries of the team's work to the broadest possible limits in order to create a kind of "suprasystem" to the entire system of family-plus-therapist-plus-all-other-involved-helpers. Attempting to go beyond the boundaries of these other systems, the team independently gleans information and creates opportunities for itself to interact with various subsystems in order to provide maximum opportunities for family structures to undergo positive transformations in the context of the consultation situation and beyond.

Finally, the team takes seriously the principle of ecological balance (Maddock, 1987). This reflects our conviction that family systems can best be helped to make changes through a series of proximate steps which permit structural transformations without threatening loss of organizational autonomy and identity. Therefore the helping environment should be characterized by efforts to facilitate both stability and change and by an exquisite sensitivity to the "fit" of the family within its ecosystem—a challenging task for families who have multiple problems and multiple helpers.

Purpose of Consultation

Three basic patterns of consultation team work have emerged in our clinical experience over the past seven years. The first is a situation in which the therapist feels somehow "stuck" in working with a family. The therapist's sense of progress in treatment, and perhaps the family's as well, has been lost. Under these circumstances, the purpose of the consultation is primarily to break up an impasse in the therapeutic system.

A second rationale for using a consultation team relates to an acute crisis in the therapeutic situation and/or in the life of the family. Use of a consultation team sends a clear message to the family that the therapist is taking these events seriously. Sometimes, the authority of a team is needed to provide the family with a sense of hope that significant help can be obtained quickly, implying "[Even more than] two heads are better than one."

The third use of the consultation team is to provide a powerful and flexible ecosystemic context around a multiproblem family whose many helpers may have lost focus and coordination, and who may even be in conflict with each other. The primary therapist may simply need help keeping track of the multiple influencing variables. Or he/she may seek aid in sorting out examples of role confusion and in coordinating the helping efforts. Sometimes, the therapist will present a situation in which the management efforts of various helpers have actually begun to interfere with the pace of therapeutic change set by the family. Or there may be evidence that a helping individual or agency is trying to manipulate the therapist to create a particular predetermined outcome. In these situations, the consultation team is challenged to adopt the broadest possible ecosystemic perspective and to create opportunities for structural transformations which don't threaten the survival of the clients individually or as a family. On some occasions, the outside perspective of the consultation team may require an evaluation of the relative merits of continuing treatment.

THE CLINICAL ENVIRONMENT

Team Design

The consultation process involves a team of six to eight members. It was originally designed to meet our training requirements. The arrangement proved so successful that it is now used routinely in our consultation work, even when trainees are not present.[1] Most consultations utilize two subteams, or consultation tiers. The first tier, or "microphone team," sits behind a one-way window, using a microphone that transmits to the primary therapist via an earpiece. This team is responsible for observing the interactions of the systems/ecosystems in the interview room and making interventions judged to be helpful.

Most of the interventions occur through input to the primary therapist, although the earpiece is sometimes passed to someone else in the interview room, such as a family member or one of the helping professionals. One team member is assigned as the team leader for a given session, and only that individual is permitted to use the microphone. Interventions are almost always a result of team consensus, although there are occasional spontaneous remarks offered by the team leader. Sometimes, too, the team is divided on the merits of a particular intervention and an informal vote must be taken. Practice is required to be able to offer interventions both concisely and effectively.

Two kinds of intervention are possible. The first are those offered directly to the primary therapist, without any explicit acknowledgement on his/her part. These interventions are typically "invisible" to the family and others in the interview room and may influence the direction of the session without their specific awareness. Other interventions are offered from the team explicitly to the family, to other professionals or to everyone in the interview room. These interventions are given to the therapist with the words, "The team would like the family (or whomever) to know . . ." These two kinds of interventions typically have very different effects on the therapeutic situation.

The second tier, or "homework team," usually observes the session from a separate adjoining office. This team has no direct method of input into the interview room during the session. Its task is to observe the interactions of the entire therapeutic ecosystem, including the impact that the microphone team is having on the course of the session. In addition, members of this team look ahead to the end of the session when various concluding comments, special interventions or homework assignments will be given to the family and/or other participants in the interview.

On rare occasions, a member of the homework team may leave the office, move to the adjoining room and confer with the microphone team. This is usually done when members of the second tier believe that the microphone team is missing some important information available in the therapy room or when it seems that the microphone team has inadvertently replicated some dysfunctional aspects of the family system and/or therapeutic system. These contacts are rare, for they run a risk of producing competition between the teams for control of the session.

On some occasions, a member of the consultation team spends part or all of a session in the interview room with the primary therapist. Rather than a co-therapist per se, this individual functions as a "team representative" in the interview and wears the earpiece so that she/he serves as a channel of communication from the microphone team. Again, our early rationale was training. However, it soon became apparent that the decision to send in a team member is best made on the basis of judging the nature of the ecological balance which the team can provide. For example, it is sometimes easier to have an unpopular or oppositional stand taken by the team through a representative in the room, to avoid "tainting" the primary therapist in the eyes of the family and/or the other professionals. Or a decision may be made to supply a gender balance, as when the helping professionals involved with a given family are either all male or all female. The decision to place a team member in the interview room is typically made in advance of the session, although it has occasionally occurred more spontaneously (after alerting the primary therapist).

When trainees are involved, each tier of the team is headed by a senior staff member. However, the composition of the tiers is not constant from session to session. The few disadvantages of this design are outweighed by the advantages and reflect some ecosystemic assumptions. The emphasis is not on team-building, but on the creation of a powerful yet flexibly cohesive ecosystemic context for the therapeutic situation. Varying team membership allows participants to focus primarily on their identities as parts of an ecosystem to the therapeutic system rather than on the internal structuring of their own team system. Efforts are made to keep the teams gender-balanced, though this varies according to the perceived needs of particular client situations.

Principles of Intervention

The ecosystemic approach is premised upon the evolution of a "therapeutic system" that creates a new context within which the family system can undergo various structural transformations considered to be positive, or useful, changes.

The principles that guide the creation of such a system have been elaborated most completely by teams of family therapists from Milan (Selvini-Palazzoli et al., 1978, 1980) and several commentators in North America and Europe (e.g., Campbell & Draper, 1985;

Hoffman, 1981; Penn, 1982; Tomm, 1984a, 1984b). The three principles guiding the Milan-style interview are now well-known:

1. *Hypothesizing*—the development of educated guesses, or descriptive hunches, about what is occurring in a family system; connecting various parts of the system and reflecting the system as a whole; judged as more or less useful on the basis of what information they yield.
2. *Circular Questioning*—the utilization of feedback from the family to further investigate the nature of interactions within the system; based upon the assumption that useful information is generated by drawing distinctions (Bateson, 1972) and that the meaning of behavior is derived from its context.
3. *Neutrality*—a behavioral stance by the therapist that does not take sides, but conveys an attitude of curious interest in all parts of the family system equally; assumes that everything somehow makes sense.

On the basis of these principles, a final intervention, or "prescription," is constructed at the conclusion of an interview. This detailed directive for action by family members can take various forms. It is often framed as an "experiment," since it, too, is based upon one or more previously-formulated hypotheses.

The Milan teams and others have speculated on the relative efficacy of circular interviewing and directive interventions in the promotion of therapeutic change. Given our emphasis on ecological balance as a dialectical relationship of stability and change in systems, we have taken a "both/and" stance on this issue. That is, we have concluded that "deciding which way to lean" in balancing a family system will determine the circumstances under which we will emphasize the circularity of the interview and those under which we will depend more upon the "lineality" of end-of-session directives. Here, too, a balance must be struck—both emphases are therapeutic.

Based upon a variety of hypotheses emerging from our interaction with a family and its helpers, we conceptually organize each therapeutic move, including the nature and timing of circular questions. We think of this as "strategizing" in the generic sense, rather than reflecting a commitment to a particular school of therapy. At the macroscopic level, we prioritize "relevant survival units" in the therapeutic ecosystem at which to direct questions and/or interventions.

Microscopically, decisions are continuously made about just where and how to balance the system/ecosystem, through questions, observations or directives. We have considered strategizing to be a regular part of the sequence of interactions in therapy. It is planning that serves as a bridge between hypothesizing and intervening, reflecting both circularity and neutrality, and is directed toward achieving ecological balance in the therapeutic system (which is, in turn, an ecosystem of the family system that will influence balancing operations in that system).[2]

In terms of the Circumplex Model, strategizing can be thought of as planning where to position the team on a moment by moment basis to intervene most effectively. Metaphorically, the team must decide in what quadrant and how close or distant from center the family can be "touched" so as to be positively influenced without skewing the system in a different direction to an equally dysfunctional degree, or—worse yet—to such an extreme degree that its centripetal balance is lost entirely and the system collapses. The following description will include strategizing as a central concept in our team's balancing efforts with multiproblem families and their helpers.

Session Structure

The typical two-hour consultation session is divided into five parts, structured along the lines of the Milan approach (Campbell & Draper, 1985; Tomm, 1984b). It can be summarized as follows:

I. Pre-Session Briefing (30 Minutes)
Team Focus: Information Gathering, Hypothesizing

The primary therapist meets with the consultation team to orient them toward the family and the therapeutic situation. Early in our work, we invited other helping professionals and/or agency representatives involved with the family to attend this meeting. However, we discovered that this altered the ecosystem in an unhelpful way and created feelings of competition and alignments between the team and various helpers, all of which could work to the disadvantage of the therapist and/or the family.

During this preparation period, individuals are assigned to one of the two consultative tiers, and specific decisions are made regarding procedures for microphone use. The exact nature and method of information transmittal between team and primary therapist is arranged, based upon a joint evaluation of the family's needs. Sometimes the therapist wishes to retain veto power over any communications from the team, including those addressed to the family. At other times, it is agreed that the therapist will always relinquish her/his perspective on the current course of the session and will activate any instructions received from the team (short of compromising personal or professional integrity).

Over the years we have learned that this negotiation process is very important. Much of the time the therapist is left in charge of his/her own therapeutic interventions and will organize material provided by the team. We have learned that, on a moment by moment basis, the primary therapist has a certain "feel" of the therapeutic process and how to implement it. It is as if the one-way window, while offering a broader "view" of the therapeutic system, also filters out elements which may be important to actually implementing the balancing processes of the team. However, to balance therapist input, the team has complete freedom to send messages directly to particular individuals in the interview room or to the group as a whole.

II. Clinical Interview (50-60 Minutes)
Team Focus: Strategizing, Intervening, Hypothesizing (Circularity)

Interviews with multiproblem families and their helpers typically begin with all participants introducing themselves to each other, and thus to the team. As the interview progresses, most individuals begin to participate. However, some may remain in the background, taking more of an "observer" role in a conscious or unconscious attempt to avoid scrutiny by the team. Often, circular questions connecting the withdrawn individual to the family will initiate some useful interaction sequences. Occasionally, a helping professional will succeed in remaining aloof and uncommitted to the process. When this occurs, the team must make a judgment about the influence of this stance and decide whether to include or ignore the individual in a final intervention.

III. Therapist-Team Consultation (10-20 Minutes)
Team Focus: Strategizing, (Re)hypothesizing

When the primary therapist excuses her/himself to join the consultation team for a meeting, family members and others are explicitly told that they will not be observed. They are free to talk privately, break for coffee, etc. The consultation meeting itself is carefully structured. It begins with a few moments of personal reaction from the primary therapist regarding the "feel" of the interview. This provides the therapist with an opportunity for some "ventilation" to relieve the stress of dealing with the complexities of both the family and the consultation process.

Members of the microphone team are permitted to ask questions or to make clarifications regarding the interview process. However, they are not to analyze, make further suggestions or otherwise continue the input process. After a few minutes, the homework team members have an opportunity to comment on the overall systemic process, including their views on the impact of the consultation on the family, the therapist and other participants. This is followed immediately by suggestions for follow-up interventions, homework assignments or other procedures that might be helpful.

At this point, all members of the consultation team may enter into the dialogue with the therapist. The hypotheses and ideas begin to be organized into an overall strategy for intervening. Typically, there is a "macro-strategy" plus several "micro-strategies" that emerge from the discussion. These are refined and clarified until the therapist and as many team members as possible have reached consensus on their utility and method of implementation (complete consensus is not always achieved). As the session ends, the therapist carefully rehearses the interventions to be certain that each suggested element has been included.

IV. Intervention Session (5-15 Minutes)
Team Focus: Implementation of Strategy, Data Gathering for New Hypotheses

The therapist returns to the interview room to present the intervention to the family and other participants. We have found it important for the therapist to avoid spending any length of time discussing or commenting on the consultation process, other than in ways previously decided during the consultation session. When conveyed to the family and/or the assembled professionals, each intervention is carefully labeled as to its origin. This is part of the balancing process. It permits the therapist to strategically disengage from selected elements of the intervention in order to maintain rapport with the family and/or various adjunctive treatment resources. Pleading time constraints, the therapist typically excuses the family and others in the midst of their reactions to the intervention, leaving them puzzled or even in consternation. Time is taken only to be certain that the intervention is understood – it is often written down – and then a future session is scheduled (a session that may or may not include the consultation team).

V. Postsession Debriefing (30-45 Minutes)
Team Focus: Hypothesizing (New Circular Sequence)

After the family and other helping professionals have left, the primary therapist and consultation team take the opportunity for a more leisurely analysis of the interactional process. The focus is usually on broad ecosystemic patterns, although specific features of an interview may occupy our attention. Additional hypotheses are generated, and possible strategies are entertained. If a follow-up consultation has been scheduled (two or three sessions at intervals of two to four weeks is typical, in our experience), then these hypotheses set the stage for further efforts by the team. However, feedback on the results of the intervention must be awaited.

Rarely are there postsessions in which significant conflict occurs. Such conflict is most often between team members rather than between the team and the primary therapist. The debriefing is redirected to focus on these issues. Given our ecosystemic approach and convictions about structural isomorphism (DeShazer, 1982;

Minuchin & Fishman, 1981), we typically find that the pattern of conflict within the team mirrors some interactive patterns of the family, the therapeutic situation, and/or various systems/ecosystems involved in the treatment process. An attempt is made to convert the conflict into data for further hypothesizing and analyzing in the consultative process.

CONSULTATION AS BALANCING

Case Description

The "Johnson" family [not the family's actual name] was brought in for consultation by a staff therapist. The case was referred to her because of allegations of incestuous contact between the children. However, sexual abuse per se was not a major focus of the therapy, although Mrs. Johnson joined the therapist's adult incest victims group to deal with her own history of sexual abuse as a child. The mother was a 32-year-old white female, recently divorced from a physically abusive alcoholic husband and now living alone. Mr. Johnson was not currently involved with the family, having been incarcerated for assault in a neighboring state. Physical abuse had occurred in the marriage, and the partners had separated intermittently. The marriage commenced following the discovery of Mrs. Johnson's nonmarital pregnancy when she was 17. Other than the mother's description of abuse, the only direct mention of the father by family members occurred when the two sons, ages eight and ten, invoked his name nostalgically (they had lived with him during several of the parental separations) or aggressively—"My dad will beat the shit out of those guys!"

The boys, Alan and Andrew, had both been diagnosed as "hyperactive." School adjustment was poor, including truancy and destructive behavior. Both were a grade behind in school and attended special learning classes. The boys were alleged to have been sexually abused by their 13-year-old sister, Allison, a quiet and withdrawn girl who was a marginal but not troublesome student. The mother reported having discovered the children in "some kind" of inappropriate sexual activity. It was also speculated by Mrs. Johnson that Allison may have been sexually molested by her father during one of the periods when he was living at home.

The Johnson family had contact with multiple clinical, social service and legal agencies. Mrs. Johnson was currently unemployed and living on public assistance, though she worked episodically. She appeared very bright and articulate, though unmotivated. None of the children was living at home. The daughter had been placed in a foster family on a temporary basis, and the boys were in a second foster home. Until recently, the mother had the younger boy, Andrew, living at home with her, having previously announced that he was her "favorite." However, when Andrew reported another incident of sexual contact with his sister when she was home on a visit, he was removed and placed with his brother's foster family.

The family was referred to the primary therapist for a "final try" at treatment prior to permanently removing the boys from Mrs. Johnson's custody. Despite the complexity of the case and the "set-up" nature of the referral, the therapist reported that there had been some very fruitful sessions with the entire family. She reported a noticeable improvement in the mother's parenting competencies with the boys and some evidence that Mrs. Johnson and Allison were beginning to develop a relationship appropriate for a mother and teenage daughter. However, progress was slow and representatives of the Department of Human Services were pressuring to conclude therapy (which had been in progress about four months) and to terminate parental rights. According to the therapist, part of the motivation for this appeared to be the interest of the foster family in adopting Alan, the older boy. Understandably, this put the mother into an adversarial position with the foster families, Child Protective Services and the school social worker. The case was further complicated by the fact that the protection worker's immediate supervisor had earlier served as Mrs. Johnson's personal therapist during her divorce when the children were also temporarily removed from her care (this social worker had then been employed at another community agency). The therapist reported that Mrs. Johnson was determined to "fight for her children," even though, behaviorally, she evidenced ambivalence about a continuing parental role. The Johnson family was brought to the consultation team at the point at which the therapist believed that the other professionals involved were managing the case in such a way as to impede positive changes in family interaction.

Presession Meeting

The team's first major hypothesis concerned the family itself, which appeared to operate at the Circumplex extreme of "chaotic disengagement." It is likely that the Johnsons had at one time been enmeshed, though probably also in a chaotic fashion, typical of a family in which there are incest dynamics and various expressions of violence. The involvement of multiple professionals and agencies, while supposedly directed toward helping the family (perhaps with positive results in the past), now had the effect of drawing family members toward further disengagement. While the family had perhaps earlier shown some capacity for adaptation to difficult circumstances, they now operated chaotically, and family survival was seriously threatened.

Professional systems in the family's ecosystem had assumed greater power and importance. Family members were now relating on a daily basis to systems with higher levels of cohesiveness than the biological family. Even Mr. Johnson's incarceration represented an ecosystemic variable – involvement with a "rigidly enmeshed" social system that coercively maintained his detachment from any part of the family! Simply put, "centrifugal forces" (Beavers & Voeller, 1983) rendered the Johnson family functionally powerless as a system.

Whatever may have been the family's adaptive capacity in the past was now not in evidence – except in the context of some of the sessions with the primary therapist. Passivity, lack of leadership, role shifts and reversals, and externally imposed rules had created chaos. The energies of family members were spent reacting primarily to their nonfamily contexts, e.g., Allison's adolescent struggles with a rather rigid foster mother, Mrs. Johnson's battles with Child Protective Services and the school social worker, and the like.

The family's capacity for effective communication was now nearly nonexistent. Partly, this resulted from externally imposed conditions. For example, Mrs. Johnson was often prevented from talking to her sons on the telephone because the foster parents believed it would "upset" the already difficult-to-handle boys. Other communication deficits were inherent in the family system. Appropriate communication between the generations had apparently never occurred, and much of the marital communication had consisted of verbal and nonverbal violence.

Ironically, though not surprisingly, the professional ecosystem surrounding the Johnson family was becoming more cohesive in its interface with family members. Aid to individuals was supplied at the expense of the family as a system. And, increasingly, various workers were purposely joining forces in opposition to the parenting efforts of the mother. Shortly before the consultation session, the primary therapist learned indirectly and accidentally that the protection supervisor was coordinating efforts by the foster family and other child workers to develop a plan for formal adoption of the boys. This was based on her conviction that therapy could be of no further benefit to this family. Her plan had begun to be implemented without the knowledge of either the mother or the family therapist. Various advocacy and helping services had successfully adapted themselves individually and collectively to the Johnson family system, assuring the survival of their respective roles and plans. Substantially more communication now occurred between family workers (except the family therapist) than between members of the family.

Thus the team's second general hypothesis was that therapy was "stuck" because the primary therapist's efforts to work with the family as a cohesive system were being countered by the efforts of the surrounding helping systems to dismantle the family. The family as a "relevant survival unit" in the helping ecosystem had been jeopardized. Clearly, the foster families and at least some of the involved professionals had already determined that disengaging members from the family unit was necessary to assure their individual survival.

On the basis of these hypotheses, the team began to strategize a variety of balancing influences which might, on the one hand, serve the interests of the therapeutic contract while at the same time testing the Johnson family's capacity to operate in a more "mid-range" fashion. The primary therapist requested specific help from the team in assessing the capacities of the mother to conduct appropriate parenting behaviors. She also expressed a desire for aid in interacting creatively rather than oppositionally with the various other service professionals (oppositional interaction only mirroring the behavior of family members, thereby adding to the cohesion of the other helpers as a system against the family). Finally, the therapist asked the team to carefully observe the behavior of the various other professionals and of foster family members, to see whether her impressions were valid or might result from some unconscious feelings of competition and performance pressure related to her designation as "the last resort" prior to dissolution of the family.

Team Clinical Interview

Eleven people attended the session. In addition to the four members of the Johnson family, included were the daughter's (group) therapist, a school social worker, the child protection worker and her supervisor, both of the boys' foster parents and the daughter's foster mother. Mrs. Johnson had also requested that her attorney be permitted to attend. However, the primary therapist had refused this request in the belief that it might increase the antagonistic atmosphere of the session. Team members expressed concern about the lack of a specific advocate for the mother and also for the gender imbalance of the session, since all of the agency representatives were female.

Therefore, it was decided that the primary therapist would be joined in the interview by a male consultation team member, who would wear the earpiece that would link him to the microphone team. This decision was based upon an underlying strategy in which the team would make its in-session interventions in a clear and assertive style and would focus them on heightening family cohesion. Thus the primary therapist would have the opportunity to assume a "mid-range" position in the event of conflict between the helpers and the family or between the helpers and the team.

With everyone together, the therapist solicited impressions of the family's current functioning as a way of helping her assess the impact of the therapy. As anticipated, nonfamily members focused most of their remarks on the individual with whom they were involved and took the position that family interactions were only disruptive and negative. Several explicitly stated that the children were better off without "interference" from their mother. Mrs. Johnson was naturally defensive. With occasional assistance from the therapist she was able to state that she was not being given ample opportunity to interact with her children in an appropriate parental fashion without encountering obstacles from either the foster parents or the child protection workers. The therapist encouraged her to document specific concerns, and she did so persuasively (from the team's point of view).

In the context of the interview, the mother was able to be articulate and reasonable, becoming argumentative only once. During the session, considerable hostility surfaced between Allison and her foster mother, particularly in response to the woman's disparaging remarks about Mrs. Johnson as a parent. Both boys were atypically quiet, apparently as a result of previous orders given them by the foster father. Based on observations during the session, the consultation team hypothesized that the boys' foster family represented a system at the opposite extreme on the Circumplex Model, i.e., rigidly enmeshed. The foster parents obviously prided themselves on their ability to keep Alan and Andrew "under control" more successfully than Mrs. Johnson.

The behavior of other participants varied, though there was a consistent underlying theme of skepticism and disapproval. The foster mother in Allison's household was quietly dogmatic about how "things have to be." The school social worker was explicitly critical and patronizing of Mrs. Johnson. The child protection workers were primarily suspicious and defensive. Only the daughter's therapist was noncommittal, occasionally asking clarifying questions.

Several major balancing strategies were utilized by the microphone team during the interview. Its spokesman in the session was directed to concentrate on facilitating an evaluation by Mrs. Johnson of the help she was receiving from the foster families and agencies while aiding her in ignoring or deflecting (without hostility) the critical judgments of her by the others. This approach was based on the team's conviction that this kind of interaction pattern would be familiar to those assembled in the room. However, this dynamic would be re-focused in a different direction, i.e., evaluating the adequacy of the helping ecosystem rather than Mrs. Johnson's competence as a parent.

In addition, the team sought to model cohesiveness by framing virtually all of its interventions in terms of "the team" rather than reflecting divisions within the team or oppositional stances (both of which can sometimes be useful when working with enmeshed families). Finally, the team sought to empower Mrs. Johnson as a parent and to reinforce intergenerational boundaries. This was done by finding ways to support the validity of her perceptions, when appropriate, and by directing that the children "take a break" and leave the interview room when certain details of their mother's past life and current personality characteristics began to be discussed. Most of the team's directives were offered in a reasonable but authoritative manner by its spokesman. Occasionally, however, the team took issue with observations of the foster parents or helping professionals that were made at Mrs. Johnson's expense. This permitted the primary therapist to be "moderate" on a number of matters and even to mediate between opposing points of view such that her neutrality in the ecosystem was reinforced and her flexibility thereby increased.

Several more specifically-focused interventions were also made in an attempt to aid the family's efforts to behave less extremely and also to maintain therapy as a balancing variable in this conflictual ecosystem. An example can be found in an incident involving the daughter: In response to Allison's complaint that she had been having considerable conflict with her foster mother just as she formerly had with her mother, the team (through its spokesman) complimented her for sacrificing some of her own happiness by living away from home and for helping the family by having some of her normal adolescent conflicts with someone other than her mother.

Carefully worded in advance, the compliment was offered to

(a) diffuse some of the conflict between the biological and foster mothers by putting them on the same side of the "generation gap"; (b) "normalize" the daughter's perception of her conflictual interactions with adults by reframing both their uniqueness and their purpose; (c) suggest the notion of a coalition rather than a conflict between Allison and her biological mother; and (d) subtly embed in all participants the idea that current events were leading to an eventual reunification of the family. This sort of intervention has been found useful by other therapists as a paradoxical means of dealing with disruptive behavior of adolescents (cf. DeShazer, 1982; Haley, 1976, 1980; Madanes, 1981; Papp, 1983; Selvini-Palazzoli et al., 1978; Weeks & L'Abate, 1982). Our consultation team conceptualizes such interventions in terms of balance – reducing the artificially-inflated importance of the behavior in the system, building meaning-systems between detached family members, restoring appropriate control previously lost by the parental generation, and the like.

Therapist/Team Consultation

Immediately following the interview, consultation team members shared their reactions to the session, largely confirming the primary therapist's impression that most of the helpers had given up on Mrs. Johnson and were working, consciously or unconsciously, against the effort at family therapy. In their attempts to counter the family's original enmeshment, the helping group had unwittingly formed an even more tightly enmeshed ecosystem. This extreme stance was influencing the family in such a way that they were moving from chaotic enmeshment to equally chaotic disengagement. The homework team believed that the structure of the session had enabled the mother to be more adult-like in her behavior and had helped minimize the intrafamilial role reversals that generally characterized this family. Further, it was felt that the direct competition between the primary therapist and the child protection workers had been somewhat reduced. The tension of opposition had been redirected away from the mother and helpers toward the interaction between the helpers and the consultation team.

Feelings of anger and frustration were voiced by members of the microphone team, who acknowledged that it was difficult to maintain a sense of balance in their interventions. Team members also acknowledged ambivalence about whether Mrs. Johnson could adequately handle the responsibility for parenting all three children. Though presented as a "united front" during the interview, opinions were actually divided about the best course of action for the family. It was noted that the team's current experience was probably isomorphic to the divisions among the various helpers at the start of their work with the Johnson family. However, the overall conclusion was positive: during the interview itself, both the family and the helping ecosystem had operated in more of a mid-range style on both cohesiveness and adaptability dimensions. The more extreme interactive processes had been successfully avoided.

The following directives were devised by the homework team for the session participants:

1. Mrs. Johnson was instructed to arrange weekend home visits for both of the boys together, rather than continuing to invite only her younger son. Plainly a balancing move directed at family cohesiveness, this action was predicated on the hypothesis that both boys had untapped resources for relationship building with each other as well as with their mother.
2. The boys' foster parents were instructed to arrange the visitations between Mrs. Johnson and her sons in the home's upstairs living room rather than in the family room with other foster family members and the TV set. This was proposed as a way to lessen the fragmenting forces that the foster parents were able to mount.
3. Mrs. Johnson and her daughter's foster mother were instructed to meet and agree on the rules that would govern Allison's behavior. It was specified that neither of them could change these rules without consulting the other, and a weekly phone call was suggested as a means to check progress on the application of the rules at each household.
4. Mrs. Johnson and the child protection worker were both instructed to privately make lists of their expectations of each other. As a balancing variable, this intervention was designed to give the mother the legitimate power to have certain expec-

tations about the nature of her interaction with the child protection system. Further, it was an attempt to concretize both the level and kind of expectations held by the worker so that she and her supervisor could not maintain impossible standards for the family. The previous lack of specificity seemed to provoke in Mrs. Johnson a kind of "crazy" reaction which led to a sense of hopelessness about her capacity to parent. In addition, the team requested that the child protection worker make a second list of her expectations for family therapy. This balancing action was designed to further empower the therapist within the helping system since she, like the mother, was constrained by a diffuse form of accountability under the label of therapy as "a last resort."

5. Finally, the daughter was instructed to continue to rebel and be difficult so that both her mother and foster mother had the opportunity to test the effectiveness of their agreed-upon rules and enforcement procedures. This paradoxical injunction made the daughter a contributor to the cooperative efforts between the two women, as well as to the appropriate parenting endeavors of the adult generation.

It was suggested that the primary therapist return to the interview room with an attitude of slight confusion and disorientation in response to the prescriptions so that she could more readily be dissociated from the team. We believed that this would permit the helping ecosystem to reduce oppositional reactions and to adapt in a more cohesive fashion to the implications of the directives.

Intervention Session

The team's comments and directives were presented to the participants by the team representative rather than by the primary therapist. The therapist spoke little, other than to clarify or express support. Reactions of the participants were as follows: quiet but obvious satisfaction on the mother's part; confusion on the part of her daughter; boisterous expressions of pleasure by the boys that they would get to visit their mother together; silence on the part of the foster parents; considerable consternation was evident in the child protection workers and social worker.

It was obvious that some helpers wanted to protest. However, the comments and directives were so reasonable and were couched in such commonsense professional language that opposition was difficult without risk of appearing foolish or obstructive. The most negative thing said was that "There's no evidence that this will help," a sentiment with which the primary therapist immediately agreed, followed quickly by an expression of her own willingness to "give it a try."

The primary therapist then moved to end the session. Immediately, the protection workers requested a private meeting with the therapist, who pleaded tardiness to a subsequent session and arranged for a later phone conversation instead. Such an attempt had been anticipated by the consultation team, who advised that, for the time being, helpers meet only when Mrs. Johnson was present, in order to reduce her distrust of the helping system and to counteract the indirect communication that characterized both the family and its ecosystem. Prior to the participants leaving, arrangements were made for another session in which Mrs. Johnson, the child protection workers and the primary therapist would meet to review the results of the directives, utilizing the consultation team at their option.

Postsession Debriefing

At the ensuing meeting (which was, in fact, brief due to time constraints), the primary therapist expressed relief at not having to individually carry the burden of responsibility she had felt for "keeping the family together." In addition, she reported that she found the session helpful in providing her with an opportunity to gain a greater understanding of the viewpoints and frustrations of the foster parents and the various other helpers. She thought she had been able to interact more reasonably with them, i.e., in a more balanced fashion. The team representative, on the other hand, reported feeling like the "bad guy" during the intervention session. At the same time, he expressed satisfaction at observing the impact of the team's interventions on the overall ecosystem. Everyone present agreed that the mother's behavior in the interview had been quite exemplary, considering her history of dysfunctional interactions with her children and with the various helping agencies.

It was hypothesized that some compensatory efforts would possibly be made by one or more of the professional helpers – most likely the child protection workers – if they recognized any signs of "success" in the therapeutic effort. The family's attempts to be more cohesive were now threatening the enmeshment of the helping system. The consultation team briefly discussed possible responses by the primary therapist to avoid the polarization that seemed to characterize so much of the work with the Johnson family. Finally, emphasis was placed on maintaining the mother's orientation toward concrete behavioral change in line with her own wishes and expectations rather than permitting her to fall back on emotional complaints and victim-like responses to the overall situation.

Case Follow-Up and Evaluation

> The Johnson family and their professional helpers responded in several ways to a total of three sessions with the consultation team. Our prediction that the child protection workers would attempt to mitigate the effects of the consultation proved to be accurate. However, this attempt did not appear to be successful, thanks to skillful handling by the primary therapist. She managed to avoid lengthy phone discussions over the two weeks prior to a subsequent consultation session. Thus the protection worker was forced to devise her lists of expectations for Mrs. Johnson and for the family therapy. This marked the first time that the therapeutic effort had been organized around possible outcomes rather than simply referred to as a time period whose implied passage would lead to termination of Mrs. Johnson's parental rights.
>
> Not surprisingly, Mrs. Johnson particularly appeared to benefit from the consultation team sessions. The therapist commented that she grew "bigger" in the system as she no longer engaged in continuous childish battles with the professionals. The developing crisis with protective services was averted, and the overall helping effort gradually shifted in the direction of once again supporting and working with the fam-

ily as a unit. Allison's behavior also moderated in response to greater cooperation between her mother and foster parents. Visits between Mrs. Johnson and her sons generally proceeded more smoothly, although both boys continued to manifest some behavior problems.

For the first time, discussions began among the various helpers about the meaning and significance of Mr. Johnson's role in the family. His previous behavior was discussed openly. His current status and possible future contacts with his sons were considered, since all of these variables appeared to play a role in their behavioral outbursts. Some plans actually began to be made for his anticipated return to the city (it was learned that he had been through chemical dependency treatment and would soon be released on parole).

Following the second consultation session, one important change occurred whose effects could not be immediately assessed: the two boys were moved to a new foster home at the instigation of the foster parents. Difficult behavior was cited as the reason. However, the consensus of others was that the boys seemed to be easier to manage than in the past. The primary therapist and team speculated that perhaps changes in rules, combined with greater competition from their mother and the recognition that immediate possibilities for adopting Alan had been eliminated—all contributed to discouraging the foster family from further efforts with these boys.

EFFECTS AND OUTCOMES OF CONSULTATION

The initial impact of the consultation team on families and their helpers is often one of consternation. Sometimes this reaction represents genuine confusion. Recently, the father of a suicidal 16-year-old girl lingered behind other family members leaving the interview room after a team assignment. He whispered urgently to the therapist, "Is this for real or are you just trying to set her (the daughter) up?" The primary therapist responded by looking directly at the father and replying in an equally earnest manner, "I know the team is very serious in its efforts to help us with their suggestions."

Occasionally, the confusion is accompanied by hostility. Some participants have been heard to mutter in disgust at a particular directive from the team or to respond with hostility to a particular line of circular questioning. A small number of participants feel "gypped" by the team experience, apparently thinking that the team has misunderstood them or believing that the team's efforts have failed to provide an immediate and complete solution to their problems. In either case, the team always takes full responsibility for the dissatisfaction of any clients, attempting to further empower the work of the primary therapist.

Viewed from the perspective of the Circumplex Model and the principle of ecological balance, the team's impact often represents an interesting paradox. Although directed toward balancing the family and/or its therapeutic ecosystem by encouraging mid-range behaviors, the team's interventions sometimes seem "extreme" to family members or other participants. This is because they are occurring at a different level of systemic/ecosystemic operation and are thereby able to be "noticed" by family members who are unaware of some of the extreme behaviors occurring within the boundaries of their own system, e.g., suicide attempts, abusive and/or violent outbursts, autistic communication, outrageous fantasies about the nature of family life. In a sense, then, change begins to occur as soon as the team forms a more flexible and extreme ecosystem around the therapeutic system and the family's behavior is reframed as more functional and meaningful, therefore somewhat more "normal" (DeShazer, 1982; Keeney, 1983; Selvini-Palazzoli et al., 1978; Watzlawick, Weakland, & Fisch, 1974; Weeks & L'Abate, 1982). This is an example of the increase in adaptability of a family system in response to the balancing interventions of the team as ecosystem.

Sometimes there are dramatic and immediate changes in family interaction patterns following a consultation team session. A couple may return home and begin to talk meaningfully about issues never before discussed. A rebellious adolescent may become docile and cooperative. Former spouses involved in longstanding custody disputes may begin working cooperatively on decisions regarding their children. Occasionally, the consultation sessions trigger a family crisis, sending things in a new and potentially more useful direction. More often, of course, changes are noticeable but gradual. Most of the effects appear within the context of the ongoing work with the primary therapist. This is particularly true with multiproblem families for whom therapy is one system within a larger ecosystem of treatment and/or management. Therapeutic efforts may have a new image of seriousness and respect among associated professionals such as attorneys or social service workers. Occasionally, a major change in therapeutic direction results, or new modalities of treatment are attempted. Rarely, is therapy itself terminated.

A small number of families get "hooked" on the consultation team process in such a way that it works to the disadvantage of the primary therapist. This is especially true when certain kinds of changes occur rapidly following a session. Clients begin to believe too much in the "magic" of the consultation effort, fostering passivity on their parts and perhaps also placing the team into a maladaptive "performance anxiety" mode. This is one of the reasons why we do not use consultation teams on a routine basis except in the context of our training program. Even then, we rely on a rotational system.

"Team-addicted" clients can be rewarding to work with; they enjoy performing for and with the consultants. For a time, a new and powerful ecosystem is formed. If the consultation team members and the primary therapist know how to use this dynamic fruitfully and when to "uncouple" from the family and the helping ecosystem, then important therapeutic gains can be made. However, there is a genuine risk of the consultation team being coopted into the helping ecosystem in such a way (via structural isomorphism) that the team, too, is rendered relatively powerless in the therapeutic process. This occurs, for example, when the team becomes merely one more competing element in the helping environment, thereby increasing the extremes of opposition and hindering ecological balance. The team's overall commitment to balance enables it to counteract the extremes of either cohesion or adaptability as well as to avoid the polarization of these dimensions to each other.

CONCLUSIONS

Overall evidence suggests that the consultation team effort does indeed produce new, and usually helpful, balances in both the family system and the therapeutic ecosystem. The very fact that families on whom some helping professionals have given up hope continue to endure as family units is considered evidence that the team's efforts can facilitate cohesiveness. Similarly, the report that therapy often takes new and more fruitful directions following consultations implies progress in adaptability, i.e., the family "uses therapy" more effectively.

Results are more ambiguous when assessing the impact of consultations on the broader helping ecosystem. Some data is positive and impressive. Certain judges, attorneys and court service workers have been impressed enough to support the team in working with entire families on a court-referred case. Some psychiatrists and other mental health professionals have joined in implementing strategies devised by the team to alter interaction between family members.

However, some negative outcomes also occur. Following a consultation, a few helping professionals and/or agencies become extremely competitive with the primary therapist. The team's efforts may constitute a threat to their roles, and we may be unsuccessful in maintaining sufficient distance or in balancing the entire ecosystem so that consultation can be experienced as beneficial for all concerned. Occasionally, a helping professional has become convinced that a subsequent family event, such as a suicide attempt by an adolescent or a drinking binge by an alcoholic spouse, has been "caused" by what the consultation team did—or, more frequently, failed to do.

Most of the negative outcomes simply take the form of pessimism: "It didn't do any good." Perhaps these professionals, like the families, are expecting therapeutic miracles or instant cures. Perhaps they simply see consultation teams as inefficient. They may even fail to recognize when genuine changes do occur, and therefore the team does not get its fair share of the credit (though the team believes that the family deserves the credit for any positive changes).

On balance, the results have been highly positive for the client units and for the primary therapists involved, even though more equivocal for the professional ecosystem. This pattern fits our stated priorities, in that the consultations are directed primarily at the therapeutic system (with clients and therapists as the most important subsystems) and only secondarily at the multi-helper ecosystem.

Our consultation team clinical program has not used formal evaluative research instruments. Elsewhere in this volume, data are cited that support the shift in family functioning on cohesion and adaptability dimensions of the Circumplex Model as a result of therapeutic effort. We believe that the consultation team is a successful extension of that effort, similarly aiding families in successfully balancing their own systems for survival, thus helping to ensure their viability within a broader ecosystem.

NOTES

1. Like other consultation teams, ours has evolved in the context of a clinical training program in a freestanding institute specializing in marital and family therapy. Individuals attending a one-day-per-week clinical practicum in systemic therapy become team members along with senior staff. The majority of trainees have Master's or Doctoral degrees in clinical disciplines. A 2-1/2 hour time period is alloted each week to the consultation team experience, in order to provide trainees with an opportunity for participant-observation in systemic therapy. Clinical facilities include three large offices with comfortable furniture, all interconnected by one-way windows and sound systems. A two-way sound system permits observation of events in the interview room, plus the capacity to pass information to the therapist and/or a selected family member. Naturally, extensive ethical and legal precautions are taken to assure client confidentiality, informed consent and related procedural matters.

2. While this article was being written, Karl Tomm (1987) published an article in which a similar notion of strategizing is advocated as a "fourth guideline" in systemic interviewing. Tomm defines strategizing as "the therapist's (or team's) cognitive activity in evaluating the effects of past actions, constructing new plans of action, anticipating the possible consequences of various alternatives, and deciding how to proceed at any particular moment in order to maximize therapeutic utility" (p. 6). He further outlines a series of "conceptual postures" which can organize the therapist's sequencing of moves in the course of an interview.

Tomm's implicit use of a balance principle is reflected in his observations on the importance of not leaning too far in either direction between neutrality—an acceptance of "what is"—and strategizing—a commitment to "what ought to be" (p. 10).

REFERENCES

Auerswald, E. H. (1968). "Interdisciplinary versus ecological approach." *Family Process, 7*, 205-215.

Bateson, G. (1972). *Steps to an ecology of mind*. New York: Ballantine Books.

Beavers, W. R., & Voeller, M. N. (1983). "Family models: Comparing and contrasting the Olson circumplex model with the Beavers system model." *Family Process, 22*, 85-98.

Berstein, R. M., Brown, E. M., & Ferrier, M. J. (1984). "A model for collaborative team processing in brief systemic family therapy." *Journal of Marital and Family Therapy, 10*, 151-156.

Campbell, D., & Draper, R. (1985). *Applications of systemic family therapy: The Milan approach*. London: Grune and Stratton.

Dell, P. F. (1985). "Understanding Bateson and Maturana: Toward a biological foundation for the social sciences." *Journal of Marital and Family Therapy, 11*, 1-20.

de Shazer, S. (1982). *Patterns of brief family therapy*. New York: The Guilford Press.

Haley, J. (1976). *Problem-solving therapy*. San Francisco: Jossey-Bass.

Haley, J. (1980). *Leaving home*. New York: McGraw-Hill.

Hare-Mustin, R. T. (1987). "The problem of gender in family therapy theory." *Family Process, 26*, 15-33.

Hoffman, L. (1981). *Foundations of family therapy*. New York: Basic Books.

Imber-Black, E. (1986). "Families, larger systems and the wider social context." *Journal of Strategic and Systemic Therapies, 5*(4), 29-35.

Keeney, B. P. (1983). *Aesthetics of change*. New York: The Guilford Press.

Keeney, B. P., & Ross, J. M. (1985). *Mind in therapy: Constructing systemic family therapies*. New York: Basic Books, Inc.

Madanes, C. (1981). *Strategic family therapy*. San Francisco: Jossey-Bass.

Maddock, J. W. (1987). "Dialectical ontology: Exploration of a theoretical basis for family therapy" (submitted for publication).

Maturana, H. R. (1985). "The biology of cognition," presentation at a conference on "Gregory Bateson: The pattern which connects." College of St. Benedict, St. Joseph, MN, May 5-7.

Minuchin, S., & Fishman, H. C. (1981). *Family therapy techniques*. Cambridge: Harvard University Press.

Olson, D. H. (1986). "Circumplex model VII: Validation studies and FACES III." *Family Process, 25*, 337-351.

Olson, D. H., Russell, C. S., & Sprenkle, D. H. (1983). "Circumplex model of marital and family systems: VI. Theoretical update." *Family Process, 22*, 69-83.

Olson, D. H., Sprenkle, D. H., & Russell, C. S. (1979). "Circumplex model of marital and family systems: I. Cohesion and adaptability dimensions, family types, and clinical applications." *Family Process, 18*, 3-15.

Papp, P. (1983). *The process of change*. New York: The Guilford Press.

Penn, P. (1982). "Circular questioning." *Family Process, 21*, 267-280.

Selvini-Palazzoli, M., Boscolo, L., Cecchin, G., & Prata, G. (1978). *Paradox and counterparadox: A new model in the therapy of the family in schizophrenic transaction*. New York: Jason Aronson.

Selvini-Palazzoli, M., Boscolo, L., Cecchin, G., & Prata, G. (1980). "Hypothesizing-circularity-neutrality: Three guidelines for the conductor of the session." *Family Process*, 193-12.

Tomm, K. (1984a). "One perspective on the Milan systemic approach: Part I. Overview of development, theory, and practice." *Journal of Marital and Family Therapy, 10*, 113-125.

Tomm, K. (1984b). "One perspective of the Milan systemic approach: Part II. Description of session format, interviewing style and interventions." *Journal of Marital and Family Therapy, 10*, 253-271.

Tomm, K. (1986). "On incorporating the therapist in a scientific theory of family therapy." *Journal of Marital and Family Therapy, 12*, 373-378.

Tomm, K. (1987). "Interventive interviewing: Part I. Strategizing as a fourth guideline for the therapist." *Family Process, 26*, 3-13.

Watzlawick, P., Weakland, J., & Fisch, R. (1974). *Change: Principles of problem formation and problem resolution*. New York: W. W. Norton & Company, Inc.

Weeks, G. R., & L'Abate, L. (1982). *Paradoxical psychotherapy: Theory and practice with individuals, couples, and families*. New York: Brunner/Mazel.

Wynne, L. C., McDaniel, S. H., & Weber, T. T. (Eds.). (1986). *Systems consultation: A new perspective for family therapy*. New York: The Guilford Press.

Cross-Generational Coalitions, Discrepant Perceptions and Family Functioning

Howard L. Barnes

SUMMARY. Family therapists rely upon the comments and perspectives of individual family members to gain insight into family functioning. Frequently, each family member reports his/her own unique view of the family life, leaving it up to the therapist to sort out the discrepancies among the varying perspectives. Such perceptual discrepancy can be confusing and misleading to therapists as they try to develop a picture of family functioning. This study used the three dimensions of the Circumplex Model of Marital and Family Systems, and the reports of three family members to identify the characteristics of families where there was a high level of perceptual discrepancy. Perceptual patterns were also used to define and examine the effects of parent-child coalitions. The amount of discrepancy was found to be related to marital and family satisfaction, communication between spouses and between parents and children. Although detrimental to the entire family, the negative impact of cross-generational coalitions registered most strongly on the marital dyad.

As therapists work with families and seek to understand how they function, their efforts are frequently hampered by the differences between the reports provided by individual family members. When asked about the nature of their family, each member may give a different description. While some family members may largely agree, others may report very different perspectives of family func-

---

Howard L. Barnes, PhD, is Assistant Professor, Human Development and Family Studies, Kansas State University, Manhattan, KS 66506.

The author wishes to thank David H. Olson for his guidance, assistance and encouragement to undertake and complete this study.

tioning. For example, some family member(s) may portray the family as close-knit, calm and relatively conflict free while another may report it to be rife with conflict and anger, which periodically boil over at unpredictable moments. A third member may describe the family group as "loners," each individual going his/her own way without interference from the others. Which view more accurately describes this family? What is to be made of the discrepancy, what does it mean? Is it significant when some members share similar perspectives of their family while others view it quite differently? How do these perceptual coalitions and discrepancies relate to the functioning of the family as a system?

One challenge to professionals working with these families is how to represent, describe, or characterize families as units when members disagree among themselves regarding the nature of their family life. For many years professionals naively relied upon the descriptions provided by a single family member. This approach was based on two assumptions. The first assumed the etiology of emotional problems had an individual rather than a relationship base. Second, when family problems were at issue, the assumption was made that individual reports reliably represented the entire family. The fallacy of these basic assumptions came into question when therapists recognized (1) the importance of including multiple components (members and their relationships) of the family system in the definition of family problems, (2) that important differences existed in the perceptions of individual family members, and (3) that these perceptions were an important component in the treatment process.

Perceptual differences among family members have been discussed in the family literature for a number of years. Safilios-Rothschild noted that if "we are interested in studying the family as a dynamic interacting unit, we have no choice but to conceptualize this unit as consisting of many points of view—as many as there are family members" (1969:295). In discussing her concept of "his" and "her" marriages, Jessie Bernard (1972) suggested the perceptual disparity may be so great in some marriages that the spouses conduct their marital interactions based on very different assumptions regarding the nature of their marital relationship.

Differing perceptions are an integral facet of family life. According to Larson, "there is no necessary reason for assuming that differential perception is not an aspect of family reality . . . perceptions of reality *are* reality to the perceiver" (1974:124). Hess and Handel similarly underscored the importance of the individual "images" when each family member "comes to have a private transcript of their common life, record through his own emotions and individual experiences" (1974:1). Thus, the perceptions of the individual family member form his/her representation of the meaning of "family."

What is the impact of these individualized views on the functioning of the family system? Based on their clinical observations, a survey of therapists indicated perceptual discrepancies among family members were a major contributor to tension in family relationships (Craddock, 1980). More specifically, the work of Satir (1964) and Bell and Bell (1982) suggested that perceptual disparity at the spousal level has a greater negative impact on family functioning than discrepancies between the parent and child generations.

Recently, the point has been made that individual's perceptions likely represent a mix of unique perceptions as well as perceptions shared by or common to other family members (Schumm, Barnes, Bollman, Jurich, & Milliken, 1985). This suggests the need to examine the patterns of perceptual similarity in families as well as the patterns and amount of discrepancy among family members.

The purpose of this study was to assess discrepant perceptions along the Circumplex Model dimensions of cohesion, adaptability and communication, to examine these discrepancies as indicators of coalitions within families, and to empirically test the impact of discrepant perceptions on family functioning. Discrepancy is defined as the disagreement or incongruence in the perceptions of family members as reflected in differences among the self-descriptions, ratings, or scores of individual family members.

FAMILY COMMUNICATION AND DISCREPANCY

The acceptance of communication as central to the well-being of family systems is evidenced by its prominence in the Circumplex Model (Olson, Russell, & Sprenkle, 1983) as well as other theoretical models of family functioning (Epstein, Bishop, & Levin, 1978; Lewis, Beavers, Gossett, & Phillips, 1976), and in enrichment programs aimed at improving family interaction and satisfaction with marital and family relationships (Wampler, 1982; Garland, 1981; Jacobson, 1978; LeVant, 1978).

Spousal communication is widely accepted as one of the most critical elements related to marital quality and satisfaction (Barnes, Schumm, Jurich, & Bollman, 1984; Olson, Russell, & Sprenkle, 1980; Lewis & Spanier, 1979). Parent-adolescent communication has been shown to be related to social and cognitive development in children (Grotevant & Cooper, 1983; Cooper, Grotevant, Moore, & Condon, 1982; Steinberg, 1981; Steinberg & Hill, 1978), and to general family functioning (Barnes & Olson, 1985).

Communication is the means through which perceptual differences among family members are reduced or maintained. Effective communication develops shared meanings among family members, thus reducing perceptual discrepancies. The result of ineffective communication patterns or a lack of communication among family members is an increase in the level of discrepancy in their perceptions of their relationships.

The marital relationship is the core or central relationship in the family (Olson, McCubbin et al., 1983; Campbell, Converse, & Rodgers, 1976). Satir noted, "The marital relationship is the axis around which all other family relationships are formed. The mates are the 'architects' of the family" (1964:1). Given the centrality of the marital relationship, discrepancy in the marriage would be expected to have a larger impact on the family than discrepancy between the generations. Also, it is developmentally appropriate for adolescents to be involved in a process of differentiating from their families. This process of differentiation often includes the redefining of relationships within the family as the adolescent attempts to psychologically distance him/herself from the family unit and test out his/her own identity as separate and distinct from the family. Given this, a greater discrepancy between the adolescent and his/her parents(s) would be expected as a natural part of differentiation.

TYPES OF FAMILY DISCREPANCY

This study examined the responses of three members, husband/father, wife/mother, and an adolescent child, in each of the families sampled. With reports from three different family members, there are at least four possible patterns of discrepancy: (1) no or *low dis-*

crepancy; (2) *spousal discrepancy* or discrepancy between the parents with the adolescent's responses fairly closely aligned with one of the parents (this could also be called *within generation* discrepancy); (3) *intergenerational discrepancy*, discrepancy between the generations with the two parents in relatively close agreement; and (4) *high discrepancy* in which all three family members are discrepant in their perceptions.

One aim of this study was to contrast families with high discrepancy and families with low levels of discrepancy, and then to examine the relative impact of within generation (or spousal) discrepancy versus intergenerational discrepancy, in terms of perceptual coalitions within families.

Another concern of this study was the impact of location or source of discrepancy. Distinctions were made between those families where the family discrepancy was primarily due to spousal differences and those where the major contributor to the family discrepancy was the difference between the generations. Specific types of generational and spousal discrepancy were examined. Discrepancy was defined as the degree or amount of disagreement or incongruence in the perceptions of family members.

There are several possible explanations for the existence of discrepancies. They may be due to different interpretations or reflect different perspectives as a result of the different developmental levels of the respondents. This would suggest larger discrepancies could be expected between the generations than between spouses. *Thus parent-child discrepancies would be expected to exceed spousal discrepancies*.

In addition to differing developmental levels, it is also possible the respondents utilize different comparators in formulating their responses. One spouse may respond in comparison to how their relationship used to be; how they viewed their own family of origin; or in comparison to other families they have observed. The other spouse may use their own family as the basis for comparison. For example, when asked to indicate their level of agreement with a statement such as, "Family members feel close to each other," the wife may think, this is not as true in her marriage as it was earlier. Using the history of her own marriage as the comparator, she would naturally be expected to express some disagreement with this statement. In contrast, the husband may use his family of origin experience as a comparator. He may perceive his current relationship to be much closer than what he experienced in his family of origin and thus would indicate some degree of agreement with the statement. Adolescents may respond in terms of what they have observed in other families. Any family member may respond in terms of some ideal family type they have envisioned, and these ideal images may differ for each family member. Discrepancies may also reflect inaccurate or incomplete communication among family members. The relationship between discrepant perceptions and communication was analyzed at both the couple and family level.

FAMILY COALITIONS VERSUS FAMILY DISCREPANCIES

The concept of family coalitions is conceptually linked to the idea of discrepancy among family members. The study of family coalitions, to some degree, reverses the perspective one adopts when studying family discrepancy. Discrepancy highlights the distance among or the magnitude of disagreement among family members whereas the concept of coalition focuses on patterns of connectedness between some family members to the exclusion of others.

Reiss (1981) has noted that families develop shared meanings or perceptual coalitions regarding the nature of the world of relationships and their place in it. Coalitions may also form at the subsystem level among individual family members. Like shared perceptions at the total family level, these inter-member coalitions are formed and/or maintained through shared perceptions. They are defined by the extent to which the meanings or perceptions of individual members interlock. Thus, a lower level of discrepancy in perceptions would be expected between members of a coalition than between a coalition member and a third family member outside the coalition.

In one of the few empirical studies of family coalitions, Bell and Bell (1982) found scapegoated girls and those involved in cross-generational coalitions scored lower on measures of psychological and social development. More specifically, they noted coalitions with low scoring girls were with their fathers but coalitions involving high scoring girls were with mothers. They cited this as evidence that cross-generational, cross-sex coalitions may be more problematic for families than same-sex, cross-generational coalitions. However, the Bell study had a very limited sample size (total N = 30 families), and was limited to families with female adolescents. These limitations suggest the need for caution in generalizing the results of that study. The study reported in this paper examined these same issues using a larger sample that included families with male and female adolescents.

SAMPLE

The sample for this study consisted of a subset of participants from a national survey of families conducted in 1981-83 (Olson, McCubbin et al., 1983). The subset used in this study is composed of the 389 families with a father, mother, and adolescent child as participants. The sample, representing 30 different states, is basically a caucasian (97%), middle class, middle income group from both rural and urban areas in the Midwest. Unlike most studies of clinical issues, this was a nonclinical sample. This group of families was randomly selected from among policy holders of a large fraternal benefits organization. These families were chosen only on the basis of their structure and thus represent a "normal" population.

In this sample husbands' ages ranged from 32 to 63 with a mean of 45.3 and wives' ages ranged from 31 to 61 with a mean of 42.8. Adolescent participants ranged in age from 12 to 20 with an average age of 16.4. Family size varied from 1 to 13 children with an average of 3. The age of the oldest child in the family ranged from 13 to 36.

Couples represent predominantly first time marriages (95%) with an average duration of 21 years. The modal (38%) family pretax income fell in the $20,000 to $29,000 range. Average family income was $34,000. Parents' educational levels showed 30% of the males and 20% of the females had at least four years of college. The sample was almost exactly divided between families with a female adolescent participant (49.6%, n = 193) and families with an adolescent male participant (50.4%, n = 196). To provide a general indication of the level of discrepancy in this sample, dyadic agreement (correlation) was computed for each of the key variables. These figures are tabled in Appendix A.

FAMILY ASSESSMENT MEASURES

This study focused on the impact of perceptual discrepancy on other key variables of family life. In order to determine the impact of discrepancy both on the marriage and on the entire family unit, issues were examined at both the couple or spousal level and at the family level. Some variables were used at both levels of analysis. These included placement on the Circumplex Model, cohesion, adaptability, stress, and satisfaction with quality of life. Other variables included in the analyses of marital couples were marital communication, conflict resolution, marital satisfaction, and marital adjustment. The family level analysis utilized measures of family satisfaction, parent-adolescent communication, the family strengths of family pride and family accord, location of discrepancy within the various subsystems of the family, and coalitions among family members. Most of the scales used to measure these variables are extensively reviewed in *Family Inventories: Inventories Used in a National Study of Families Across the Family Life Cycle* (Olson, McCubbin et al., 1982). These are all self-report, paper and pencil measures. Appendix B summarizes the variables, instruments and instrument reliabilities.

CASE EXAMPLES OF FAMILY DISCREPANCY

To more clearly illustrate family discrepancy, four case examples of families who completed *FACES III* are presented. (See Figure 1 for a graph of these four families.) In each of the first three cases family members responded to *FACES III* in a manner that indicated substantial discrepancy in their perceptions of their family life. Keep in mind the range of possible scores on *FACES III* is 10-50 on each of the two scales, cohesion and adaptability. The mean, based on national norms, is 39.8 for cohesion and 24.1 for adaptability (Olson, Portner, & Lavee, 1985).

The Scherles family came into therapy through a referral from their son's school counselor. Tom, 41, and Janice, 35, had been

Figure 1: Discrepancy of Family Members Scores on the Circumplex Model

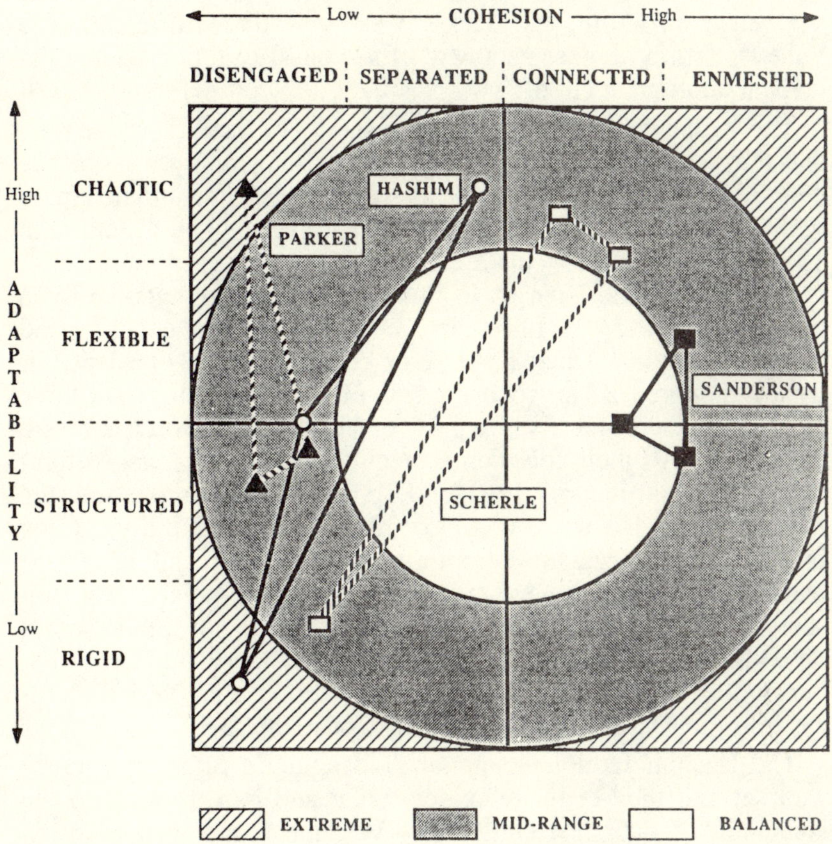

married for 17 years and had one son, Jack, a 15-year-old freshman. On *FACES III*, Tom's scores were 42 for cohesion and 33 for adaptability. Janice had 44 on cohesion and 30 on adaptability. Jack's scores were very different, with a 24 on cohesion and a 17 on adaptability. Tom and Janice viewed their family life as high on adaptability, to the point of being Chaotic and quite close or Connected on cohesion. In contrast to his parents, Jack perceived his family as Rigidly Disengaged.

In this case, the marital pair indicated the family fell in the mid-range area of the Circumplex Model, but their son perceived the family as low in their emotional ties and rigid in their functioning. Also notice Tom and Janice were quite similar in their perceptions of their family life, but Jack's view was quite different. The Scherles family represents a case of a spousal coalition with a discrepant adolescent child.

The Parker family was seen because Steve, the father (age 46), was referred for alcohol abuse treatment by the employee assistance counselor at the company where he worked. He came into treatment with Diane (age 35) his second wife, and her daughter, Patti (age 13), who lived with them. Steve and Diane had been married for two years. He had been an institutional sales representative for a computer company for five years. Steve scored 19 on cohesion and 35 on adaptability. Diane had a 33 on cohesion and 22 on adaptability. Patti scored 27 on cohesion and 21 on adaptability. All three family members perceived a lack of emotional connectedness to each other. All their cohesion scores indicated a Disengaged family. This is particularly true for Dad/Steve whose score was the most extreme. His score was also extreme on adaptability, falling into the Chaotic category. Contrary to Steve's perceptions, Diane and Patti both viewed the family as Structured as indicated by their scores in the low middle range. Diane and Patti, with similar scores on both cohesion and adaptability, form a mother-daughter, cross-generational coalition. Steve Parker's perceptions are very discrepant from those held by his wife and stepdaughter.

The Hashim family thought their daughter's future was fairly well set and they could relax somewhat and look forward to the launching of their last child. However, the found themselves in therapy following their daughter's suicide attempt during her last semester of high school. Sarah (age 18), the youngest of four children, viewed the family as extremely rigid and family members as very emotionally distant from one another. She scored a 17 on cohesion and 14 on adaptability. Jacob, her 59-year-old father, saw more flexibility and closeness in the family with a 24 on adaptability and 33 on cohesion. Ruth, 56, saw even greater flexibility and connectedness with scores of 42 and 39 on adaptability and cohesion, respectively. Sarah's perceptions indicated her family fell in the lower right or Rigidly-Disengaged area of the Circumplex

Model. Her father's scores were also characteristic of low family cohesiveness or Disengaged but right at the mean between Structured and Flexible on adaptability. Ruth's responses indicated a Chaotic and emotionally Separated family.

The Hashims are very discrepant in their perceptions of their relationships. Each of the three family members holds a distinctly different view from each of the other two. Not only is this family highly discrepant, but each reports their family as extreme on one or both dimensions of the Circumplex.

In all three of these families there is a high level of discrepancy. In the first two families one member was relatively more discrepant in his/her perceptions and there was a coalition between the other two members. In the Scherles' case, the adolescent was relatively more distant from the spouses, and in the Parker's case, the father's perceptions were relatively more discrepant. The Hashims were each distinctly different from the other two family members in their perceptions.

The Sandersons illustrate a family with high agreement or low discrepancy in the perceptions of the family life they share. Jon, Ginny, and Phil had cohesion and adaptability scores of 45, 45, 43, and 23, 26, and 24 respectively. The cohesion scores for all three are typical of Connected families. Their adaptability scores place Jon and Phillip in the Structured area while Ginny's score signifies a Flexible family style. All of these scores are in the Balanced range. Additional discussion of these four cases will be presented in a later section.

THE IMPACT OF DISCREPANCY

This study examined the impact of discrepant perceptions on marital and family life using discriminant analyses to distinguish between high and low discrepant couples and high and low discrepant families. First, high and low groups were defined according to the level of discrepancy on *FACES III*. In the second set of analyses, groups were defined according to high or low communication scores to see if the level of discrepancy on the other variables could discriminate between effective and ineffective communicators. The final analyses examined family coalitions. A series of chi square analyses were used to test the relative significance of various gender patterns of parent-child coalitions. This was followed by discriminant analyses to examine the impact of coalitions on other variables of marital and family life. The groups compared in these final discriminant analyses were couples or families with a parent-child coalition versus those with a marital coalition. The discriminant analyses were completed twice, once using couples and couple variables (such as marital communication and marital satisfaction) and then again using families and family variables (such as parent-child communication and family satisfaction).

The results indicated discrepancy is most highly correlated with communication for couples and families. Satisfaction with marital or family relationships, and family pride were also significantly related to discrepancy. For marital pairs, the analysis of discrepancy on *FACES III* ($N = 103$ couples), especially discrepancy on cohesion, revealed that high levels of discrepancy were related to poorer marital communication ($p < .003$), less adequate conflict resolution ($p < .03$), and lower levels of marital satisfaction ($p < .03$). A similar pattern emerged from the analyses at the family level where higher discrepancy was related to significantly poorer parent-adolescent communication (Total scale $p < .003$; Openness, $p < .005$; and Problem Free, $p < .02$; $N = 40$), lower family satisfaction ($p < .02$) and lower family pride ($p < .02$).

To further explore the relationship between discrepancy and family communication, a discriminant analysis ($N = 57$) was completed separating families with effective communication from those reporting ineffective patterns of communication. This analysis revealed that families with poor communication, especially those who lacked openness between parent and child, had significantly *greater discrepancy* in family members' perceptions of cohesion ($p < .0009$) and family strengths ($p < .007$), particularly family pride ($p < .0001$).

Families with poor communication also had significantly *lower levels* of cohesion ($p < .0001$), family satisfaction ($p < .0001$), satisfaction with quality of life ($p < .0001$), family pride ($p < .0001$), and family accord ($p < .0001$). They also had significant greater family stress levels ($p < .0008$). Thus families with ineffective patterns of communication had greater levels of discrepancy and lower levels of functioning in other areas of family life.

Based on the family level variables, family discrepancy scores discriminated between poorly and effectively communicating families in 86% of the cases. Family mean scores on these same variables correctly distinguished between poor communicators and families with good communication in 100% of the 75 cases where complete data were available for all family members.

THE IMPACT OF PARENT-CHILD COALITIONS

In the final phase of this study, the issue of discrepancy was examined from the perspective of family coalitions or connectedness with dyads to the exclusion of the third family member. As with discrepancy, the definition of coalitions was based on the relative distances between dyads within the family. Coalitions were defined by the relative differences among the three family members. *Spousal coalitions* included all cases where the husband-wife difference was substantially less than the difference between either parent and the adolescent child. In *parent-child coalitions*, the distance between the child and one of the parents was relatively smaller than the distance between the child and the other parent and smaller than the distance between the spouses.

Although only three coalitions were possible in each family (husband-wife, mother-child, and father-child), these can be combined with gender differences to form a variety of patterns. In order to more fully explore these possible permutations, a series of chi square analyses were completed. The coalitions tested using chi square analysis were mother-son versus mother-daughter and father-son versus father-daughter (each parent with children of different genders), mother-son versus father-daughter (cross gender coalitions), mother-daughter versus father-son (same gender coalitions), mother-son versus father-son and mother-daughter versus father-daughter (contrasting the two parents with gender of the child held constant).

The series of chi square analyses using the various possible combinations of family dyads showed no significant differences among any of the groups with the exception of husband-wife versus parent-child coalitions and the single variable of openness in communication which indicated mother-son coalitions were less open than mother-daughter combinations (see Table 1). Contrary to what the literature suggests (Bell & Bell, 1982), these analyses indicated there were no differences based on either the gender of the child or the gender of the parent. The impact on family functioning is attributable to the presence of parent-child coalitions in the family rather than the gender of the coalition members.

When there are parent-child coalitions, regardless of the gender

TABLE 1: Chi-square Analyses of Parent-child Coalitions Utilizing Varied Gender Combinations

	COALITIONS*						
	1	2	3	4	5	6	7
VARIABLES							
Openness	.69(52)[a]	.04(20)	.56(38)	.39(28)	.13(30)	.34(32)	.31(26)
Problem Fr	.26(47)	.86(20)	.19(37)	.15(27)	.68(30)	.66(32)	.43(25)
Pride	.84(53)	.52(19)	.43(39)	.20(27)	.45(31)	.65(34)	.60(24)
Accord	.03(53)[b]	.10(20)	.32(39)	.20(28)	.06(31)	.70(35)	.45(24)
Family Satisfac.	.86(45)	.07(15)	.55(36)	.62(27)	.06(24)	.27(29)	.16(22)
Stress	.19(44)	.53(15)	.17(33)	.36(24)	.65(24)	.54(27)	.77(21)
Quality of Life	.48(43)	.90(18)	.06(29)	.32(22)	.97(25)	.78(27)	.20(20)
Marital Communica.	.02(55)[b]	.69(22)	.71(39)	.83(29)	.97(32)	.45(34)	.91(27)
Locke-Wall.	.02(48)[b]	.78(19)	.64(34)	.78(26)	.36(27)	.73(32)	.64(21)
Marital Sat. ENRICH	.003(55)[b]	.95(22)	.08(39)	.72(29)	.12(32)	.20(34)	.66(27)

* Legend for Coalitions

1 = Husband/Wife vs. Parent/Child
2 = Mother/Male teen vs. Mother/Female teen
3 = Father/Male teen vs. Father/Female teen
4 = Mother/Male teen vs. Father/Female teen (cross gender)
5 = Mother/Female teen vs. Father/Male teen (same gender)
6 = Mother/Male teen vs. Father/Male teen
7 = Mother/Female teen vs. Father/Female teen

a Level of significance with 2 degrees of freedom (N)
b Families with a parent/child coalition scored lower on these

of the parent or the child, the result is lowered family functioning in some aspects of family life. When *FACES III* was used to define the coalitions, families with parent-child coalitions had significantly lower marital satisfaction (Locke-Wallace, $p < .01$) and lower satisfaction with quality of life ($p < .001$). With coalitions defined on parent-adolescent communication, families with parent-child coalitions again showed lower marital satisfaction (Locke-Wallace, $p < .0005$) using the total communication scale and lower family accord ($p < .01$) when the problems subscale was used. These results are in the predicted direction even though most of the variables did not show such differences.

Parent-child coalitions seem to be most detrimental to the marital relationship. Husband-wife versus parent-child coalitions (as defined on the Circumplex Model) were tested using discriminant analyses with couple variables and then repeated with family variables. Coalitions defined on *FACES III* showed about the same level of predictability using couple (67%, $N = 78$) or family (69%, $N = 71$) variables. As Table 2 shows, when a parent-child coalition was present, scores on the following aspects of family life were low; family satisfaction ($p < .01$), quality of life ($p < .003$), pride ($p < .03$), marital communication ($p < .02$), conflict resolution ($p < .02$), and marital satisfaction (*ENRICH*, $p < .003$, Locke-Wallace, $p < .03$). Although parent-child coalitions negatively impact family satisfaction, they are even more strongly related to lower marital satisfaction. Similarly, the presence of a parent-child coalition was closely related to poorer marital communication and conflict resolution but appeared statistically unrelated to parent-child communication. Thus the negative effects of parent-child coalitions register most dramatically on the spousal relationship.

IMPLICATIONS FOR PRACTICE

With the increased recognition of the validity of a family systems approach to therapy, clinicians increasingly work with multiple family members. As with individual therapy, family assessment scales offer the clinician an additional diagnostic tool. The Circumplex Model of Marital and Family Systems offers a theoretical/conceptual base for understanding family functioning, for planning ap-

TABLE 2: Families with Husband-Wife Coalitions versus Families with Parent-Child Coalitions: Discriminant Analysis

	Husband-Wife Coalitions Group Mean	Parent-Child Coalitions Group Mean	F	p of F
FAMILY LEVEL VARIABLES				
Parent-Adol. Communication	69.90	68.73	.28	.60
Openness	36.85	35.90	.58	.45
Problem Free	33.05	32.84	.03	.85
Family Sat.	48.16	44.22	6.9	.01
Stress*	.034	-.157	1.0	.31
Quality of Life*	.296	-.312	9.4	.003
Family Pride	29.39	27.30	5.2	.03
Family Accord	16.75	16.06	1.0	.32
Level of Predictability = 68.60%				
COUPLE LEVEL VARIABLES				
Communication	35.67	32.31	5.8	.02
Conflict Resolution	34.95	31.82	5.5	.02
Marital Sat.	38.28	34.00	9.3	.003
Locke-Wallace	52.33	48.71	4.8	.03
Stress	134.38	133.56	.51	.48
Quality of Life	136.68	126.02	7.2	.009
Level of Predictability = 66.67				

* scores based on z-score units

propriate interventions and for mapping the changes in families as they progress through therapy. As the field of family therapy matures, more instruments become available for assessing family functioning. *FACES III* (Olson, Portner, & Lavee, 1985), the Clinical Rating Scale (Olson & Killorin, 1985), and scales to measure both marital and family communication (Olson, Fournier, & Druckman, 1982; Barnes & Olson, 1982) are now available to aid the practitioner in assessing family functioning on the dimensions of the Circumplex Model. However, assessment of multiple family members will frequently result in disagreement among the family members about their family life. Rather than assuming these differences are an indication of psychometric problems with the scales, such discrepancies can provide insight into family functioning by underscoring areas where family members differ in their perceptions.

The results of this study show high levels of discrepancy among the reports of different family members are related to difficulties in several facets of couple or family functioning. In cases like the Parker family (see case studies), where there was a high level of marital discrepancy, a therapist would find lower levels of marital satisfaction for one or both partners and less effective spousal communication and conflict resolution skills. The likelihood of a combination of ineffective communication patterns and low relationship satisfaction increased with the recognition that the Parkers not only had high discrepancy, but there was a coalition between mother and daughter. In this stepfamily, the coalition between mother and daughter may or may not have predated the marriage, but the coalition functioned to keep Steve as an outsider. Even though a close relationship was evident between Patti and Diane, this coalition maintained a distance between Steve and Diane. Steve viewed the family as chaotic and disengaged. Diane and Patti reported it as structured and somewhat closer, although they agreed with Steve that they were disengaged. Given a coalition's tendency to function as a unit within the larger system, Diane and Patti Parker had more structure and a little more closeness in their own relationship than what they shared with Steve. Thus, when he was outside the coalition for two years of marriage, he did not understand the relationship rules or how they functioned and therefore perceived the relationship as having few rules or little stability. Steve's drinking appeared related to a sense of isolation from the other family members.

The Scherles family presented quite a different situation. Like the Parker family, they had a high level of discrepancy but much of it was attributable to Jack's perceptions, which differed greatly from both his parents. Tom and Janice were in much closer agreement in their perceptions. While the high level of discrepancy appeared related to dissatisfaction and problems in some areas of family functioning, the closeness between the spouses suggested a coalition that would serve as a buffer to some of the difficulties the family was experiencing. Jack's extreme representation of the family was a concern. However, it is typical for adolescents to view their family life somewhat differently from their parents. Unlike the Parker case, a therapist working with the Scherles family might expect better spousal communication and a higher likelihood of spousal cooperation and motivation toward resolving the family problems. The problems likely revolve around some difficulty in parent-adolescent communication and the adolescent's perception of the rigid quality of his family life versus his parents' view.

Ruth and Jacob Hashim and their daughter Sarah each provided distinctly different descriptions of their family life. Constraints on spousal and parent-adolescent communication as well as lower satisfaction with marital and family relationships would be characteristic of the wide perceptual discrepancy reported by this family on *FACES III*. The results of this study indicated the Hashims likely experienced higher levels of stress, difficulty in communicating between the generations as well as between the spouses, and lower levels of satisfaction derived from their relationships with each other. Sarah reported feeling the family had very little emotional bonding and a great deal of rigidity. In a family such as this, there is very limited openness in the communication between the generations and likely poor conflict resolution skills between the spouses. Futile attempts to openly share, form caring bonds, and resolve conflicts decrease the motivation for future efforts at improving relationships and frequently lead to increasing isolation in families like this. The lack of communication means each family member's own private perceptions of family life go unchallenged and unchanged.

Parent-child coalitions represent a specific pattern of family discrepancy. In these cases there is some commonality in perceptions within the coalitions. Contrary to some of the earlier work on coalitions (Bell & Bell, 1982), this study provides no evidence to support the notion that coalitions which cross gender as well as crossgenerational boundaries are particularly detrimental to family functioning. The results of this study underscore that a parent-child coalition, regardless of the gender of either the parent or the child, is related to decreased family functioning. The impact primarily relates to lower satisfaction derived from marital and family relationships, less effective patterns of communication among spouses and family members, and a higher level of stress. The effect seems greatest on the marital subsystem.

Unlike other studies which have examined coalitions in terms of their relationship to individual functioning, here the focus was on family functioning and family relationships. It should come as no surprise to therapists that from the relationship vantage point, the marriage appears to be most vulnerable to the negative impact of a parent-child coalition. While the child who is overinvolved with a parent may pay an emotional price in the long run, the existence of a parent-child coalition is most clearly related to ineffective or impaired functioning in the marital dyad.

In contrast, a strong marital coalition provides the foundation for both effective parenting and satisfying marital relations. Higher marital satisfaction, more satisfying spousal communication and conflict resolution, more effective parent-child communication, a greater sense of family pride and higher levels of family satisfaction and satisfaction with overall quality of life were reported by couples and families with strong marital coalitions.

As therapists engage families in the process of therapy using the variety of assessment tools available, it is useful to note not only the specific responses of each family member, but the pattern of responses among them. Examination of the pattern of responses will indicate the level of congruence or discrepancy among family members' views. The results of this study indicated high discrepancy is related to lower levels of relationship satisfaction and poorer communication between spouses and between parents and their children.

Perceptual coalitions in families represent a special case of perceptual discrepancy. Coalitions represent a convergence of perspective between two family members relative to the exclusion of a third member. While parental coalitions are considered appropriate for effective family functioning, parent-child coalitions were shown to be detrimental. Although detrimental to the functioning of the entire family, the negative impact of parent-child coalitions registered most strongly on the marital relationship with lower marital satisfaction, impaired conflict resolution skills, ineffective spousal communication, and lower levels of general life satisfaction.

Contrary to earlier findings, this study noted the detrimental effects related to parent-child coalitions are not linked to the gender of either the parent or the child involved in the coalition. Tests of different gender combinations of parent-child coalitions yielded no significant differences. The results of this study indicated the detrimental effects of parent-child coalitions on family functioning are related to the crossing of generational boundaries alone, rather than the crossing of both gender and generation boundaries.

REFERENCES

Barnes, H. (1985). Discrepancy in family perceptions: Conceptual and methodological issues (Doctoral dissertation, University of Minnesota, 1985). *Dissertation Abstracts International, 46*, 3873A.

Barnes, H., & Olson, D. (1985). Parent-adolescent communication and the circumplex model. *Child Development, 56*, 438-447.

Barnes, H., & Olson, D. (1982). Parent-adolescent communication scale. In Olson, D., McCubbin, H., Barnes, H., Larsen, A., Muxen, M., & Wilson, M. *Family inventories: Inventories used in a national survey of families across the family life cycle*. St. Paul, MN: Family Social Science, University of Minnesota.

Barnes, H., Schumm, W., Jurich, A., & Bollman, S. (1984). Marital satisfaction: Positive regard versus effective communication as explanatory variables. *Journal of Social Psychology, 123*, 71-78.

Bell, L., & Bell, D. (1982). Family climate and the role of the female adolescent. Determinants of adolescent functioning. *Family Relations, 31*, 519-527.

Bernard, J. (1972). *The future of marriage*. New York: World.

Campbell, A., Converse, P. E., & Rodgers, W. L. (1976). *The quality of life: Perceptions, evaluations and satisfactions*. New York: Russell Sage Foundation.

Cooper, C. R., Grotevant, H. D., Moore, M. S., & Condon, S. M. (1982). *Family support and conflict: Both foster adolescent identity and role taking*. Paper presented at the meeting of the American Psychological Association, Washington, DC.

Craddock, A. (1980). The effect of incongruent marital role expectations upon couples' degree of goal-value consensus in the first year of marriage. *Australian Journal of Psychology, 32*(2), 117-125.

Epstein, N., Bishop, D., & Levin, S. (1978). The McMaster model of family functioning. *Journal of Marriage and Family Counseling, 4*, 19-31.

Garland, D. R. (1981). Training married couples in listening skills: Effects on behavior, perceptual accuracy, and marital adjustment. *Family Relations, 30*, 297-306.

Grotevant, H. D., & Cooper, C. R. (1983). *The role of family communication patterns in adolescent identity and role taking*. Paper presented at the meeting of the Society for Research in Child Development, Detroit, MI.

Hess, R., Handel, G. (1974). *Family worlds: A psychosocial approach to family life*. Chicago: University of Chicago Press.

Hull, C. H., & Nie, N. H. (1981). *SPSS update: New procedures and facilities for releases 7-9*. New York: McGraw Hill Book Co.

Jacobson, N. S. (1978). A review of the research on the effectiveness of marital therapy. In T. J. Paolino & B. S. McCrady (Eds.), *Marriage and marital therapy*. New York: Brunner/Mazel.

Larson, L. (1974). System and subsystem perception of family roles. *Journal of Marriage and the Family, 36*, 123-138.

LeVant, R. F. (1978). Client-centered approaches to working with the family: An overview of new developments in therapeutic, educational, and preventive methods. *International Journal of Family Counseling, 6*(1), 31-44.

Lewis, R. A., Beavers, W. R., Gossett, J. T., & Phillips, V. A. (1976). *No single thread: Psychological health in family systems*. New York: Brunner/Mazel.

Lewis, R. A., & Spanier, G. B. (1979). Theorizing about the quality and stability of marriage. In W. R. Burr, R. Hill, F. I. Nye, & I. Reiss (Eds.), *Contemporary theories about the family* (Vol. 1). New York: Free Press.

McCubbin, H., Patterson, J., & Wilson, L. (1981). *Family inventory of life events and changes (FILE) form A*. St. Paul, MN: Family Social Science, University of Minnesota.

McCubbin, H., Patterson, J., Bauman, E., & Harris, L. (1981). *A-FILE Adolescent-family inventory of life events and changes*. St. Paul, MN: Family Social Science, University of Minnesota.

Olson, D., & Barnes, H. (1982). Satisfaction with quality of life scale. In D. Olson, H. McCubbin, H. Barnes, A. Larsen, M. Muxen, & M. Wilson, *Family inventories: Inventories used in a national survey of families across the family life cycle*. St. Paul, MN: Family Social Science, University of Minnesota.

Olson, D., Fournier, D., & Druckman, J. (1982). Enriching and nurturing relationship issues, communication and happiness (ENRICH). In D. Olson, H. McCubbin, H. Barnes, A. Larsen, M. Muxen, & M. Wilson, *Family inventories: Inventories used in a national survey of families across the family life cycle*. St. Paul, MN: Family Social Science, University of Minnesota.

Olson, D.; & Killorin, E. (1985). *Clinical rating scale*. St. Paul, MN: Family Social Science, University of Minnesota.

Olson, D., Larsen, A., & McCubbin, H. (1982). Family strengths scale. In D. Olson, H. McCubbin, H. Barnes, A. Larsen, M. Muxen, & M. Wilson, *Family inventories: Inventories used in a national survey of families across the family life cycle*. St. Paul, MN: Family Social Science, University of Minnesota.

Olson, D., McCubbin, H., Barnes, H., Larsen, A., Muxen, M., & Wilson, M. (1982). *Family inventories: Inventories used in a national survey of families across the family life cycle*. St. Paul, MN: Family Social Science, University of Minnesota.

Olson, D., McCubbin, H., Barnes, H., Larsen, A., Muxen, M., & Wilson, M. (1983). *Families: What makes them work*. Beverly Hills, CA: Sage Publications.

Olson, D., Portner, J., & Lavee, Y. (1985). *FACES III*. St. Paul, MN: Family Social Science, University of Minnesota.

Olson, D., Russell, C., & Sprenkle, D. (1980). Marital and family therapy: A decade review. *Journal of Marriage and the Family, 42*(4), 973-993.

Olson, D., Russell, C., & Sprenkle, D. (1983). Circumplex model VI: Theoretical update. *Family Process, 22*, 69-83.

Olson, D., Sprenkle, D., & Russell, C. (1979). Circumplex model of marital and family systems I: Cohesion and adaptability dimensions, family types and clinical application. *Family Process*, *18*, 3-28.

Olson, D., & Wilson, M. (1982). Family satisfaction scale. In D. Olson, H. McCubbin, H. Barnes, A. Larsen, M. Muxen, & M. Wilson, *Family inventories: Inventories used in a national survey of families across the family life cycle*. St. Paul, MN: Family Social Science, University of Minnesota.

Reiss, D. (1981). *The family's construction of reality*. Cambridge, MA: Harvard University Press.

Russell, C. S. (1979). Circumplex model of marital and family systems: III. Empirical evaluation with families. *Family Process, 18*, 29-45.

Safilios-Rothschild, C. (1969). Family sociology or wives' family sociology? A cross-cultural examination of decision-making. *Journal of Marriage and the Family, 31*, 290-301.

Satir, V. (1964). *Conjoint family therapy*. Palo Alto, CA: Science and Behavior Books, Inc.

Schumm, W. A., Barnes, H. L., Bollman, S. R., Jurich, A. P., & Milliken, G. A. (1985). Approaches to the statistical analysis of family data. *Journal of Home Economics Research, 14*, 112-122.

Steinberg, L. D. (1981). Transformations in family relationships at puberty. *Developmental Psychology, 17*(6), 833-840.

Steinberg, L. D., & Hill, J. P. (1978). Patterns of family interaction as a function of age, the onset of puberty, and formal thinking. *Developmental Psychology, 14*(6), 683-684.

Wampler, K. S. (1982). Bringing the review of literature into the age of quantification: Meta-analysis as a strategy for integrating research findings in family studies. *Journal of Marriage and the Family, 44*(4), 1009-1023.

APPENDIX A: Agreement Between Family Members (correlations)

	Husband-Wife	Husband-Adolescent	Wife-Adolescent
Family System			
FACES III			
Family Cohesion	.44	.44	.38
Family Adaptability	.24	.21	.14
Parent-Adolescent Communication	.26	.31	.34
Open Communication	.24	.31	.29
Problem Free Comm.	.17	.16	.29
Family Inventory of Life Events and Changes (FILE)	.32	.30	.34
Family Satisfaction	.37	.31	.29
Satisfaction with Quality of Life	.38	.29	.24
Family Strengths	.43	.40	.34
Family Pride	.33	.39	.29
Family Accord	.39	.25	.22
Marital System			
Marital Satisfaction (ENRICH)	.50		
Marital Satisfaction (Locke-Wallace)	.57		
Marital Communication (ENRICH)	.36		
Conflict Resolution (ENRICH)	.40		

APPENDIX B: Summary of Variables, Instruments, and Instrument Reliabilities for Couples and Families.

VARIABLE	INSTRUMENT	RELIABILITY Alpha	RELIABILITY Test-retest
FAMILY SYSTEM			
Family Type	FACES III	.68	.90
Communication	Parent-Adolescent Communication Scale		
	Open Communication	.87	.78
	Problem Free Comm.	.78	.77
Family Satisfaction	Family Satisfaction Scale	.92	.75
Quality of Life	Satisfaction with Quality of Life Scale		
	Adult form	.92	.65
	Adolescent form	.86	.55
Family Strengths	Family Strengths Scale		
	Family Pride	.88	.73
	Family Accord	.72	.79
Stress	FILE	.81	.80
	A-FILE	.82	.84
Discrepancy	Discrepancy scores on all instruments		
Location of Discrepancy	Cutting points established according to the nature of the analysis		
MARITAL SYSTEM			
Communication	Communication (ENRICH)	.68	.90
	Conflict Resolution (ENRICH)	.75	.90
Marital Satisfaction	Marital Satisfaction (ENRICH)	.81	.86
	Locke-Wallace Marital Satisfaction Scale	not available	

Ethnic Families in the Circumplex Model: Integrating Nuclear with Extended Family Systems

Carol E. Woehrer

SUMMARY. This article compares ethnic families on the cohesion and adaptability dimensions of the Circumplex Model from the perspective of intergenerational and extended family systems. Recent studies unexpectedly found that rigid enmeshed families function well when they have high expectations for togetherness. These findings probably occurred because enmeshment in extended families, in contrast to nuclear families, increases the resources available for alleviating problems and moderates the effects of low adaptability.

The Circumplex Model predicts that families with central levels of cohesion and adaptability function more adequately across the family life cycle than those at the extremes of these dimensions. However, in recent discussions of the Circumplex Model, Olson and McCubbin (1982) and Olson, Russell, and Sprenkle (1984) add the qualification of cultural relativity to the model.

> In general, the hypothesized curvilinear relationship between effective family functioning and the cohesion-adaptability dimensions applies to families that accept the current cultural norms that support both family togetherness and individual development. The general hypothesis would not apply, however,

Carol E. Woehrer, MA, is a doctoral student in American Studies at the University of Minnesota, St. Paul, MN.

> for families that have very high expectations for family togetherness. (Olson & McCubbin, 1982, p. 56)

This qualification raises important questions regarding the range of family cultures to which the model can be applied. How might the Circumplex Model be expanded to include families with a wider range of norms or expectations? How do families of different cultural backgrounds vary in their placement on the model? Why is it that families with high expectations for family togetherness show a different relationship between family functioning and the cohesion-adaptability dimensions than families that support greater individualism?

The Circumplex Model has been used mainly to study the effects of family cohesion, adaptability, and communication in nuclear families. Clinical work and research on ethnic families, on the other hand, indicates that for many ethnic families, family functioning cannot be understood simply in terms of the nuclear unit. Rather, to understand the nuclear family, one must understand the extended family, particularly when the extended family is high in cohesion. Families that have very high expectations for family togetherness are probably most often families with high extended family cohesion. The nuclear family is frequently supported by and integrated with the extended family. A highly cohesive extended family might share religious beliefs and occupational involvement as well as emotional support, interests and activities, family customs, meals, and celebrations. Thus, when the cohesion scale shows an enmeshed level of cohesion for the nuclear unit of an enmeshed extended family, it is probably often measuring enmeshment in the larger extended family system rather than simply in the nuclear family unit.

While studies of clinical samples demonstrate that problem families are much more likely to be one of the extreme types on the Circumplex Model than are nonsymptomatic families (Clarke, 1984; Carnes, 1985; Garbarino, Sebes, & Schellenbach, 1985), in an extended family, enmeshment has different causes and effects family functioning in quite different ways than in a nuclear family. Enmeshment in the extended family is probably most often a result of intentional commitment to family customs and traditional expectations of sharing practical and emotional support, activities, and values. Enmeshment in the nuclear family, on the other hand, is probably more often unintentional, a result of family skills and approaches to certain situations, stages, or problems in the family. While enmeshment in the nuclear family can limit a family's resources, as family members become overinvolved with each other or with a problem situation, an enmeshed extended family can often contribute to alleviating problems because of its wider range of resources.

This paper integrates nuclear with extended family systems by comparing extended ethnic families in terms of their dispersion on the Circumplex Model. The placement of ethnic families is not based on research using FACES and is not meant to be definitive. The placement is based rather on varied research on ethnic families and on descriptions of ethnic families by family therapists, historians, and ethnic family members.

Generalizations regarding ethnic families, particularly when they are simplified, are often referred to as stereotypes. This paper discusses ethnic families in reference to the Circumplex Model and in terms of the insights the extended family contributes to the hypotheses of the Model. Its purpose is not to give a comprehensive description of ethnic families. While the descriptions of ethnic families are brief and might sound like stereotypes, research has shown that people of different ethnic backgrounds vary in occupational choice, political involvement, community participation (Greeley, 1974), child rearing values, extended family interaction (Greeley, 1971), and drinking subcultures (Greeley, McCready, & Thiesen, 1980).

As McGoldrick and Rohrbaugh (1987) point out, until recently researchers' discussion of differences among American ethnic families has been virtually taboo. Thus the research on ethnic families is sparse and uneven. McGoldrick and Rohrbaugh (1987) used statements which embody common cultural stereotypes to construct an ethnicity questionnaire. In a sample of 220 mental health professionals with three of their four biological grandparents belonging to a particular group, 92 percent of the items differentiated between the mean of one ethnic group and the mean of all the others. Differences were in the direction predicted. In comparing Irish and Irish American respondents in a second study, McGoldrick and Rohrbaugh (1987) found the two groups had almost identical significant items on the questionnaire. Thus, the fact that a description of an ethnic family fits commonly held stereotypes does not mean that it is inaccurate. Rather, stereotypes are often shorthand descriptions of cultural differences between families. As the discussion of rigid enmeshed families in this paper will show, stereotypes are incomplete and inadequate descriptions. Nevertheless, they often contribute useful suggestions regarding family phenomena which deserve more thorough research.

This, of course, does not mean that all families of a particular ethnic background are the same. Such families would be dispersed among all types on the Circumplex Model. Families are influenced by many other variables besides ethnicity such as education, occupation, income, mass media, geographic propinquity of family members, neighborhood, church, rural or urban residence, individual characteristics of the family members, stage of the family life cycle, and family problems and crises. A distinctive pattern of dispersion for ethnic families is more likely to emerge if families of that background are highly concentrated in a geographic area. One might expect, for example, to find a distinctive pattern of dispersion for German families in St. Cloud, Minnesota, which has a high percentage of people of German background, whereas German families in Los Angeles, California would be less likely to be differentiated from other families. Distinctive patterns of dispersion are probably more likely to emerge during child rearing and adolescent stages of the family cycle when parents are trying to teach family values to their children.

This article first compares ethnic families on the dimensions of cohesion and adaptability and places ethnic families on the Circumplex Model. It then discusses this placement in terms of the problems therapists frequently encounter in various ethnic families. Finally, it suggests modifications and additions to the hypotheses of the Model based on the analysis of ethnic families.

EXTENDED FAMILY COHESION

Family cohesion varies greatly in American families – from the independence and self-reliance characteristic of Anglo, Scandinavian, German, and Irish families to the extensive exchange of help, frequent visits, and emotional support found in Italian, Mexican, and Jewish families. First, ethnic families will be placed on the levels of the cohesion dimension on the basis of their traditional extended family characteristics. Second, contemporary changes and variation in ethnic families will be discussed. Third, the relationship between nuclear and extended family cohesion will be analyzed. (See Figure 1.)

Traditional Extended Ethnic Families

In *disengaged families*, nuclear units are independent from each other. Individuals do not expect to receive aid or emotional support from one another. Individual pursuits of the nuclear units take precedence, and allegiance to the extended family is not expected. Though family members visit, these visits tend to be less frequent than for families at other levels.

The disengaged family is more common in modern urban settings, and it is probably not appropriate to place any traditional ethnic families at this end of the cohesion dimension. It is appropriate to note, however, that due to traditional values of independence and self-reliance held by Anglo Americans, one would find a larger number of Anglo American families at the low end of the cohesion dimension. McGill and Pearce (1982) describe Anglo Americans as self-reliant, taking responsibility for their own problems by not complaining or involving other people.

> Keeping a stiff upper lip, muddling through, and taking it all like a man, all reflect English values, which British Americans have maintained as the desired responses to pain, suffering, and life's difficulties. (p. 458)

McGill and Pearce note that Anglo American couples rely on their families of origin as resources in childbirth or child rearing

Figure 1: Traditional Extended Ethnic Families

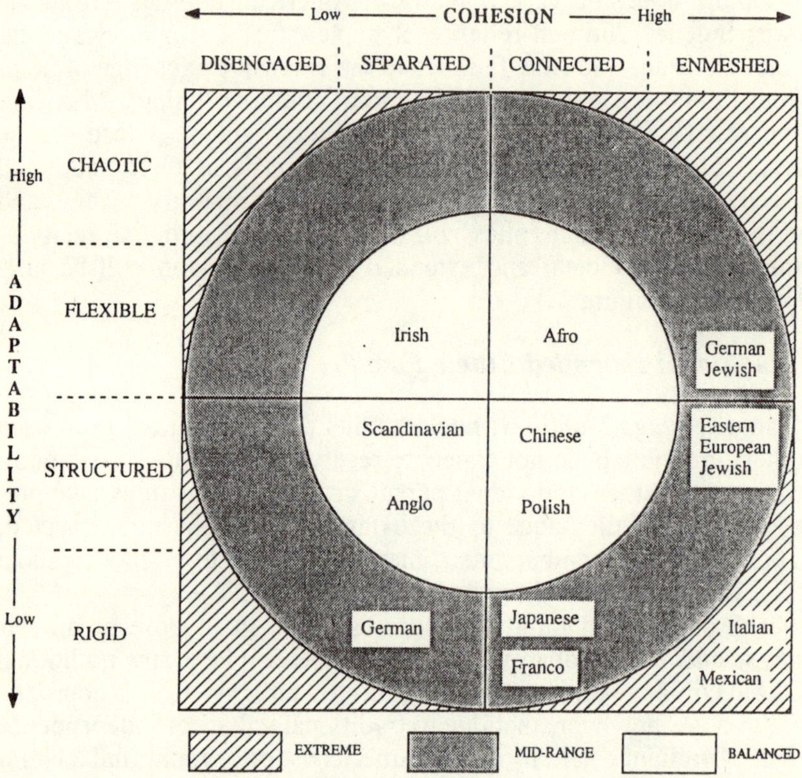

less frequently than families of many other cultural backgrounds. In studying urban neighborhoods, Greeley found that fewer young Anglo American adults visited their parents weekly than young adults of other ethnic groups (1971, p. 77).

In *separated families*, nuclear units define their status in terms of the success of the nuclear unit. Though the units are independent from each other, they recognize obligations to extended family members. Nuclear units are reluctant to ask for help and do not expect help from each other, but help is usually given in times of crisis. Help may also be exchanged on the basis of mutual interest and reciprocity. The frequency of visits between parents and children and between brothers and sisters depends on common interests and enjoyment. Thus interaction with different parts of the extended family may vary. For example, one's relationship to some siblings could be at the connected level and to others at the disengaged level. Close family relationships are valued, but individuals' inclination and choice determine the actual relationships. The modal level of cohesion for Anglo, German, Irish, and Scandinavian American extended families is hypothesized to be the separated level.

Emotional restraint and independence of the nuclear unit are characteristic of all of these ethnic families. Warmth, affection, grief, and anger are not easily expressed in their family cultures. The boundaries between nuclear and extended families are clear in German American families (Winawer-Steiner & Wetzel, 1982). Boszormenyi-Nagy and Ulrich (1981) report that German Americans rely less on what they regard as the transient nature of feelings than on the fair and honest give and take of established family relationships.

The Irish are also reported to be enormously sensitive to each other's right to privacy. Their family relationships tend to be governed by loyalty and a sense of duty or obligation (McGoldrick, 1982). Cohler and Lieberman (1979) describe older Irish Americans as having a more independent view of themselves than the elderly of many other ethnic backgrounds. Scandinavian Americans recognize mutual obligations in the kinship network, but asking for help is uncommon. When necessary, help is given "with a minimum of words and excuses as it is shameful both to need help and to suggest that someone is incapable of managing on his or her own" (Midelfort & Midelfort, 1982, p. 441).

In *connected families*, nuclear family units define their status in terms of the extended family. The accomplishments of the extended family as a whole determine one's own status. Nuclear units are expected to live close to one another when possible and to exchange aid. This aid is reciprocal, and everyone is expected to contribute. Visits with family members are frequent. However, emotional dependency and emotional expression are discouraged, and family members usually do not expect to share their feelings. These families thus encourage instrumental interdependence based on reciprocity together with emotional independence. Hypothesized to have a modal level of connectedness the cohesion dimension are Japanese, Chinese, French Canadian, Polish, and Afro American families.

For example, regarding Asian families, Shon and Ja (1982) explain:

> These systems do not stress the independence and autonomy of the individual, but rather that the individual is superceded by the family. Rules of behavior and conduct are formalized. An individual's response and adherence to the code of conduct becomes not a reflection of the individual, but of the family and kinship network to which he or she belongs. (p. 209)
>
> This is not to say that individuation does not occur or is not promoted, but it is constantly tinged with the subconscious knowledge of the relationships and obligations between the individual and other family members. (p. 224)

First generation Japanese Americans report frequent visiting with their children and grandchildren and often live with them (Modell, 1968). Their culture emphasizes "gaman," the endurance or suppression of emotion, and "enryo," being reserved. Japanese American respondents recognize that one is indebted to others and that one should return favors (O'Connor, 1977).

French Canadian and Polish American families also reportedly discourage the strong expression of emotion. Franco Americans tend not to be demonstrative. Rather they express feelings of intimacy and attachment nonverbally through family reunions and get-togethers (Langelier, 1982). Parents and adult children visit each other frequently and often live close to one another (Greeley, 1971, p. 77). Franco Americans regard reciprocal family, kinship, and religious obligations as more important than the individual's self-interest (French, 1981).

In the Polish family, respect rather than love was traditionally the binding tie (Thomas & Znaniecki, 1920). Polish American families are characterized by mutual respect, support, cooperation, financial and spiritual help, and sacrifice (Mostwin, 1980, p. 110). They tend to live close together and to exchange aid frequently (Greeley, 1971, p. 77). However, emotional dependency is highly disapproved. Feelings of need are not seen as normal, and being taken care of implies weakness and inability to pull one's own weight (Mondykowski, 1982). Status is based on a family's position in the local community, and families compete with each other to attain a high position (Lopata, 1976). Each family member is expected to contribute to maintaining his own family's status (Lopata, 1981; Finestone, 1967).

Scholars studying both African and Afro American families emphasize that these families cannot be understood by studying nuclear units (Sudarkasa, 1980; Tetteh, 1967). An open system, the Afro American family is not primarily based on a conjugal relationship or on a single household. Rather, it is based on a wide ranging group of parents, children, siblings, friends, neighbors, and fictive kin involved in relationships of exchange and coparenting (Aschenbrenner & Carr, 1980; Aschenbrenner, 1978; Billingsley, 1968; Dougherty, 1978; Ladner, 1971) Implicit understandings exist between people who participate in the exchange referred to as "reciprocity" (Stack, 1974; Malson, 1982) or "kin insurance" (McAdoo, 1978). Nonkin are often absorbed into existing family structure and are seen as part of the family because they function in family-type roles.

In *enmeshed families*, individuals' identities are defined in terms of their role in the family. There is much greater emphasis on emotional expression and emotional support of family members than in connected families. Nuclear units are expected to live close to one another when possible and to visit frequently. Both instrumental help and emotional support are exchanged. Help is based on need and on one's ability to give it rather than on reciprocity. One's right to receive help is derived from being a member of the family and is not based on one's ability to contribute. Dependency is not feared because family members are available for help and encouragement. Hypothesized to have the highest percentage of extended families at the enmeshed level of the cohesion dimension are Mexican, Italian, and Jewish American extended families.

Keefe (1980) describes the Mexican American extended family

as offering protection, advice, nurturance, and support both during major crises and in day-to-day problems. Grandparents, uncles, aunts, and godparents provide individual attention for children and guide adolescents. Children have siblings and cousins for their playmates and often have few friends outside the family (Falicov, 1982).

Similarly, for Italian Americans, the family is reported to be the primary orientation (Tomasi, Tomasi, & Engles, 1970; Gambino, 1973, 1975). Mutual rights and obligations are strong and binding on all members of the family (Quadagno, 1981). Within the family context itself, all emotions are viewed as acceptable. Once settled, Italian Americans often spend their whole lives in the same neighborhood, close to family members (Rotunno & McGoldrick, 1982). Upward mobility and education are viewed as secondary to the security and affection of the family (Ragucci, 1981; Vecoli, 1978; Papajohn & Spiegel, 1975; Marjoribanks, 1982).

Jewish Americans are hypothesized to be somewhat less cohesive than Italian and Mexican American families. Their emphasis on education and social status often leads family members to live at greater distances from each other. Yet, they still regard family as central in their lives. Obligations to the extended family are of great importance (Herz & Rosen, 1982). A comparison of religious groups in the Phoenix metropolitan area showed that Jewish respondents have the greatest amount of contact with parents and brothers and sisters when they live in the area and have the most frequent contact by phone and mail when they live out of state (Farber, Mindel, & Lazerwitz, 1981).

High family cohesion influences family support throughout the life cycle. Wake and Sporakowski (1972) reported that Jewish families are more willing to support aged parents than other ethnic families. Italian families prefer to care for older relatives at home rather than place them in a nursing home, even when caring for them at home puts great strain on the family (Fandetti & Gelfand, 1976; Ragucci, 1981; Johnson, 1978). In a study of hospitalized patients, Zborowski (1969) found that Irish Americans contrasted with Jewish and Italian Americans. While Irish Americans preferred to be alone when ill and saw no point in burdening others with their discomfort, Jewish and Italian Americans regarded withdrawal from family members as inconceivable. They saw suffering as an experience to be shared with others just as the entire process of living is shared.

Contemporary Ethnic Families

The emphasis on individual choice in American society, together with education and occupational and geographic mobility, tends to lower cohesion in intergenerational family relationships. (See Figure 2.) Thus, many people of Anglo American, Irish, Scandinavian, and German backgrounds may have a disengaged intergenerational family. Many traditionally connected families would evolve

Figure 2: Contemporary Extended Ethnic Families

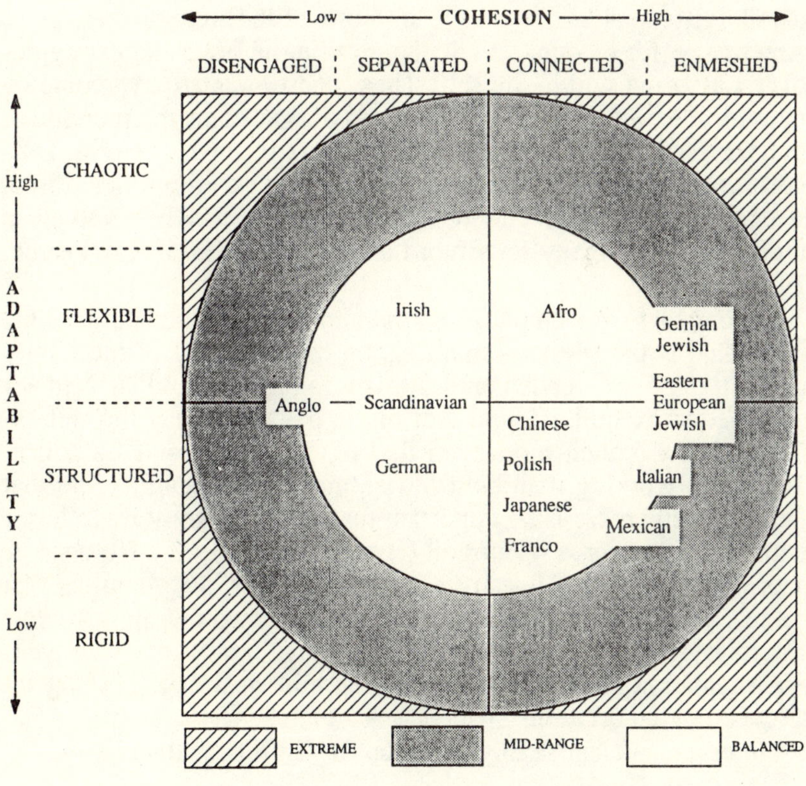

into a separated type and enmeshed into a connected type. Though there is a general change toward less cohesion, this change is not uniform. Even within the same family, some members of younger generations have a family type very similar to that of their grandparents, while others change quite dramatically. In addition, family stage and life circumstances can result in movement in both directions especially for families in the midrange on the cohesion dimension. However, one would usually not expect change from one end of the scale to the other. *Thus, contemporary ethnic families are hypothesized to show considerable dispersion along the cohesion dimension.*

Nuclear versus Extended Families

In general, cultural patterns of cohesion in the nuclear family parallel extended family cohesion. Gorer (1964) reports that Anglo Americans, for example, view the meaningful issues and struggles of life as being within the self. Thus, constraints are overcome by individual effort. The family is valued as it sustains the individual, as a facilitator of success and achievement in the wider world. During their children's adolescence, Anglo American families do not struggle to keep their children at home or as closely involved in family life as do many Jewish or Italian families (McGill & Pearce, 1982).

In contrast to this emphasis on the family as a springboard for the individual is the primary emphasis on the centrality of the family characteristic of Jewish and Italian families. Brodbar-Nemzer (1986), for example, found that marital stress affects the self-esteem of Jews much more than that of Protestants and Catholics. Therapists working with both Jewish and Italian families find that family togetherness is so important that children rarely leave home without some degree of turmoil (Herz & Rosen, 1982; Rotunno & McGoldrick, 1982). It can be expected that ethnic families that value close intergenerational relationships throughout the life cycle would have higher cohesion in the nuclear family units as well. Such higher cohesion would socialize children for the lifelong intergenerational relationships.

However, nuclear family cohesion for families with cohesive extended family relationships is more complex than the cohesion of nuclear families which function more independently from their extended families. The cohesion of nuclear families closely integrated with their extended families might be regarded as multifaceted. Their overall cohesion is influenced not only by the direct relationships between nuclear family members, but also by the multiple indirect relationships which result from their common participation in the extended family. Thus, for example, the time nuclear family members spend only with each other does not reflect their complete shared experience. What is shared as a result of their common experiences in the extended family also contributes to their family cohesion. The degree to which they share problems and consult directly with one another does not fully reflect their understanding of each other or their participation in decision making. Getting to know each other's parents and siblings and participating in discussions with other family members is an indirect way of understanding one another and sharing in decision making.

Because of the multifaceted nature of cohesion in connected and enmeshed extended families, it would seem possible for a family member to complete the family version of FACES with a score at the enmeshed level and to complete the couples version of FACES with a score at the disengaged level with neither score accurately reflecting cohesion in the nuclear family. For instance, while the Italian family is often described as enmeshed, intimacy in marriage is not characterized as having a high priority in Italian families (Arenson, 1979). The mutual support and complementarity of roles between husband and wife relate to the intergenerational family, rather than to the marital sharing of emotions (Rotunno & McGoldrick, 1982). In such a family, a disengaged couple score reflects the direct contribution of the couple's interaction to the couple's cohesion, but not the contribution of the shared commitment and experience in the extended family. The enmeshed family score, on the other hand, probably reflects enmeshment in the extended family rather than in the nuclear family.

Many nuclear families with traditionally higher expectations for extended family cohesion become separated from the extended family. Do these families maintain high cohesion in the nuclear family? When the extended family is no longer high in cohesion due to geographic mobility, nuclear family cohesion probably depends mainly on the marital dyad. When marital communication and shared decision making is important, as in the modal Jewish family, one would expect high nuclear family cohesion to be maintained. However, when communication between husband and wife is not as important and roles of men and women in the family are highly differentiated, the couple would probably often not have an approach to decision making, communication, and sharing activities which enables them to maintain higher levels of family cohesion. For example, Flores and Sprenkle's (1987) recent study comparing Mexican American and white middle class Lutheran families showed a higher number of Mexican American families were dispersed at the lower levels of the cohesion dimension.

High extended family cohesion contributes to cohesion in the nuclear family. However, when extended family cohesion is low, the nuclear family is, in a sense, left to its own devices. Thus, it can be hypothesized that ethnic nuclear families with lower extended family cohesion will be rather similarly dispersed on the cohesion dimension with a higher concentration at the middle levels.

While the enmeshed nuclear family is probably not typical for any ethnic group, enmeshment in the nuclear family might well occur more frequently in nuclear family units low in extended family cohesion. Such independent nuclear families might become enmeshed in response to geographic and occupational mobility which reduces ties to friends and a community or in their attempts to cope with problems of the family members on their own. In those nuclear families separated from an extended family traditionally high in cohesion, emotional energy formerly directed to other relatives may become focused on a child, and enmeshment may result.

NUCLEAR FAMILY ADAPTABILITY

As can be noted from the previous discussion, the ties that bind American ethnic families vary in their nature, length, and strength. Ethnic family patterns for adaptability can be described somewhat more simply as the extent to which men, women, and children in the family share areas of responsibility and decision making or are differentiated.

All societies structure roles and responsibilities based on women's function of bearing and nurturing children. However, the extent to which men and women share in one another's responsibilities and in decision making in regard to various aspects of their family life differs from one culture to another. For example, while Jewish women in Eastern Europe and unmarried women in Ireland worked outside the home, Italian women almost never worked (Yans-McLaughlin, 1977).

Families also differ in the extent to which children are encouraged to participate in decision making, in expressing their own ideas, and in having a say regarding household rules and their own discipline and responsibilities. Some families expect children to obey parents on the basis of their greater knowledge, wisdom, and authority. These families use punishment more frequently as a method of socialization. Other families want children to guide their behavior on the basis of understanding the rationale behind rules. These families use reason and persuasion more frequently as a method of socialization. Ethnic families are placed on an adaptability level based on the extent to which husbands and wives traditionally shared areas of responsibility, activities, and decision making, on the extent to which children were encouraged to express their views, and on their approaches to children's socialization.

Rigid Families

Many traditional European, Latin, and Asian cultures have been described as having rather strict role segregation in the family, with women responsible for home and children and men responsible for economic support. In Japanese (Kitano & Kikumura, 1981; O'Connor, 1977), Mexican (Falicov, 1982; Panitz, McConchie, Sauber, & Fonseca,1983; Triandis, 1983), Italian (Gambino, 1973, 1975; Rotunno & McGoldrick, 1982; Johnson, 1982), German (Parsons, 1976; Winawer-Steiner & Wetzel, 1982; Schelsky, 1954), and French Canadian (Woolfson, 1975; Langelier, 1982) American families, the father was regarded as head of the family and economic provider. Authority was his prerogative. The mother's life centered on caring for her children and home. In the German American family, for example, the mother's domain was "Kinder, Kirche, and Kuche" – children, church, and kitchen.

Though Japanese, Mexican, Italian, German, and French Canadian women might work outside the home in times of economic necessity, wives', and especially mothers', employment was avoided when possible, and their careers were not considered important. Husbands were links to the community, and wives reportedly were not encouraged – and were often discouraged – from participating in educational, political, and community affairs as well as in economic activities. In a comparison of seven ethnic groups, Greeley (1972) found German and Italian respondents highest in valuing obedience for children. Children did not have a say in their discipline or in the rules of the house. They were to be polite and to avoid disagreements with parents. Because of the clear role segregation, women's low participation in the world of work, the strong authority of the father, and expectations of obedience and compliance for children, these ethnic families are hypothesized to be traditionally low on the adaptability dimension with the mode at the rigid level.

Structured Families

Placed at the structured level of adaptability are those ethnic families that encourage and value women's participation in employment outside the home. Though these families still regard men as head of the household, their authority is less absolute, and wives tend to have a higher status with greater participation in decision making. Though the Chinese American wife, for example, is not regarded as having a totally equal relationship with her husband, her career is valued, and many Chinese women engage in professional work (Huang, 1981). Also included at the structured level are Polish, Scandinavian, Anglo, and Orthodox Jewish American families of Eastern European origin.

While the Polish American father and husband was traditionally regarded as head of the household, the dominance of the Polish man is regarded as more theoretical than real (Bloch, 1976). The Polish wife worked along with her husband in planting and harvesting, and this gave her a higher status than Western European wives (Sanday, 1974). Similarly, present day Polish American wives expect to contribute to family income and to assert themselves in the family (Mondykowsky, 1982). Child rearing in the Polish family, however, appears similar to that in rigid families. Mostwin (1980) observes that children are expected to respect their parents and are often physically punished for disobedience.

Traditional Scandinavian socialization of children, in contrast, provides a foundation for a flexible level of adaptability in contemporary families. Norwegian children, for example, were taught to guide their conduct more by objective rules than by personal authority (Gronseth, 1964). In comparing ethnic groups, Greeley (1972) found Scandinavians to be lowest in their emphasis on obedience and highest in valuing independence and self-reliance. Calmness and reason were traditionally central to child rearing. Norwegian parents think that children should not be physically punished. Instead, parents should explain to their children why their behavior is wrong (Rodnick, 1955). In comparing Norwegian and Italian families, Gronseth (1964) found that Norwegian children saw their parents as more equal than Italian children. Eliot and Hillman (1960) note that in the mid-nineteenth century, although Norwegian women were under their husband's authority, they still had high status in the family, and a woman who worked outside the home was perceived as industrious and useful.

While traditional Anglo American sex roles were divided with the father the breadwinner and the mother the homemaker, Anglo Americans' emphasis on egalitarian relationships moderated the rigidity of these roles. While Anglo American women did not traditionally value working outside the home, McGill and Pearce (1982) observe that Anglo Americans view marriage as a contract for the negotiation and meeting of individual needs and Anglo American children are usually not subject to strict control. Anglo American respondents ranked intermediate in valuing obedience for children in a comparison of ethnic groups (Greeley, 1972).

Flexible Families

The Jewish American family is somewhat more difficult to place on the adaptability dimension than other ethnic families. On the one hand, Gordon (1959) notes that even among immigrant families there was a considerable degree of equality between husbands and wives. There was a high degree of interchangeability in family roles, and wives were trained to be ready to support the family. Women often had opportunities to conduct business or seek employment (Landes & Zborowski, 1968). Furthermore, Herz and Rosen (1982) describe Jewish Americans as considering family problems from every angle. Father, mother, and children are encouraged to express their ideas and feelings. Jewish families rank low in valuing obedience for children (Greeley, 1972). Thus, the Jewish American family might be placed at the flexible level of adaptability.

However, the Eastern European Jewish community was a male-oriented culture. Women were regarded as subordinate, and men greeted each day by offering thanks to God "that Thou hast not made me a woman" (Hertz, 1969, p. 21). In the "shtetl," families prayed that their offspring would be boys, and the study of Torah was considered the lofty pursuit of men alone (Zborowski & Herzog, 1952; Herz & Rosen, 1982). Thus, traditional Jewish American families with an Eastern European Orthodox background would probably more often be at the structured level of adaptability and families with a German Reform Jewish background closer to the flexible level.

The Afro American and the Irish American families are also placed at the flexible level. Flexibility of family roles and the participation of both husband and wife in child rearing, household tasks, and employment are characteristic of the Afro American family (Hill, 1972; Hines & Boyd-Franklin, 1982). Research on Afro American families supports the diffusion of sex roles and relative equality between husband and wife (Millham & Smith, 1981; DeJarnett & Raven, 1981). Black children also share in family responsibilities by taking care of younger siblings and performing household tasks (Staples, 1981; Malson, 1980).

Irish women have enjoyed a greater degree of independence than women in most other cultures. Irish American families often pay as much attention to the education of daughters as to that of sons, and Irish American women are overrepresented in professional and white collar jobs (Blessing, 1980). Though women officially defer to the authority of men, a relatively equal relationship is probably found in most families, with mothers sometimes dominant in the family if fathers are distant due to family tensions or overinvolvement in work (Lidz, 1968; McGoldrick, 1982; Biddle, 1981). Both Irish American men and women are often involved in social roles outside the home—such as education, employment, volunteer work, political involvement, and friendships. Irish Americans rank low in valuing children's obedience and children's agreement with parents' ideas (Greeley, 1971, 1972, 1974).

Chaotic Families

No American ethnic families were placed at the chaotic level of adaptability. As will be noted later, though a very high level of change does not seem to be a cultural mode for families, ethnic families can be found at this level of the adaptability dimension under certain circumstances.

In summary, ethnic families were assigned a modal level of adaptability with an eye to their potential for change. Cultural norms, sex roles and responsibilities, authority, the distribution of resources in the family, children's roles, and children's socialization were kept in mind in assigning a modal level on the adaptability dimension to varied ethnic families. However, even families with a high potential for change often choose more structured roles, responsibilities, and decision making. During certain stages of the life cycle, such as child rearing stages, a more structured division of responsibility may be desirable. In addition, the contemporary emphasis on a more equal relationship between spouses and the dramatic increase in women's employment outside the home have resulted in a change toward higher adaptability.

Ethnic Families on the Circumplex Model

Figures 1 and 2 place traditional and contemporary extended ethnic families on the Circumplex Model. This placement is not definitive since it is not based on research using FACES, but rather on descriptions of ethnic families by therapists and historians and on a variety of studies of ethnic families. The placement of ethnic families does not mean families of a particular ethnic group are not expected to be other types on the model. Families of any particular ethnic group would be dispersed among all types on the Circumplex Model. However, as shown on Figures 3 and 4, if one were comparing Irish, German, and Italian extended families, one would expect a higher proportion of Irish families in the upper left portion of the model, a higher proportion of German families in the lower left,

Figure 3: Traditional Irish, German, and Italian Extended Families

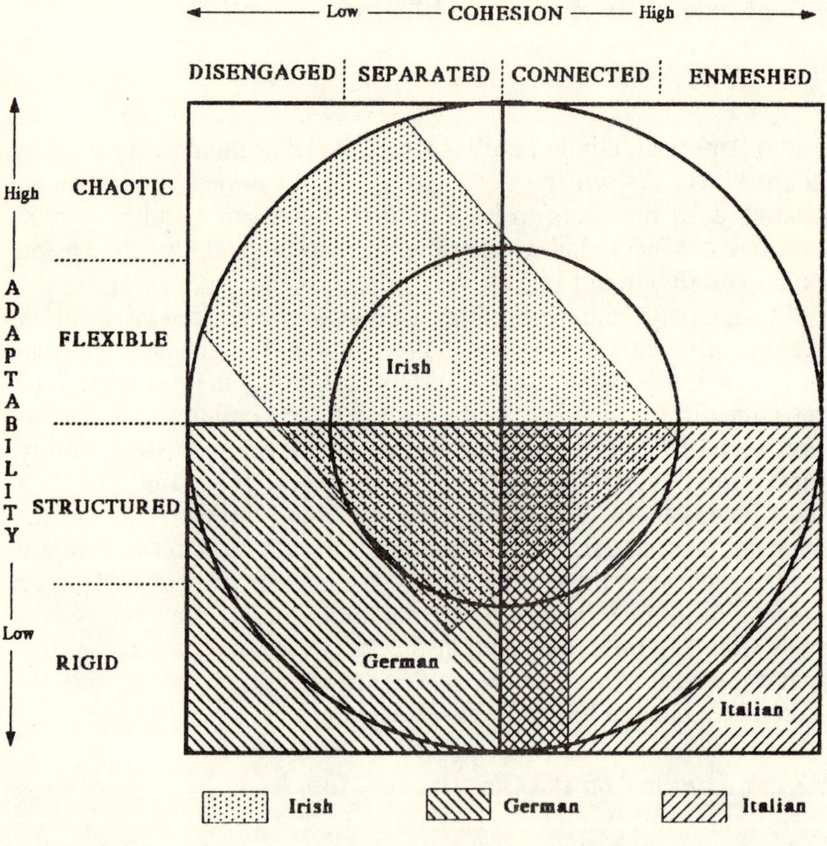

and a higher proportion of Italian families in the lower right section of the Model.

A comparison of Figures 1 and 2 and of Figures 3 and 4 in general reflects a decrease in extended family cohesion and an increase in adaptability. These changes result in a movement toward the balanced central region of the Circumplex Model for contemporary ethnic families. Change probably affects the distribution of ethnic families on the Circumplex Model in somewhat different ways. For example, contemporary Italian families would probably be dispersed more widely over the Model. Irish families, on the other

Figure 4: Contemporary Irish, German, and Italian Extended Families

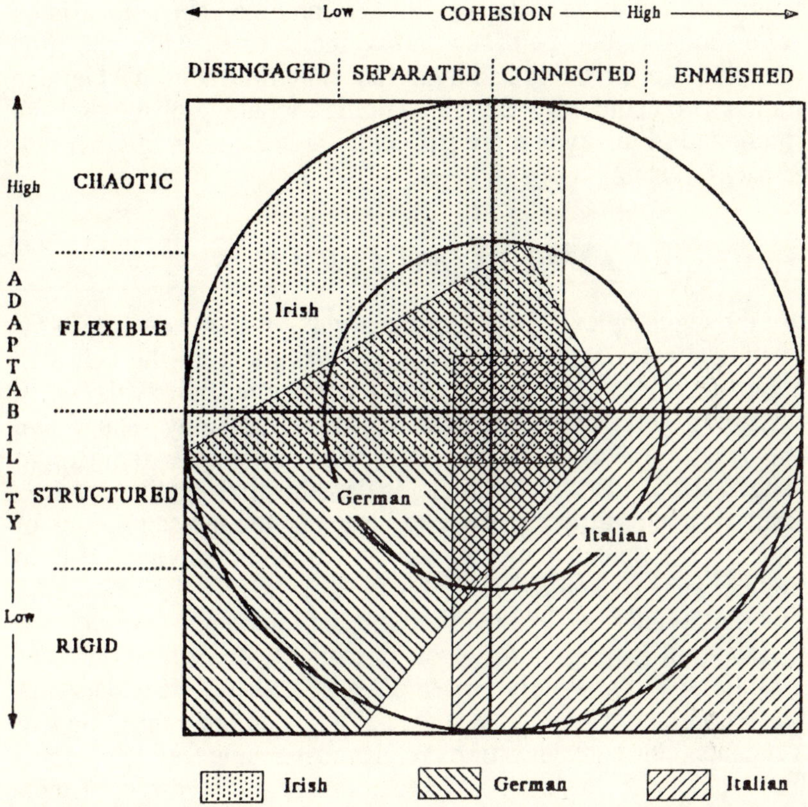

hand, would probably show high dispersion among the same types on the Model. However, a greater number of traditional families, especially those rural in background, would be of the structured connected type. The dispersion of contemporary German families is expected to shift toward the balanced central portion of the Model with few families represented in the rigid connected type and a significant number in the flexible separated and flexible connected types. Two assumptions are made for German families. First, it is assumed that the German extended family higher in cohesion is connected by choice rather than by expectation. Second, it is assumed that families connected by choice are probably those with better communication skills and would be more likely to increase their adaptability, particularly with the contemporary emphasis on greater equality between men and women. Thus, while the rigid connected type probably had high frequency for traditional German families, contemporary German families would probably not be represented in this type more frequently than families of other ethnic backgrounds.

FAMILY COMMUNICATION

In the Circumplex Model, family communication serves as a facilitating dimension which influences movement on the cohesion and adaptability dimensions. Positive communication skills—such as sending clear and congruent messages, empathy, supportive statements, and effective problem solving—enable families to change their levels of cohesion and adaptability. Negative communication—such as incongruent and disqualifying messages, lack of empathy, negative statements, and poor problem solving—tend to inhibit change (Olson & McCubbin, 1983).

Research and descriptions of ethnic families report more on the expression of feelings and support in ethnic families than on problem solving skills. Within any ethnic group, there is a wide variation in communication skills, especially since communication can be enhanced through education. While most people tend to communicate adequately in day-to-day life and may not be aware of their communication skills, these skills influence one's effectiveness in meeting crises, working through emotional problems, resolving family conflicts, and negotiating with family members about new goals and the needs of changing identities.

It is probably not even appropriate to categorize ethnic families according to communication skills in general. However, ethnic communication skills related to emotional expression and support are listed below and will be referred to in the discussion of problems and resources in ethnic families. Note especially the more positive support reported for families at the enmeshed level of cohesion and the negative verbal skills described for ethnic families hypothesized to be higher in adaptability.

Negative:

Irish	Ridicule, shame, belittling (Biddle, 1981; Greeley, 1972; McGoldrick, 1982)
British	Criticism (McGill & Pearce, 1982)
Japanese	Shame (Doi, 1973; O'Connor, 1977; Shon & Ja, 1982)
Jewish	Criticism, condescension, guilt (Herz & Rosen, 1982)

Discipline, Punishment:

German (Winawer-Steiner & Wetzel, 1982), Polish (Mondykowski, 1982), and French Canadian (Langelier, 1982)

Explanation, Reasoning:

Scandinavian (Gronseth, 1964; Rodnick, 1955; Kandel & Lesser, 1969; Greeley, 1972) and Jewish (Herz & Rosen, 1982)

Lack of Support, Nonexpression of Feeling:

French Canadian (Langlier, 1982), Scandinavian (Midelfort & Midelfort, 1982; Rodnick, 1955; Greeley, McCready, & Thiesen, 1980), British (McGill & Pearce, 1982), Irish (Zborowski, 1969; McGoldrick, 1982; Greeley, McCready, & Thiesen, 1980), and German (Winawer-Steiner & Wetzel, 1982)

Support for Instrumental Activities, Praise for Skills:

German (Winawer-Steiner & Wetzel, 1982) and Polish (Mondykowski, 1982)

Emotional Support, Expression of Feeling:

Mexican (Falicov, 1982; Keefe, 1980), Italian (Gambino, 1974; Zborowski, 1969; Rotunno & McGoldrick, 1982; Greeley, McCready, & Thiesen, 1980), and Jewish (Zborowski, 1969; Herz & Rosen, 1982; Zborowski & Herzog, 1952; Greeley, McCready, & Thiesen, 1980)

THE INFLUENCE OF EXTENDED FAMILIES ON NUCLEAR FAMILY FUNCTIONING

Ethnic variation in the dispersion of families on the Circumplex Model has important implications for family functioning throughout the life cycle. This section analyzes the kinds of problems that bring ethnic families to family therapists in terms of the three dimensions of the Circumplex Model: family cohesion, family adaptability, and family communication. In trying to gain insight into the relationship between the dimensions of the Circumplex Model and family functioning, it is important to assess whether families which have problems are typical of families in their ethnic group or whether they are families which have moved to different levels on the dimensions. As will be noted, due to life circumstances and poor communication skills, families in a particular ethnic group sometimes diverge from more typical levels on the dimensions of cohesion and adaptability and encounter problems related to the divergence.

In general, the following analysis of problems in ethnic families supports research on the Circumplex Model indicating that nuclear families with central levels on the cohesion and adaptability dimensions function more adequately across the life cycle than those at the extremes. However, the dimensions of cohesion and adaptability have a quite different effect for the extended family. Because questions on the Family Adaptability and Cohesion Evaluation Scales can be answered from either a nuclear or extended family frame of reference, the scales do not distinguish between nuclear and extended family cohesion. The apparent divergence in the model's predictions for rigid enmeshed families probably occurs because, in contrast to nuclear families, high cohesion in intergenerational families is often beneficial to family functioning.

Family Cohesion

Extremes on the cohesion dimension for *nuclear* families are hypothesized to contribute to problems in family functioning. However, *extended* families with higher cohesion offer a richness in kin resources which families at the lower levels of cohesion often lack. Descriptions and research on ethnic families indicate that the disengaged level of cohesion is not a cultural ideal or modal type for either nuclear or extended families. However, due to endeavors outside the family, geographic mobility, and limited communication skills, quite a few families from cultural backgrounds valuing the separated level of cohesion would actually be disengaged.

Disengaged Families

As already noted, Anglo American values of self-reliance probably result in a higher percent of Anglo American families at the disengaged level. Family therapists describe these families as vulnerable to major external catastrophes such as accidents, serious illness, or economic depression. The complaint of children in therapy often is that their parents relate to them in a detached manner. Anglo American families often do not try to keep children at home or closely involved in family life. They sometimes have difficulty dealing with a child's dependency needs and withdraw physical, financial, or emotional support before an adolescent is ready for independence. Therapists observe that couples often respond to conflict by distancing and avoidance rather than direct confrontation. Thus, they sometimes drift apart emotionally. Fear of incapacity and dependency make Anglo American elderly vulnerable to loss of self-esteem and depression.

> British American families carry self-determination to an extreme. They are good at promoting separation but a little lost when it comes to providing guidance and support. . . . They cope easily with success, not with troubles or failure. (McGill & Pearce, 1982, pp. 469-470)

Similarly, Stein (1971) observes that some Irish Americans neither have nor want much contact with their extended family and, even in situations of extreme need, they do not solicit help from family members. In contrast to Anglo American norms of independence, however, Irish distancing from extended family may be related to tensions and anger which build up over time and lead to emotional cutoff (Spiegel, 1971). Researchers and family therapists note that Irish American alienation from their families is accompanied by pain and a sense of isolation. It evolves from negative communication patterns of ridicule and belittlement. These may be used as gentle teasing in some families, but they serve to undermine self-esteem and family cohesion in others. Ridicule, combined with the lack of support and emotional expression reported to be characteristic of many Irish American families, can alienate family members from each other (Zborowski, 1969; McGoldrick, 1982; Greeley, McCready, & Thiesen, 1980).

Separated Families

Like Anglo American and Irish families, Scandinavian and German American families were placed at the separated level of family cohesion. Therapeutic problems of these families do not seem to be directly related to their level on the cohesion dimension. As already noted, however, the expression of feeling and emotional support are closely related to the cohesion dimension. Communication problems can influence German and Scandinavian families to move from the separated level to the disengaged level of family cohesion or to fail to ask for help when it is needed.

> Norwegians believe that they should not burden their family or even their closest friend with personal problems or feelings of inadequacy. (Midelfort & Midelfort, 1982, p. 443)
>
> In treating families of German heritage, we are sometimes struck by the lack of expression of feelings despite the severity of their problems. (Winawer-Steiner & Wetzel, 1982)

Connected Families

For most people, the connected family is a source of help and support that allows considerable participation in the wider society. Because the extended family is often viewed as a source of status, however, the individual who deviates significantly from family values or embarrasses the family in some way can be rejected (Finestone, 1967). An individual or nuclear unit can then become disengaged from the extended family. In addition, the loosening of family ties can occur throughout the life cycle as people go away to school, change occupations, receive transfers and promotions, and change their residences. As a result, a connected extended family often evolves into a separated one.

Some ethnic families traditionally at the connected level, such as Polish and French Canadian, emphasize neighborhood, church, and local community as a source of identity. These families often experience problems during the launching stage, especially if adolescents and young adults have aspirations which might separate them from the family and community. Polish American children, for example, "were told they were stuck up if they sought higher education or mobility out of the neighborhood. To call a person 'stuck up' was a serious charge that isolated them from the community" (Kuniczak, 1978).

Enmeshed Families

For parents in families at higher levels of cohesion, the loss or feared loss of family ties makes the launching stage of the family life cycle even more stressful.

> Enmeshment is a frequent characteristic of Jewish American families. However, the family will not usually be aware that they are upset about the child's leaving. Since Jews tend to be liberal and open to ideas, the last thing they would want is to be seen as unsophisticated, uneducated, or boring. (Herz & Rosen, 1982, p. 385)

Parents in Italian American families often perceive their children's involvement in relationships and activities outside the family as equivalent to leaving the family. Thus, they sometimes define their children's marital, residential, or occupational choices as abandonment and rejection (Rotunno & McGoldrick, 1982). This stress during the launching stage is related to the attempts by parents to assure life-long cohesion in the intergenerational family.

While enmeshed extended families usually function well, nuclear families separated from their extended families often experience problems. In the enmeshed extended family, emotional expression tends to be encouraged. However, since such a family involves many people, the emotion expressed is diffused. Other family members respond to one's feelings and problems with insights and empathy, and one likewise responds to them. When individuals are separated from their extended family, they can experience a profound sense of loss. As a result, they sometimes focus their emotional expression on their spouse and children. The focusing of intense emotion can lead to emotional and psychological problems, especially between parents and children, since parent-child relationships are usually close in these families. In addition, since these families are not accustomed to turning to people and resources outside the family for help, crises and problems can become especially stressful and difficult to resolve when extended kin are not available.

> Some of these family changes are related to the fact that immigration usually involves separation from extended family and friends. These losses prompt a regrouping to accomplish nurturance and instrumental functions and may increase the cohesiveness of the nuclear family to compensate for the initial sociocultural isolation. While initially crucial for survival, this cohesiveness may lead to a dysfunctional enmeshment. (Falicov, 1982, p. 144)

Family Adaptability

Chaotic Families

As can be seen by the placement of ethnic families on the Circumplex Model, no families were placed at the chaotic level of the dimension. This indicates that the highly changeable family is not typical for a culture. Ethnic families which are described in a way which fits the chaotic level tend to be dysfunctional families which have key members missing. For example, in the Hispanic family, the father is often the definitive enforcer of limits and rules. When the father is absent, other males in the extended family, such as brothers, take his place. Hardy-Fanta and MacMahon-Herrera (1981) note that roles and rules often are unclear, and authority shifts back and forth between family members, perhaps between a mother, grandmother, and older siblings, when the father is absent and the extended family is not close by.

Black families are reported to be more open. Reciprocal relationships with kin and friends may change as new people come into the family network or as people in the network change their roles.

When key members are not available to fill their previous roles, the family may go through a period of disorganization with no clear leadership (Aponte, 1976; Hines & Boyd-Franklin, 1982).

Flexible Families

In general, flexibility is considered a family strength. Roles and rules are adjusted to meet family members changing preferences and needs. Wives and mothers contribute to family income through employment, and husbands and fathers contribute to household tasks and child rearing. In reality, in many ethnic families assigned to the flexible level, women's roles are flexible while men's roles remain more structured. In other words, women are encouraged to pursue careers and take on roles outside the home, but men are not equally flexible in taking on household responsibilities. In these "semi-flexible" families, women experience considerable stress and inner conflict.

> An additional conflict for Jewish women is the dual emphasis on her place in the home and on academic achievement and financial success. . . . The manifestations of this conflict may range from the inability to make a decision about career to considering divorce the only way to open the door to a career. (Herz & Rosen, 1982, p. 386)

Because the flexible level of adaptability involves considerable interchange of roles and responsibilities and the sharing of decision making, it requires higher communication and organizational skills. When these skills are lacking, families tend to become either structured or chaotic even though they prefer the flexible level. Flexible families also tend to value the equal opportunity for members' education and participation in work and activities outside the home. The paradox of equality is that when people are given equal opportunities, they view themselves and others in terms of their skills and accomplishments. This can give rise to intense competition between family members, including the use of negative verbal skills to maintain or enhance an individual's own position (Biddle, 1981; Greeley, 1972; McGoldrick, 1982; Herz & Rosen, 1982).

Structured Families

Nuclear ethnic families at the lower levels of adaptability experience problems, particularly at the stressful period when children are adolescents. However, as will be explained, high intergenerational family cohesion often reduces the marital and family problems of families represented in the bottom right quadrant of the Circumplex Model while poor communication patterns may accentuate the problems of families represented in the bottom left quadrant.

Midelfort and Midelfort (1982), for example, describe Scandinavian American families as using words sparingly and avoiding confrontation. Though Scandinavian Americans value individual freedom highly and accord women a quite high status, their family life is structured, and resentment may smolder within outwardly "cheerful" obedient family members. Lack of communication may increase the perception of rigidity and injustice in the family and may lead to a strained family life.

Rigid Families

Similarly, wives in traditional German American families often do not express the rage they feel at their subservient roles. Fathers as head of the traditional German family were expected to make just and fair decisions for their families without much discussion (Winawer-Steiner & Wetzel, 1982). Without discussion, of course, family members would often not know the rationale for father's decisions nor would he have gotten all the information relevant for making the decision.

Family therapists note that German American families often do not teach children to air feelings or negotiate disagreements. Winawer-Steiner and Wetzel (1982) observe that the struggles of increasing autonomy for children are discussed less than in many other ethnic groups, particularly those with expectations for higher cohesion such as Italian, Polish, and Jewish families. If parents and children do not relate well, parents or children may give up their contact rather than negotiate differences.

High intergenerational family cohesion tends to diminish the family problems encountered by structured and rigid families. Traditional Japanese, French Canadian, Italian, and Mexican families have clearly defined roles, with authority invested in the father as head of the family. However, studies indicate that when nuclear families are part of a larger extended family, family members do not regard the authority structure and decision making as rigid. Though these groups also do not have a tradition of negotiation between husband and wife, discussion on controversial issues often takes place with extended family members. Thus husband, wife, and often children have opportunities to hear the pros and cons on an issue and to express their opinions to others in the family. When decisions are made, one is more likely to have contributed to them and to know the reasons for them. Mexican American wives, for example, perceive themselves as having an equal role in decision making (Zapata & Jaramillo, 1981).

The extended family also buffers the effect of rigid family structure and rules on the socialization of children. Extended family members serve as role models for children and adolescents and supervise them. When extended family members are not available, parents supply their missing influence through restrictions on children's activities, selection of their friends, and increased discipline. These parental restrictions tend to increase intergenerational conflicts (Falicov, 1980). Descriptions of Asian families also show the essential contribution of the extended family to good relationships in family systems low in adaptability.

> For example, changes for the family may result from the loss of the extended family network. Relatives and close friends are no longer available to provide support to the nuclear family. . . . Without close friends, relatives, or extended family, interpersonal relations are limited to the nuclear family. Given the rigidity of family roles, the problems experienced within the family may have little or no outlet for expression or resolution. (Shon & Ja, 1982, p. 219)

In general then, the literature which describes problems of ethnic families supports the Circumplex Model's hypothesis that families operating at the extremes on the adaptability dimension function less well than those in the mid-range. While families at the chaotic level of the adaptability dimension tend to lack leadership and guidance for their younger members, families at the rigid level are more likely to experience alienation, unresolved tensions, and confrontations.

However, the effects of low adaptability are considerably diminished when extended family relationships are high in cohesion. A close intergenerational or extended family system greatly increases avenues of communication, role models for traditional values, help in everyday life and crises, and emotional support. Looking at the extended family system, then, explains the unexpected high level of functioning found in many rigid enmeshed families.

IMPLICATIONS FOR CIRCUMPLEX HYPOTHESES

This comparison of ethnic families emphasizes the importance of looking at the family from the perspective of several family systems: the extended family, the nuclear family, the marital dyad, parent-child, and sibling relationships. Particular attention has been given to the influence of rigid enmeshed extended families. The discussion of these families reveals the complexity behind the stereotype of the highly cohesive Italian or Mexican family as well as the complex dynamics of the cohesion and adaptability dimensions of the Circumplex Model.

In the Italian family, for instance, nuclear family cohesion was traditionally rooted in the extended family cohesion. Describing his own Italian family, Richard Gambino (1975) wrote, "I was raised simultaneously by my immigrant grandparents and by my parents" (p. 38). While husband and wife shared the same family values, commitment, and extended family experiences, cohesion in the marital dyad itself did not arise primarily from direct discussion and the shared activities of husband and wife.

> The father exercised responsibility without confiding its problems or details to his wife. They were simply *fatti soui*, his business. He would discuss them only when necessary, and then only with close male relatives, most often the clan's elders. (Gambino, 1975, p. 7)

What then happens to the nuclear unit of such a family when it becomes separated from the extended family through geographic mobility? While some observers suggest Mexican nuclear families frequently become enmeshed (Falicov, 1982), other research suggests they frequently become disengaged (Flores & Sprenkle, 1987). Given the highly differentiated roles of men and women in these families, fewer enmeshed marital dyads could be expected. It would seem that enmeshment, when it occurs, would be between parents and children. In the rigid enmeshed extended family, parents are expected to be role models for children of the same sex. When the father is not able to provide adequately for his family because of low income or discontinuous employment, his value as a role model, especially for adolescent and young adult sons, is diminished. This can result in awkwardness and intergenerational distancing in both nuclear and extended families. Such distancing could account for the high percentage of Mexican Americans who scored toward the rigidly disengaged area of the Circumplex Model in Flores and Sprenkle's comparison of Mexican and white Lutheran families. These scores in the rigid disengaged area came mainly from respondents living in an economically depressed area of San Antonio.

The rich network of relationships for sharing and mutual help in the enmeshed extended family suggests modifications in Hypotheses I and V of the Circumplex Model to take into account extended family relationships. Though the age hierarchy and roles of family members are rather rigidly defined, the rigidly enmeshed extended family system has quite a bit of flexibility because of its larger network of relationships. To take into account both the extended and nuclear family systems, Hypothesis I could be divided into the two modified hypotheses which follow it.

> I. Couples/families with balanced (two central levels) cohesion and adaptability will generally function more adequately across the family life cycle than those at the extremes of the dimensions.
>
> I. A. Nuclear families connected to or enmeshed with their extended families will generally function more adequately across the family life cycle than nuclear families disengaged or separated from their extended families.
>
> I. B. If couples/nuclear families are disengaged or separated from their extended families, those with balanced (two central

levels) cohesion and adaptability will generally function more adequately across the family life cycle than those at the extremes of these dimensions.

The comparison of ethnic families indicated that skills of emotional support and emotional expression were related to the cohesion dimension, with enmeshed extended families highest in these communication skills. Descriptions and research on ethnic families indicate that extended families high in cohesion have more positive affective communication skills than other families. The comparison of ethnic families suggests that communication skills might be too broad for inclusion in one hypothesis and could be divided into two categories with separate hypotheses for each.

V. Balanced couples/families will tend to have more positive communication skills than extreme families.

V. A. Extended families higher on the cohesion dimension tend to have more positive affective (emotional support and expression of feelings) communication skills.

V. B. Nuclear families central on the adaptability dimension tend to have more positive instrumental (negotiation and decision making) skills than families extreme on this dimension.

This paper has attempted to demonstrate that the Circumplex Model is a useful model for studying a wide range of families. While not all families within an ethnic group are the same type on the model, families in different ethnic groups probably vary in their dispersion on the model. Comparing those ethnic families which traditionally differ on the dimensions of the model can increase the range of variation on cohesion and adaptability.

REFERENCES

Aponte, H. (1976). In P. Guerin (Ed.), *Family therapy: Theory and practice*. New York: Gardner Press.

Arenson, S. J. (1979). Rankings of intimacy of social behaviors by Italians and Americans. *Psychological Reports*, 44, 1149-1150.

Aschenbrenner, J. (1978). Careers of black youth in the metro-east area. In J. Aschenbrenner & L. Collins (Eds.), *Processes of urbanism: A multidisciplinary approach* (pp. 267-295). The Hague: Mouton.

Aschenbrenner, J. & Carr, C. H. (1980). Conjugal relationships in the context of the black extended family. *Alternative Life-Styles*, 3(4), 463-484.

Biddle, E. H. (1981). The American Catholic Irish family. In C. H. Mindel & R. W. Habenstein, (Eds.), *Ethnic families in America: Patterns and variations* (pp. 86-114). New York: Elsevier.

Billingsley, A. (1968). *Black families in white America*. Engelwood Cliffs, NJ: Prentice-Hall.

Blessing, P. J. (1980). Irish. In S. Thernstrom (Ed.), *The Harvard encyclopedia of American ethnic groups*. Cambridge: Harvard University Press.

Bloch, H. (1976). Changing domestic roles among Polish immigrant women. *Anthropological Quarterly,* 40(1), 3-10.

Boszormenyi-Nagi, I. & Ulrich, D. (1981). Contextual family therapy. In A. Gurman & D. Kniskern (Eds.), *Handbook of family therapy*. New York: Brunner/Mazel.

Brodbar-Nemzer, J. Y. (1986). Marital relationships and self-esteem: How Jewish families are different. *Journal of Marriage and the Family*, 48(1), 89-98.

Carnes, P. (1985). *Counseling sexual abusers*. Minneapolis: CompCare Publications.

Clarke, J. (1984). *The Family Types of Schizophrenics, Neurotics and "Normals."* Unpublished doctoral dissertation, Family Social Science, University of Minnesota, St. Paul, Minnesota.

Cohler, B. J. & Lieberman, M. A. (1979). Personality change across the second half of life: Findings from a study of Irish, Italian, and Polish-American women. In D. E. Gelfand & A. J. Kutzik (Eds.), *Ethnicity and aging* (pp. 227-245). New York: Springer.

DeJarnett, S. & Raven, B. (1981). The balance, bases and modes of interpersonal power in Black couples: The role of sex and socioeconomic circumstances. *Journal of Black Psychology*, 1, 51-66.

Devereux, E. C. (1972). Authority and moral development among German and American children: A cross national experiment. *Journal of Comparative Family Studies*, 3(11), 99-124.

Doi, T. (1973). *The anatomy of dependence.* New York: Harper and Row.

Dougherty, M. C. (1978). *Becoming a woman in rural Black culture*. New York: Holt, Rinehart and Winston.

Elliot, T. D. & Hillman, A. (1960). *Norway's families: Trends, problems, and programs*. Philadelphia: University of Pennsylvania Press.

Falicov, C. J. (1982). Mexican families. In M. McGoldrick, J. K. Pearce, & J. Giordano (Eds.), *Ethnicity and family therapy* (pp. 134-163). New York: Guilford Press.

Fandetti, C. V. & Gelfand, D. E. (1976). Care of the aged: Attitudes of white ethnic families. *Gerontologist*, 16, 544-549.

Farber, B., Mindel, C. H., & Lazerwitz, B. (1981). The Jewish American family. In C. H. Mindel & R. W. Habenstein (Eds.), *Ethnic families in America: Patterns and variations* (pp. 350-385). New York: Elsevier.

Finestone, H. (1967). Reformation and recidivism among Italian and Polish criminal offenders. *American Journal of Sociology*, 72(6).

Flores, Maria T. & Sprenkle, Douglas (1987). Can therapists use FACES III with Mexican Americans? A preliminary analysis. Family Therapy Program, Department of Child Development and Family Studies, Purdue University, West Lafayette, Indiana.

French, L. (1981). The French Canadian American family. In C. H. Mindel & R. W. Habenstein (Eds.), *Ethnic families in America: Patterns and variations* (pp. 326-349). New York: Elsevier.

Friedman, E. H. (1982). The myth of the shiksa. In M. McGoldrick, J. R. Pearce, & J. Giordano (Eds.), *Ethnicity and family therapy* (pp. 499-526). New York: Guilford Press.

Gambino, R. (1973). La famiglia: Four generations of Italian-Americans. In J. Ryan (Ed.), *White ethnics: Life in working-class America* (pp. 42-51). Englewood Cliffs, NJ: Prentice-Hall.

Gambino, R. (1975). *Blood of my blood: The dilemma of the Italian-Americans*. Garden City, NY: Anchor Books.

Garbarino, J., Sebes, J., & Schellenbach, C. (1985). Families at risk for destructive parent-child relations in adolescents. *Child Development*, 55, 174-183.

Gordon, A. I. (1959). *Jews in suburbia*. Boston: Beacon Press.

Gorer, G. (1964). *The American people: A study in national character*. New York: Norton.

Greeley, A. M. (1971). *Why can't they be like us?* New York: Dutton.

Greeley, A. M. (1972). *That most distressful nation: The taming of the American Irish*. Chicago: Quadrangle.

Greeley, A. M. (1974). *Ethnicity in the United States*. New York: Wiley.

Greeley, A. M., McCready, W. C., & Thiesen, G. (1980). *Ethnic drinking subcultures*. Brooklyn, NY: Praeger.

Gronseth, E. (1964). Research on socialization in Norway. *Family Process*, 3, 302-322.

Hardy-Fanta and MacMahon-Herrera. (1981). Adapting family therapy to the Hispanic family. *Social Casework*, 62(3), 138-148.

Hertz, J. H. (Ed.). (1969). *The authorized daily prayer book*. New York: Bloch.

Herz, F. M., & Rosen, E. J. (1982). Jewish families. In M. McGoldrick, J. K. Pearce, & J. Giordano (Eds.), *Ethnicity and family therapy* (pp. 364-392). New York: Guilford Press.

Hill, R. (1972). *The strengths of Black families*. New York: Emerson Hall.

Hines, P. M. & Boyd-Franklin, N. (1982). Black families. In M. McGoldrick, J. K. Pearce, & J. Giordano (Eds.), *Ethnicity and family therapy* (pp. 84-107). New York: Guilford Press.

Huang, L. J. (1981). The Chinese American family. In C. H. Mindel & R. W. Habenstein (Eds.), *Ethnic families in America: Patterns and variations* (pp. 115-141). New York: Elsevier.

Johnson, C. L. (1978). Family support systems of elderly Italian Americans. *Journal of Minority Aging*, 3-4, 34-41.

Johnson, C. L. (1982). Sibling solidarity: Its origin and functioning in Italian-American families. *Journal of Marriage and the Family*, 44(1), 155-167.

Kandel, D. & Lesser, G. S. (1972). *Youth in two worlds: United States and Denmark*. San Francisco: Jossey-Bass Publishers.

Keefe, S. E. (1980). Personal communities in the city: Support networks among Mexican-Americans and Anglo-Americans. *Urban Anthropology*, 9(1), 51-74.

Kitano, H. H. & Kikumura, A. (1981). The Japanese American family. In C. H. Mindel & R. W. Habenstein (Eds.), *Ethnic families in America: Patterns and variations* (pp. 43-60). New York: Elsevier.

Kuniczak, W. S. (1978). *My name is million*. New York: Doubleday.

Ladner, J. (1971). *Tomorrow's tomorrow: The Black woman*. Garden City, NY: Doubleday.

Landes, R. & Zborowski, M. (1968). The context of marriage: Family life as a field of emotions. In H. K. Geiger (Ed.), *Comparative perspectives on marriage and the family* (pp. 77-102). Boston: Little, Brown.

Langelier, R. (1982). French Canadian families. In M. McGoldrick, J. K. Pearce, & J. Giordano (Eds.), *Ethnicity and family therapy* (pp. 229-246). New York: Guilford Press.

Lidz, T. (1968). *The person*. New York: Basic Books.

Lopata, H. Z. (1976). *Polish Americans: Status competition in an ethnic community*. Englewood Cliffs, NJ: Prentice-Hall.

Lopata, H. Z. (1981). The Polish American family. In C. H. Mindel & R. W. Habenstein (Eds.), *Ethnic families in America: Patterns and variations* (pp. 17-42). New York: Elsevier.

Malson, M. (1982). The social support systems of Black families. *Marriage and Family Review*, 5(4), 37-57.

Marjoribanks, K. (1982). Sibling and family environment correlates of children's achievement: Ethnic group differences. *Journal of Biosocial Science*, 14(1), 99-107.

McAdoo, H. (1977). Family therapy in the Black community. *American Journal of Orthopsychiatry*, 47.

McAdoo, H. (1978). Factors related to stability in upwardly mobile Black families. *Journal of Marriage and the Family*, 40, 761-776.

McGill, D. & Pearce, J. K. (1982). British families. In M. McGoldrick, J. K. Pearce, & J. Giordano (Eds.), *Ethnicity and family therapy* (pp. 457-479). New York: Guilford Press.

McGoldrick, M. (1982). Irish families. In M. McGoldrick, J. K. Pearce, & J. Giordano (Eds.), *Ethnicity and family therapy* (pp. 310-339). New York: Guilford Press.

McGoldrick, M. & Rohrbaugh, M. (1987). Researching ethnic family stereotypes. *Family Process*, 26, 89-99.

Midelfort, C. F. & Midelfort, H. C. (1982). Norwegian families. In M. McGoldrick, J. K. Pearce, & J. Giordano (Eds.), *Ethnicity and family therapy* (pp. 438-456). New York: Guilford Press.

Millham, J. & Smith, L. E. (1981). Sex role differentiation among Black and White Americans: A comparative study. *The Journal of Black Psychology*, 1, 77-90.

Modell, J. (1968). Japanese American family: A perspective for future investigations. *Pacific Historical Review*, 36(1), 67-81.

Mondykowski, S. M. (1982). Polish families. In M. McGoldrick, J. K. Pearce, & J. Giordano (Eds.), *Ethnicity and family therapy* (pp. 393-411). New York: Guilford Press.

Mostwin, D. (1980). Social dimensions of family treatment. Washington, DC: National Association of Social Workers.

O'Connor, J. (1977). *Tradition and change in three generations of Japanese Americans*. Chicago: Nelson-Hall.

Olson, D. H. & McCubbin, H. I. (1982). Circumplex model of marital and family systems V: Application to family stress and crisis intervention. In H. I. McCubbin, A. E. Cauble, & J. M. Patterson (Eds.), *Family stress, coping, and social support* (pp. 48-68). Springfield, Illinois.

Olson, D. H., McCubbin, H. I. et al. (1983). *Families: What makes them work*. Beverly Hills: Sage Publications.

Olson, D., Russell, C. S., & Sprenkle, D. H. (1984). Circumplex model of marital and family systems: VI. Theoretical update. In D. H. Olson & B. C. Miller (Eds.), *Family Studies Review Yearbook*, Volume 2 (pp. 59-73). Beverly Hills: Sage Publications.

Panitz, D. R., McConchie, R. D., Sauber, S. R., & Fonseca, J. (1983). The role of machismo and the Hispanic family in the etiology and treatment of alcoholism in Hispanic males. *The American Journal of Family Therapy*, 11(1), 31-44.

Papajohn, J. & Spiegel, J. (1975). *Transactions in families*. San Francisco: Jossey-Bass.

Parsons, W. T. (1976). *The Pennsylvania Dutch*. Boston: Twayne.

Quadagno, J. S. (1981). The Italian American family. In C. H. Mindel & R. W. Habenstein (Eds.), *Ethnic families in America: Patterns and variations* (pp. 61-85). New York: Elsevier.

Ragucci, A. T. (1981). Italian Americans. In A. Hargood (Ed.), *Ethnicity and medical care*. Cambridge: Harvard University Press.

Rodnick, D. (1955). *The Norwegians: A study in national character*. Washington, DC: Public Affairs Press.

Rotunno, M. & McGoldrick, M. (1982). Italian families. In M. McGoldrick, J. K. Pearce, & J. Giordano (Eds.), *Ethnicity and family therapy* (pp. 340-363). New York: Guilford Press.

Sanday, R. R. (1974). Female status in the public domain. In M. Z. Rosaldo & L. Lamphere (Eds.), *Women, culture, and society*. Stanford, CA: Stanford University Press.

Schelsky, H. (1954). The family in Germany. *Marriage and Family Living*, 16(4), 331-335.

Shon, S. P. & Ja, D. Y. (1982). Asian families. In M. McGoldrick, J. K. Pearce, & J. Giordano (Eds.), *Ethnicity and family therapy* (pp. 208-228). New York: Guilford Press.

Spiegel, J. (1971). Cultural strain, family role patterns, and intrapsychic conflict. In *Theory and practice of family psychiatry*. New York: Brunner/Mazel.

Stack, C. B. (1974). *All my kin*. New York: Harper and Row.

Staples, R. (1981). The Black American family. In C. H. Mindel & R. W. Habenstein (Eds.), *Ethnic families in America: Patterns and variations*. New York: Elsevier.

Stein, R. F. (1971). *Disturbed youth and ethnic family patterns*. Albany: State University of New York Press.

Sudarkasa, N. (1980). African and Afro-American family structure. *The Black Scholar*, 11(8), 37-59.

Tetteh, P. A. (1967). Marriage, family, and household. In W. Birmingham (Ed.), *A study of contemporary Ghana*, Volume 2. London: Allen and Unwin.

Thomas, W. I. & Znaniecki, F. (1920). *The Polish peasant in Europe and America*. New York: Octagon Books, 1974 (republished).

Tomasi, S. M., Tomasi, C. S., & Engles, M. (Eds.). (1970). *The Italian experience in the United States*. New York: Center for Migration Studies.

Triandis, H. C. (1983). Some dimensions of intercultural variation and their implications for community psychology. *Journal of Community Psychology*, 11(4), 285-302.

Vecoli, R. J. (1978). The coming of age of the Italian Americans: 1945-1974. *Ethnicity*, 15, 119-147.

Wake, S. B. & Sporakowski, M. J. (1972). An intergenerational comparison of attitudes toward supporting aged parents. *Journal of Marriage and the Family*, 34, 42-48.

Winawer-Steiner, H. & Wetzel, N. A. (1982). German families. In M. McGoldrick, J. K. Pearce, & J. Giordano (Eds.), *Ethnicity and family therapy* (pp. 247-268). New York: Guilford Press.

Woolfson, P. (1975). Traditional French-Canadian family life patterns and their implications for social services in Vermont. In *A Franco American Overview*, Volume 2. Cambridge: National Assessment and Dissemination Center for Bilingual/Bicultural Education.

Yans-McLaughlin, V. (1977). *Family and community: Italian immigrants in Buffalo, 1880-1930*. Ithaca: Cornell University Press.

Zapata, J. T. & Jaramillo, P. T. (1981). Research on the Mexican-American family. *Journal of Individual Psychology*, 37(1), 72-85.

Zborowski, M. (1969). *People in pain*. San Francisco: Jossey-Bass.

Zborowski, M. & Herzog, E. (1952). *Life is with people*. Hew York: Shocken Books.

Can Therapists Use FACES III with Mexican Americans? A Preliminary Analysis

Maria T. Flores
Douglas H. Sprenkle

SUMMARY. A stratified, random nonclinical sample of 959 Mexican Americans completed FACES III. Results were compared with the normative Anglo American sample of Olson et al. (1983). Results indicated that although there were statistically fewer balanced and more extreme family types among the Mexican Americans, FACES III scores were much more similar than different. The stereotype of the Mexican American family as highly enmeshed was not confirmed. There was a modest relationship between acculturation and family structure and a stronger and consistent relationship with family income. Specifically, high income respondents were more likely to have balanced scores on FACES III and lower income subjects were more likely to have extreme scores. Overall, results suggest that therapists can use existing norms for FACES III with Mexican Americans, especially if they are *not* poor and have become bicultural.

Since FACES III was normed on a predominantly Anglo, middle-class, Lutheran population, it has heretofore not been known if it is appropriate for clinicians to utilize the same norms for clients with differing cultural characteristics. For this reason, the authors administered FACES III to a large sample of Mexican American families. Research questions addressed by the study included:

Maria T. Flores, PhD, is an instructor and Douglas H. Sprenkle, PhD, is Professor and Director, Family Therapy Program, Department of Child Development and Family Studies, Purdue University, MFT Building, 523 Russell Street, West Lafayette, IN 47906.

(1) Would the basic structure of the Mexican American family (as measured by cohesion and adaptability scores and patterns) be substantially different from Olson et al.'s (1983) normative Anglo American sample? (2) Would the results corroborate or disconfirm certain cultural stereotypes about Mexican American families that are frequently reported in the literature, but have not been verified empirically? (3) Would certain family characteristics, specifically acculturation and family income, be associated with Mexican American family structure? (4) Given these findings, under what circumstances would it be appropriate to utilize established norms for FACES III when it is used as a diagnostic tool with Mexican American families?

The study has significance because of (1) the exponential growth of the Hispanic population (of whom 59% are Mexican American) which is predicted to be the largest U.S. minority by the year 2000 (Gallup Poll, 1986; Rodriguez, 1987) and (2) the lack of mental health services for Hispanics due, in part, to inaccurate understanding of this population (Acosta and Evans, 1982; Dillard, 1983).

SAMPLE AND METHOD

Questionnaires were distributed to a nonclinical (to parallel Olson et al., 1983) sample of 600 Mexican American families residing in San Antonio, Texas. A stratified-random procedure was utilized. Every third family in a randomly selected grade level in three high schools, and every family with an adolescent in one large Roman Catholic church was asked to complete questionnaires. The sample was stratified to include an economically depressed as well as a middle-class area. Responses were procured from 333 families (a response rate of 55.5%). Fifty-four percent (n = 180) were from the middle-class area and 46% (n = 153) from the depressed areas. There were 959 total respondents which included 626 parents and 333 adolescents. Two hundred and ninety-three were intact families and 40 were single-parent families.

The mean age of the parents was 44 years (husbands – 46 years, wives – 43 years). The mean age of the single parents was also 44 years. Parents in the intact families had been married an average of 22 years and the vast majority (90%) had never been divorced. The mean number of children per family for the entire sample was three to four. Virtually all respondents were Roman Catholic.

Data was collected from 217 male and 101 female adolescents. Adolescent participants ranged from 13 to 19 years with a mean age of 15.3 years. Based on self-reports by the parents, the adolescents were generally well-behaved at home, at school, and in the neighborhood. Parents reported that only 2% had been in trouble in school, 2% had been in trouble within their own neighborhoods, and 3.7% had been in trouble with the police.

Eighty-three percent (n = 127) of the families in the depressed area had yearly incomes in the $0-$19,999 bracket. Eighty-five percent (n = 153) of the middle-class families were in the $20,000-$49,499 bracket. The remaining 15% (n = 53) had total yearly incomes in excess of $50,000. Looking at the sample as a whole, like the Olson et al. (1983) sample, mean yearly income fell into the $20,000-$30,000 category.

Social class was computed utilizing Hollingshead's Two Factor Index of Education and Occupation. Fifty-eight percent of the total sample could be characterized as "lower middle-class" with the remaining 42% designated as "middle-class."

A rigorous process was followed to translate FACES III and the demographic information sheet into Spanish. Two independent translation teams were assembled from the teaching faculty of the Mexican American Cultural Center in San Antonio. Minor differences between the two teams were resolved before data collection commenced.

The Acculturation Rating Scale for Mexican Americans (ARSMA) was utilized to categorize respondents on an acculturation continuum ranging from Mexican/Spanish to Anglo/English. The developers of this instrument report impressive evidence for reliability and validity (Cuellar, Harris, and Jasso, 1980).

Questionnaires were distributed to the families through targeted adolescents. A cover letter and return envelope were included in an initial packet. One week later, a postcard was sent by the on-site investigator to all subjects thanking those who returned the questionnaire and reminding those who had not. A third contact, through a reminder postcard or telephone call, or both, was conducted three weeks later. These contacts yielded a response rate of 55.5%.

RESULTS

Figure 1 compares the Olson et al. (1983) breakdowns for balanced, mid-range, and extreme scores for parents with the parents of the adolescents in the current study on FACES III "real" scores. Although the Chi-square is statistically significant, it should be noted that the Mexican Americans as well as the Anglo Americans overwhelmingly fell into the balanced and mid-ranged groups: 88.7% of the Anglo Americans and 83.3% of the Mexican Americans. Extreme family structures were found only among 11.3% of the Anglo Americans and 16.7% of the Mexican Americans. Al-

Figure 1: Anglo American and Mexican American Parents: Circumplex Model

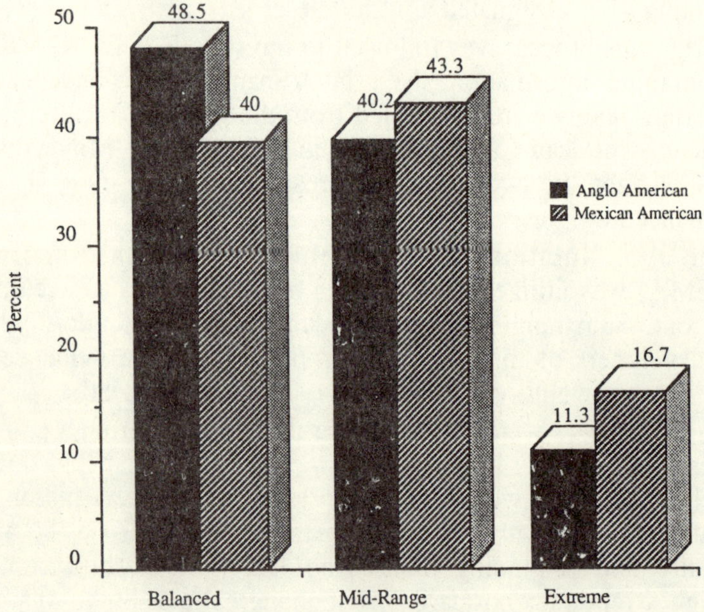

though there are statistically fewer balanced and more extreme family types among the Mexican Americans, these differences were not dramatic. Preliminary T-test analyses showed there were no differences between Mexican American males and females, between adolescents and their parents, between adolescent males and females, and between intact and single parent families on these dimensions.

Figures 2 and 3 compare the norms and cutting points for the four levels of cohesion and adaptability in the Anglo American and Mexican American samples. Contrary to the stereotype of the Mexican American family as highly enmeshed (Padilla and Lindholm, 1984), the major Anglo versus Mexican American differences (for families with adolescents) on the cohesion dimension were found at the "disengaged" end of this continuum rather than on the "enmeshed" side.

On the adaptability dimension, the largest difference showed up on the "rigid" end of the continuum. Indeed, subsequent analysis demonstrated that it was the higher percentage of Mexican Ameri-

Figure 2: Parents and Adolescents Norms for Four Levels of Cohesion

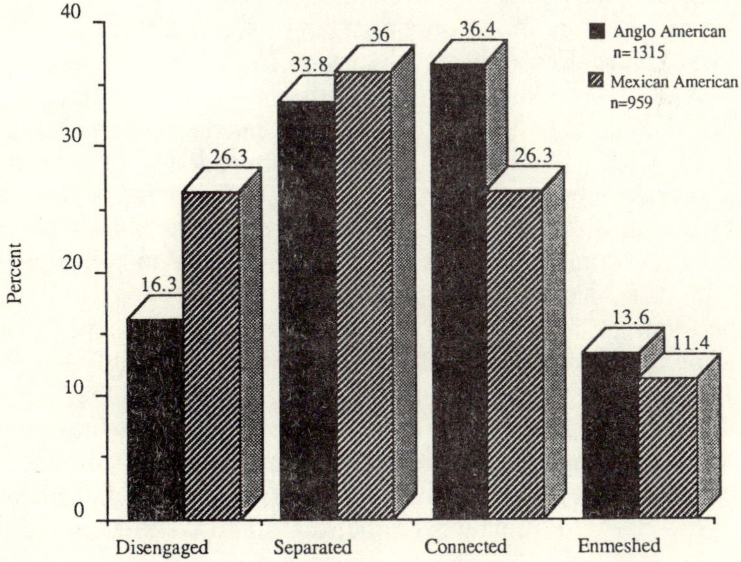

Figure 3: Parents and Adolescents Norms for Four Levels of Adaptability

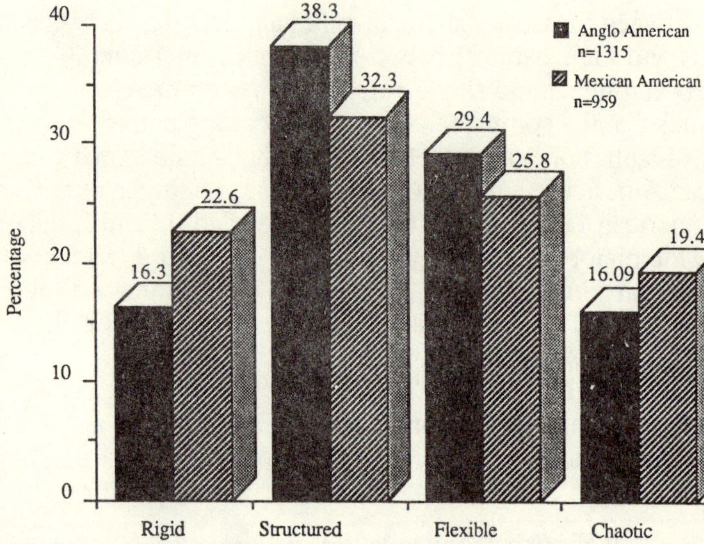

cans who scored toward the "rigidly disengaged" area of the Circumplex that accounted for the significant Chi-square in Figure 1.

There was only a modest relationship between acculturation and family structure. Respondents who had become bicultural were neither less nor more likely to produce extreme scores than those who had not become bicultural. However, respondents who had become bicultural were statistically significantly more likely to have balanced scores on both adaptability and cohesion. Therefore, becoming bicultural did enhance the likelihood of balanced scores even though such family members were equally likely to fall into the minority of subjects with extreme scores.

The relationship between joint family income and family structure, however, was consistent and rather dramatic. Table 1 cross-tabulates family structure (balanced and extreme) with total yearly family income. The cells indicate whether the actual values (number of subjects in each cell) were less than or greater than the expected number of subjects which by "chance" would fall in each cell if there were no relationship between family structure and in-

Table 1: Balanced and Extreme Family Structures by Income Level: Expected (in parenthesis) and Actual Frequencies

1st: (expected frequency)* 2nd: actual frequency	Balanced	Extreme***
$000-999	(7.3) 2 less than expected**	(2.7) 7 more than expected**
$10,000-19,999	(25.8) 20 less than expected	(9.7) 11 more than expected
$20,000-29,999	(34.7) 34 less than expected	(13.0) 18 more than expected
$30,000-39,999	(25.8) 28 less more than expected	(9.7) 4 less than expected
$40,000-49,999	(14.5) 21 more than expected	(5.5) 4 less than expected
$50,000+	(19.8) 23 more than expected	(7.4) 4 less than expected

* Indicates number of subjects expected to be in the cell if income and structure were not related.

** Indicates actual frequency is less or more than the expected frequency.

*** for ease in following the table, the mid-range cells are omitted. They show an alternating pattern in terms of being less then and more than the expected values. The Chi-square for the full table is 34.44 which exceeds the .05 critical value of 21.02.

come. The reader will note that actual frequencies exceeded expected frequencies for subjects with balanced scores with incomes greater than $30,000 per year and actual frequencies were less than expected frequencies for "balanced" respondents with incomes below this figure. The exact reverse is true for subjects with extreme scores. Actual frequencies were less than expected in the higher income categories and greater than expected in the lower income brackets. These results clearly suggest that income was a significant predictor of family structure in the sample. Indeed, subsequent analysis demonstrated that most of the extreme scores came from respondents in the economically depressed area.

CONCLUSIONS AND IMPLICATIONS FOR THE THERAPIST

Overall, the results suggest that existing norms for FACES III can be used with Mexican Americans. Although there were statistically significantly fewer balanced and more extreme scores among the Mexican Americans than among Olson and McCubbin's (1983) Anglo American sample, the norms were far more similar than different. Similarities between Anglo American and Mexican American families are greater if clients are "middle-class" and not poor, and they have also become bicultural. FACES III results can probably not be explained by any unique dimensions or attributes related to being a Mexican American.

Since acculturation appears to have a modest relationship to family structure, the therapist should consider how cultural aspects of the client's context influence the problems being brought to therapy. Based on this data, however, one should *not* interpret an extreme score as being reflective of the degree of acculturation.

Because family income was consistently related to family structure, the therapist needs to note family income level before assuming there is another "source" of "family dysfunction." Perhaps utilizing a social worker or enhancing job skills may be as important as psychotherapy. In any event, especially when clients are poor, the therapist needs to be cautious about interpreting an extreme score.

Although it has potentially significant implications, the results of this study must be considered preliminary for the following reasons:

1. Subjects were sampled from only on phase of the family life cycle. Perhaps the tendency of extreme subjects to score toward "rigidly disengaged" may be related to their being an adolescent in the household.

2. No attempt was made to investigate the respondents' relationships with their extended families.
3. Analysis was based only on the "real" and not the "ideal" version of FACES III. It is possible, for example, that Mexican American respondents' "ideal" family cohesion scores might be closer to the cultural stereotype.
4. The sample, while random and relatively large, was taken from a limited geographical region.
5. Since only a nonclinical population was utilized, it is not known if the instrument will discriminate troubled from non-troubled Mexican American families.

Even with these caveats, however, the authors believe the study can be interpreted as a "green light" for the use of FACES III with the Mexican American population. Naturally, further research is necessary to support this preliminary conclusion.

REFERENCES

Acosta, F. & Evans, L. (1982). The Hispanic American patient. In F. Acosta, J. Yamamoto, & L. Evans (Eds.), *Effective psychotherapy for low income and minority patients* (pp. 51-81). New York: Plenum Press.

Cueller, I., Harris, L. C., & Jasso, R. (1980). An acculturation scale for Mexican American normal and clinical populations. *Hispanic Journal of Behavioral Sciences, 2*(3), 199-217.

Dillard, J. (1983). *Multicultural counseling*. Chicago: Nelson-Hall.

Dillman, D. (1978). *Mail and telephone surveys: The total design method*. New York: A Wiley-Interscience Publication.

Gallup Poll (1986). New York: New York Times Press.

Olson, D. H., McCubbin, H. I., Barnes, H. I., Larsen, A. S., Muxen, M. J., & Wilson, M. A. (1983). *Families: What makes them work*. Beverly Hills, CA: Sage Publications.

Padilla, A. M. & Linholm, K. J. (1984). Hispanic behavioral science research: Recommendations for future research. *Hispanic Journal of Behavioral Science, 6*, 13-32.

Rodriquez, B. (1987). *Research America*. Washington, DC: Res. America.

The Circumplex Model with Adjudicated Youths' Families

Peter E. Maynard
Anna Hultquist

SUMMARY. The Circumplex Model has been integrated into the diagnostic and treatment of families of juvenile offenders at an alternative treatment facility. The model has proven helpful in setting treatment goals, designing therapeutic interventions and assessing changes in the family systems. A case study describes how the model was incorporated into the diagnosis and treatment of a multi-problem family. The use of the FACES III and the Clinical Rating Scale allowed both an insider and outsider view of the families. Implications and outcomes using the model with juvenile offenders' families in a restricted setting are discussed.

Juvenile delinquency is a longstanding problem in our society. It was recognized long ago that mere incarceration of deviant youths for the protection of society was inadequate and a treatment/rehabilitative approach was needed (Tolan, Cromwell, & Brasswell, 1986). The treatment/rehabilitative approach itself with its psychological underpinnings is now being viewed with skepticism (Flicker, 1977) and is often seen as costly and ineffective (Johnson, Bird, & Little, 1979; Romig, 1978).

While the credibility of the psychological treatment approach has generally declined within the juvenile justice system, family focused interventions are showing promise (Johnson, 1977; Johnson, 1978) and are gaining support (Janeksela, 1979; Kogan, 1980; Millard & McLogan, 1972; Travisiono & O'Neill, 1969).

Tolan, Cromwell, and Brasswell (1986) in a major review of the

---

Peter E. Maynard, PhD, is Professor, University of Rhode Island.

Anna Hultquist, MS, was formerly Family Therapist at Ocean Tides Treatment Center and is now in independent practice.

research of the use of family therapy with delinquency asked three main questions: (a) Is there evidence that family therapy is effective with delinquents? (b) Is family therapy more effective than other approaches? (c) What factors influence effectiveness? Their review revealed that basic studies of the effect of family therapy on delinquency provide general support for linking poor family functioning to the development of delinquency and improved family functioning and reduced delinquency to interventions with family therapy. They also found family therapy was more effective than individual therapy in improving communications (Parsons & Alexander, 1972) and in reducing recidivism. Maskin (1976) found communications-oriented family treatment resulted in significantly less recidivism than a work oriented program in which individual responsibility was emphasized. There were three categories of factors that were influential in determining the effects of family therapy with delinquents: the type of family therapy used, the therapist variables (characteristics and skills), and client variables (characteristics).

While the current research shows promise for family therapy as an effective method for treating juvenile delinquency, further research and study is needed. Particularly, Tolan, Cromwell, and Brasswell (1986) suggest further elucidation of major systems theories is needed to explain adequately delinquent behavior as a function of the family system and its context. The purpose of this paper is to examine the introduction and use of the Circumplex Model into an ongoing juvenile delinquency treatment program. Previously, the family treatment component of the program at Ocean Tides, an alternative residential treatment program for male delinquents, had been seen as important but each member of the counseling staff operated independently. This article will describe how the Circumplex Model has provided a theoretical base for the family treatment component. A case study will describe the practical uses of the model with a multi-problem family. Implications of the use of the model at Ocean Tides will be discussed.

TREATMENT SETTING

Ocean Tides, a residential program in Rhode Island, is designed to serve male adolescent delinquents between the ages of 13 and 17. Founded in 1975, Ocean Tides has been successfully working with this client population for more than a decade, earning the respect and admiration of the family court system and state Department of Children and Their Families. All residents must be adjudicated delinquent by the family court system. The only such youngsters not considered for acceptance are those involved in serious crimes against the person, including murder, rape, armed robbery; youngsters with serious emotional disorders and/or having been diagnosed as psychotic; or youngsters who have a history of arson or are, de facto, addicted to narcotics. Youngsters complete the treatment program in 9 to 12 months.

FAMILY TREATMENT PROGRAM

To meet the needs of this client population, the treatment plan is centered on a three-faceted approach; educational, residential, and counseling. The educational focus includes an accredited jr./sr. high school attended by each boy in residence. Small class size and individualized instruction plans are featured in this educational environment. The residential component provides supervised guidance for the residents for all the hours they are not involved in school.

An integral part of the treatment effort is the individual and family therapy conducted by the social service department. Individual sessions are held weekly and family sessions are scheduled bimonthly. The Ocean Tides' program is committed to including the family as a critical part of the change process for a youngster, since it is found that when the family itself is dysfunctional, then the family as a whole system needs assistance in making change. Although the department focuses on a social work approach, the development of a more defined family therapy model has been evolving as the program continues to progress. Incorporated into this developmental process has been the addition of the Circumplex Model into diagnostic assessment and treatment plans. The model has been in use in the counseling department for a year. In this time it has proven to be most valuable in providing insight into family dysfunction and guidance in developing therapeutic interventions.

THE CLIENT POPULATION

To date, the FACES III instrument has been used in the treatment of 12 residents and their families. Pretreatment scores (Figure 1) find the majority of families (75%) falling within the mid-range to extreme range, while 25% scored in the balanced range. Interestingly, the majority of family scores fell in the disengaged range of

Figure 1: Family Scores of Clinical Families on the Circumplex Model

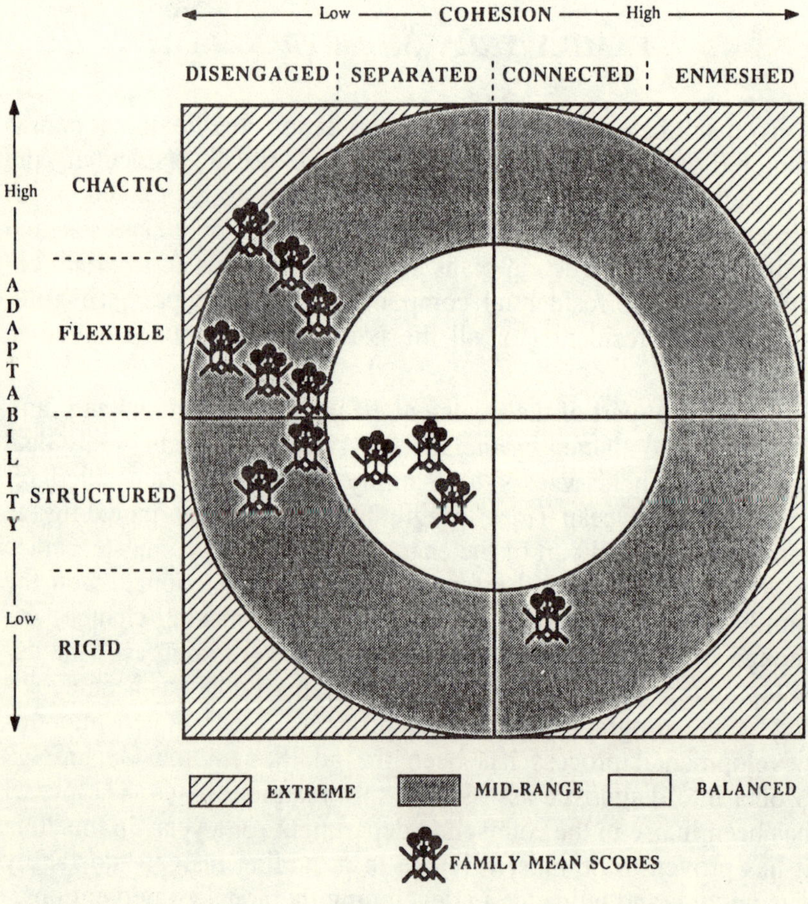

the cohesion scale, distributed between flexible and structured in the adaptability scale. This is in sharp contrast to a study done by Rodick, Henggeler, and Hanson (1986) using FACES which found delinquent family scores clustered in the chaotically enmeshed area of functioning. The difference may well be due to the physical disengagement of the Ocean Tides' residents from their families. However, further variables that may contribute to this difference may center around ethnicity, regional variation in family style, or age of the offender.

An analysis of individual scores (N = 27) (Figure 2) shows 12 family members (44%) fell in the extreme range, 13 (48%) were into mid-range, and 2 (8%) in the balanced range. The juveniles themselves showed the following pattern: 2 balanced, 10 mid-range, and none located in the extreme ranges. From this sampling it would seem that the deviant behavior of the youths may be indicative of overall family dysfunction.

Of the dozen cases studied indepth, it was found that 11 were single-parent households brought about by divorce or by the mother never marrying. Of these, nine were headed by females.

Drug and alcohol use have been found to be common recreational substances used by the residents while on their weekend passes. Two of the youths in this study were found to have serious alcohol/drug addiction. Analysis of the previous generation showed 50% of the residents had an alcohol or drug abusing parent. Of the parents who were not in serious trouble with substances, the majority of them used alcohol socially.

Finally, two additional background variables were looked at. It was found that 33% of the youngsters in this study had experienced serious and prolonged physical abuse during their formative years. Aggressive family patterns were evident in the interactional style of the boys and their families during initial treatment. Also, it was noted that two-thirds of these residents came from the low income bracket—many living in subsidized housing. This overview of general case backgrounds provides a description of the types of families who are serviced at Ocean Tides. The following case study demonstrates how the Circumplex Model was used to diagnose and treat one of these families.

Figure 2: Family Members and Individual Scores of Clinical Families

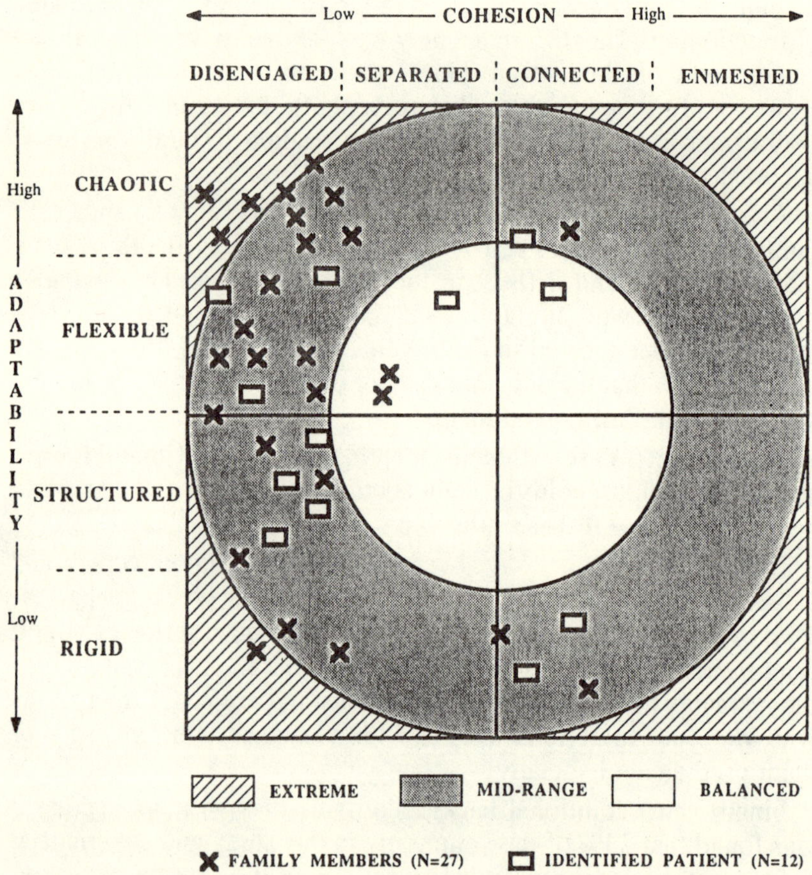

SINGLE FATHER AS CUSTODIAL PARENT

Wayne Billingham came to Ocean Tides with a record of breaking and entering. Before his admission to the program, Wayne spent a month at the state Juvenile Diagnostic Center and was placed in a foster care group home due to his parent's refusal to allow him home following his charges.

His parents had a highly conflictual marriage relationship that ended in separation when Wayne was 3. The parents had married in their late teens and Wayne was born within the year. Several long-distance moves, along with school and job changes, characterized their early relationship. The level of marital satisfaction had been deteriorating for some time. In the fourth year of marriage Susan had an affair and eventually left the family. It was several months before she made contact, and then David rejected her attempts at reconciliation. A lengthy court battle ensued, and David was awarded sole custody of Wayne.

Since the initial separation, Susan had maintained regular contact with Wayne. Tension between the parents remained high. Susan once took Wayne for his regular weekend visit, and failed to return him. David had trouble locating them, and when he did, he took legal action to force Wayne's return.

The conflict between David and Susan continued and Wayne became more involved in their angry exchanges. This was evidenced in his growing hostility toward both David and Susan. A pattern of house hopping developed as Wayne's defiant behavior grew. When conflict at one parent's home was intense, Wayne would quickly enlist the support of his other parent who would then care for him until conflict developed there as well. This pattern became cyclical, with Wayne rotating between both homes at will. Both David and Susan were sensing the chaos of their situation, yet felt powerless. Compounding the internal family dysfunction was chronic truancy that began when Wayne was in seventh grade, as well as using and dealing drugs.

At the onset of treatment, Wayne was a very angry and hurt youngster who saw reconciliation with his parents impossible. He could not envision living with either parent again. Wayne's early behavior at Ocean Tides revealed a highly unmotivated 16-year-old who appeared unable to take on the normal responsibilities for his age group. He developmentally typified a much younger child.

Initial contact with the family consisted of home visits to both Susan's and David's separate residence. At the initial meeting, Susan was defensive and skeptical of our family therapy approach. However, after this session wherein some family systems issues were explored, Susan was more willing to try family therapy to help

Wayne. Barry, Wayne's stepfather, although not present, said he would be available in the future.

David was the owner of a highly successful manufacturing business and had a hectic schedule. However, he said he could accommodate the time demands of our treatment outreach. In this initial meeting, David expressed his extreme ambivalence toward Wayne as well as feelings of being victimized by his son. David expressed a keen interest in beginning family work. Therefore, a conjoint session was scheduled for him, Susan, and Wayne.

Susan and Wayne attended the first family session but David did not show. This initial meeting did allow the close observation of the dydactic interaction between mother and son. While Wayne sought to engage his mother on an emotional level through anger and tears, Susan remained disengaged.

All three attended the second family session. This meeting allowed the therapist to join and engage the family and begin assessment of the family's functioning. At the close of this session the FACES III was given to each member. A Clinical Rating Scale was completed by the therapist.

From the "outsider's" perspective (Figure 3), the overall family functioning was seen as structured—with some evidence of rigidity and separated—with some aspects of being disengaged. Overall communication patterns were rated in the "low" range. This assessment was then compared to the "insider's" perspective given by the family members themselves. The FACES instrument (Figure 4) found David in the extreme range of rigidly disengaged; Wayne scored in the mid-range of structurally disengaged; and Susan, saw the family's functioning as balanced-flexibly separated. This difference in Susan's perspective was anticipated due to her position as noncustodial parent. The averaged family score placed the overall level of functioning in the mid-range as structurally disengaged. The "insider"-"outsider" perceptions were similar in the way both perceived the family's functioning. This consensus confirmed the therapist's initial assessments, while providing specific direction for treatment.

Several working hypotheses were formulated from the data obtained through the Circumplex Model. Susan and David rated their perception of the family's adaptability in strikingly different ways.

Figure 3: Circumplex Clinical Rating Scale (Pre & Post Treatment)

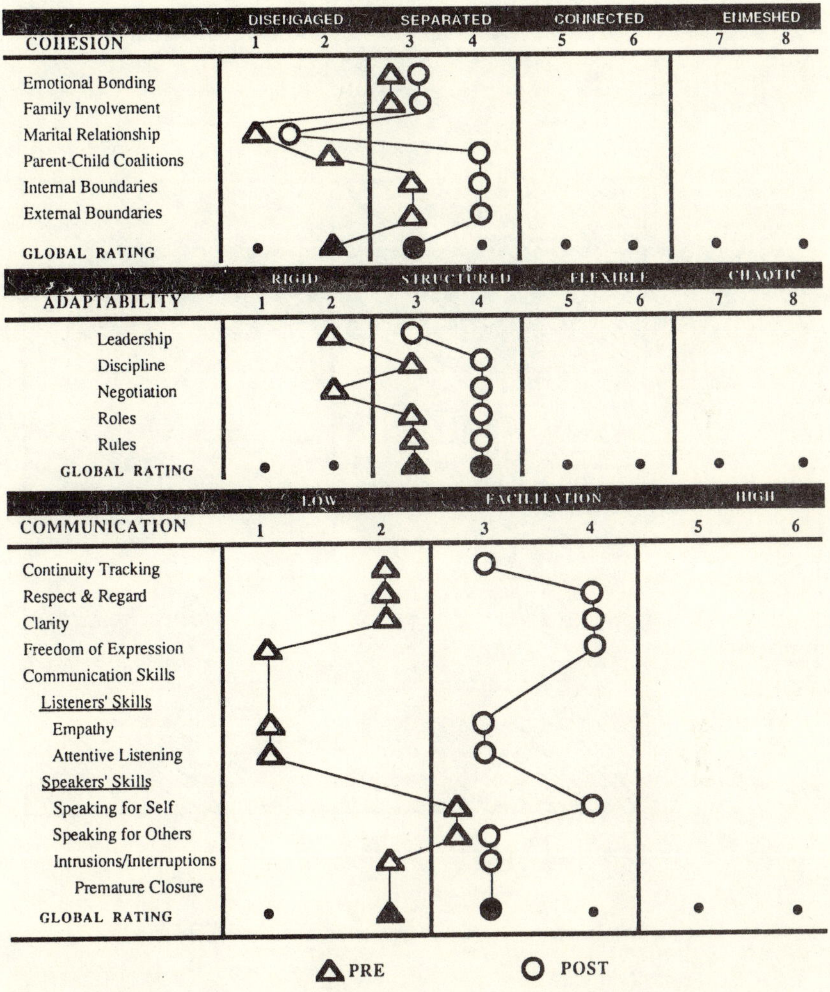

David saw the family as rigid, and Susan scored the family as flexible, tending toward the chaotic side of the range. This large difference between parents may be indicative of a family dynamic that may be aiding Wayne in his controlling behavior. It was hypothesized that a cyclical pattern may be in play, whereby David's rigid style of handling Wayne may, in fact, push Susan toward greater

Figure 4: Billingham's Family (Pre-Mid-Post) on the Circumplex Model

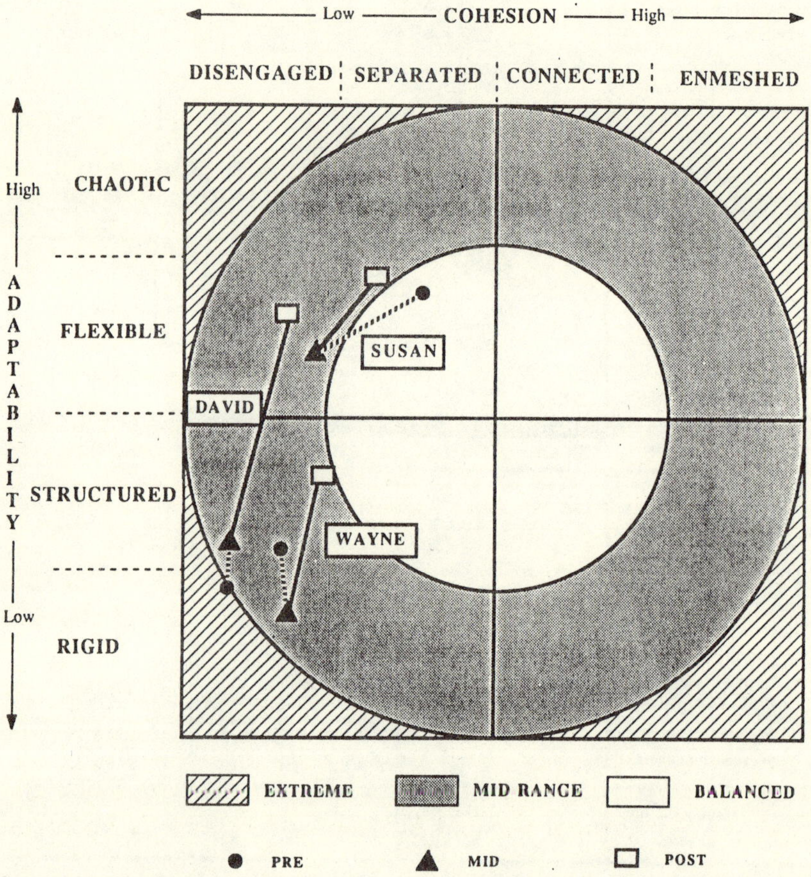

flexibility as a parent. At the same time, Susan's lack of consistency in controlling Wayne may be driving David into greater rigidity. This discrepancy between the parents was perhaps giving Wayne the opportunity to play one parent off against the other. Since neither parent was aware of this pattern, Wayne manipulated both parents to achieve his goals. Therefore, an initial therapeutic strategy was to align David and Susan in their parental roles to increase their effectiveness.

In reviewing the perceived and ideal FACES scores, it became clear that all three family members wanted to see change on the adaptability dimension, moving toward the flexible/chaotic ranges. Desired movement on the cohesion dimension was not as dramatic. Since this was a divorced family, this was in line with the family's structure. The treatment plan was designed to concentrate on the adaptability dimension—working to bring the family toward a greater consensus on their perception of and execution of rules and roles.

Some specific strategies were developed to facilitate changes in adaptability. Household rules were negotiated, and consequences for infractions planned by both parents. These limits were to be effective in either home, governing the time Wayne spent with them. Since both parents were hesitant to allow Wayne to stay with them during his imminent weekend passes, these guidelines provided some assurance of Wayne's cooperation. Each parent agreed to host him one of the next two weekends on a trial basis. The therapist then instituted a final guideline which prohibited Wayne from transferring households within one weekend pass. This was introduced in efforts to decrease Wayne's effectiveness in manipulating his parents.

The first few weekends with David and Susan proved to be successful. Both parents were pleased with Wayne's behavior. This positive experience increased their investment in the therapeutic process. After Wayne had consistent contact with his parents, the next phase of treatment was initiated. In the third complete conjoint session, training in communication skills was begun. Role play techniques were used to assist the family in negotiating areas of disagreement and achieving conflict resolution. In the next several family sessions there was less hostility expressed between the parents, as well as between Wayne and each parent. However, Wayne was less cooperative during his weekend passes, and both parents were ineffective in handling his defiance. Wayne was also attempting to regain control of the family by abandoning his host parent for the weekend and staying with "unknown" friends. This was seen as an attempt to pressure Susan and David into allowing him to go back and forth between their homes as he had done in the past.

This regression disclosed the highly resistant nature of this family's dysfunctional patterns. Apparently each member was highly dependent upon the conflict cycle they had engaged in over the years. Therefore, it was hypothesized that the negative confrontations characteristic of this system must be serving a function in maintaining the family's homeostatis. It was clearly seen that periodically Wayne and his parents allowed conflicts to escalate to the point of tantrum behavior. Perhaps this ritual allowed for the release of otherwise pent-up emotions. Wayne provided the negative behavior that justified each parent's angry reaction. This gave Susan and David a suitable target for their aggressive feelings. At the same time, this exchange provided Wayne with a release and the opportunity to leave the home he was in to engage the other parent in a similar exchange. Within this system, it could be equally hypothesized that each parent would cue Wayne, through various verbal and nonverbal behavior, when they were reaching their emotional limit and needed some release. Wayne would then provide the issue to fight over. This conflict cycle also allowed each family member to have intense emotional contact with one another.

This dysfunctional pattern did appear to be serving an important mechanism whereby the family could have an emotional release while maintaining some interpersonal contact albeit at a pseudomutual level. To diffuse this negative pattern, which was maintaining much of the masked residual anger within the family, the therapist prescribed less destructive means of achieving personal contact. The family's turbulent history had revealed to the therapist several of the major troublesome issues around which to build these prescriptions. Wayne's confusion concerning his parents' separation had never been resolved. Nor had the rejection and anger felt by Susan, David and Wayne been ameliorated. The therapist designed the family therapy so the family members could process these sensitive issues and thereby reduced their emotional baggage.

A review of the first ten conjoint sessions showed Wayne's acting out not only provided emotional release for the family, but also gave the parents reason for continued contact. Susan and David had greatly increased their time together, both in person and on the phone, when Wayne began escalating his negative behavior. Wayne was triangled into his parents' unresolved marital issues. To remove Wayne structurally from this role, therapy turned to Susan and David's relationship.

The divorced parental dyad was invited to several conjoint sessions without Wayne. These meetings allowed the couple to review the reasons behind their divorce. This intervention provided a cathartic environment that permitted Susan and David to sort out the emotion-laden events of the past. The intensity of their approach/avoidance relationship decreased. Along with this progress, both parents began to exhibit more effectiveness in handling Wayne. In response to these changes, Wayne increased his defiant behavior in an attempt to maintain the previous pattern of family functioning. Both parents met this new round of conflict with improved abilities in enforcing house rules and negotiation without escalating the disagreements.

The family system appeared to be making significant shifts as therapy progressed. The three family members who had been attending treatment were exhibiting signs of improved functioning. However, midway through Wayne's placement, Wayne became increasingly hostile toward Barry, Susan's second husband. Self-reports indicated that Susan and Wayne would escalate in their disagreements to the point where Barry would step in and settle things. Barry was now invited to attend several all-member family meetings. In these sessions all three parents discussed their hardships in dealing with Wayne, and what was working for them now. Barry explored the specific problems of stepparenting as he sought to find a comfortable relationship with Wayne. In his discussion, Barry expressed his intolerance of conflict in his home, and his need to support Susan in handling Wayne. Should a conflict get out of hand, Barry admittedly stepped in to help Susan. Wayne was providing a reason for Susan and Barry to be more united. Apparently, Wayne was triangled into this new marriage relationship as he had been with his parents. To reduce this effect, Susan was given full responsibility for handling Wayne, while Barry was to remain supportive. This strategy pulled Wayne from his triangled role in this marital dyad (Visher & Visher, 1979).

The family was still struggling to gain longstanding progress 6 months into treatment. To provide insight into the systemic shifts that may have occurred, FACES III was readministered. It was clear that therapy had exerted pressure on the family system. Therefore, it was anticipated that the scores would reveal a family somewhat off-balance, seeking to find a homeostatic balance. This projection was clearly seen in the new FACES scores (Figure 4). David shifted from the extreme range into the mid-range area of structurally disengaged. He had made positive movement along the adaptability dimension. In contrast, Wayne's scores moved opposite to David – from structurally disengaged into the extreme range of rigidly disengaged. These two family members switched places in the system, perhaps in attempts to keep the family in balance. Susan, feeling the stress of change, moved out of the balanced area into the mid-range section of flexibly disengaged. The family clearly showed signs of internal movement along with what appeared to be the attempts to rebalance the altered system.

The family was still experiencing conflict after more than a dozen therapy sessions. At this point, a strategic intervention was designed to help push the system toward a release of their dysfunctional pattern. Rather than encourage the family to reduce the fighting between them, a simple technique of prescribing the symptom was incorporated into therapy. It was explained to the family that their need to have intense personal contact with one another was a deep need they all possessed. To allow a nondestructive way for this need to be met, the family was asked to schedule a fight each morning Wayne stayed in their homes. The exchange should last no more than 15 minutes, and should take place in private. Each parent agreed to this plan, and Wayne concurred as well.

Susan and David did not carry through on the scheduled fights with Wayne. However, all three were functioning with more positive affect and less hostile interchange. As is common in using a paradoxical technique, the family refused to follow the suggestion of the therapist and thereby gave up its dysfunctional pattern. In the ensuing weeks, both parents began to demonstrate the ability to monitor Wayne's behavior without escalating. Sporadic acts of defiance, initiated by Wayne, became part of the family's attempt to find a balance in their interactional patterns. As Wayne continued to test the system, the parents were better able to handle the disruptive behavior.

Subsequent sessions focused on self-monitoring techniques that enabled the family to maintain its progress. The year-long treatment period was nearing completion. Family sessions began to incorporate goal-setting for Wayne's return to home and community. In direct contrast to his initial decision not to live with either parent, Wayne now agreed to move in with his father upon release. The family was prepared for this reunion through negotiation of overall house rules, expectations for work and school achievements, and leisure activities.

A final administration of FACES III was given to assess the overall systemic changes. The family's movement on the Circumplex Model (Figure 4) revealed positive shifts in the overall functioning. David continued to make progress along the adaptability dimension. He moved two levels—reaching structurally disengaged. Wayne's score was in the structurally disengaged range and revealed his adjustment to the family's internal changes. Susan perceived the family much like she had prior to therapy. Her position as noncustodial parent had been reestablished. The foundational treatment goals had been achieved as David moved into the mid-ranges of the adaptability dimension. Wayne and Susan saw the family within the mid-range as well. With David's significant movement, the parental dyad had been brought closer in establishing and enforcing rules and roles within their homes.

The posttreatment clinical rating scale confirmed this systemic movement (Figure 3). The "outsider's" perspective rated the family's overall functioning as flexibly disengaged with mid-range communication skills. This coincided with the averaged family score from the FACES at posttreatment. These factors, along with clinical observation, indicated that positive changes had occurred in this separated family system enabling it to function without destructive symptomology.

PREDICTIVE QUALITIES

The use of the Circumplex Model with this client population has shed light on several vital aspects of treatment within a residential setting.

Individual and Family Progress

The Circumplex has proven to be valuable in initial assessment and treatment planning. It allows the therapist to establish therapy goals based on data generated from family members and allows both therapist and family to focus on areas perceived as needing change via the "insider" and "outsider" analysis.

The periodic use of the FACES III and Clinical Rating Scale throughout therapy allows the therapist to monitor changes as these are occurring and to provide feedback as to the effectiveness of the therapeutic interventions. As treatment goals are realized, the family begins functioning in a healthier manner, the Circumplex Model provides a vehicle for reporting progress and describing systemic changes. This is particularly helpful since this treatment facility has to interface constantly with the correctional and court systems.

During the time the Circumplex Model has been in use with this client population, it has become apparent that the data contains some predictive qualities. A family demonstrating positive changes on the FACES III in line with the treatment goals have demonstrated their ability to sustain the desired moves toward healthier functioning. In contrast, when a family makes general movement away from the outlined treatment goals over the course of therapy, they have exhibited chronically dysfunctional family patterns while in treatment as well as upon release.

Highly discrepant scores among family members on the initial administration of the FACES III have been a useful indicator of a youth's inability to function effectively in the Ocean Tides residential program. When the youth's initial rating of the family on both the perceived and idea scales are highly discrepant than those of the other family members, it has been an indicator the youth will not complete the program. Similar results with youths in the post-residential phase of the program can be predictive of inability to maintain positive family relationships.

DISCUSSION

The Circumplex Model has been favorably received by those on the clinical staff at the Ocean Tides facility. Its value in treating the highly dysfunctional, multi-problem families characteristic of this client population has been seen repeatedly. The FACES III and Clinical Rating Scale provide valuable assessment data at the onset of treatment, and provide the therapist with direction in developing therapeutic strategies. As therapy progresses, systemic change can be monitored, and interventions prepared accordingly. Such data then provides another tool with which to determine the progress and prognosis for a youngster and his family's rehabilitation.

Within the confines of the residential facility itself, the Circumplex Model provides worthwhile insight into the youngster's style of interaction as characterized by the intra-familiar patterns revealed in the FACES scores. High levels of discrepancy in family scores, particularly when the youngster's scores do not align in the direction of a parent, indicate systemic dysfunction that may be at higher risk for prolonged difficulty. Such scores may give early insight into the prognosis for successful individual and family treatment.

Finally, the "insider"-"outsider" perspectives have proven to be of great benefit in achieving an accurate picture of the family's true condition and areas of dysfunction. In working with extreme multi-problem systems, it can often be difficult to make accurate assessments and design treatment plans to focus on areas of primary concern. The "insider" perception as revealed in the FACES III scores provides an internal look at how the family views their current and ideal levels of functioning in adaptability and cohesion. This data, when compared to the therapist's own perception of the family's functioning as seen in the Clinical Rating Scale, provides a thorough assessment of the system from within and without. Discrepancies between the "insider" and "outsider" viewpoints provide valuable clinical information to assist the therapist in gaining a realistic perspective of the family's underlying dysfunctions. When dealing with a client population where multi-problem families are the norm, such a reality check is beneficial for therapists.

The Circumplex Model has proven to be a valuable addition to the clinical assessment and treatment of delinquent youths and their families. It provides concise data as to the family's system dysfunction, and gives immediate direction for the formation of treatment plans. This tool provides an effective means of monitoring progress within therapy, and sheds light on the prognosis for sustained improvement.

REFERENCES

Flicker, B.D. (1977). *Standards for juvenile justice: A summary and analysis*. Cambridge, MA: Vallinger.

Janeksela, G.M. (1979). Mandatory parental involvement in the treatment of delinquent youth. *Juvenile and Family Court Journal*, 30; 47-54.

Johnson G., Bird, T., & Little, J.W. (1979). *Delinquency prevention: Theories and strategies*. Washington, DC: U.S. Gov. Printing Office.

Johnson, T.F. (1977). The results of family therapy with juvenile offenders. *Juvenile Justice*, 28; 29-34.

Johnson, T.F. (1978). A contextual approach to treatment of juvenile offenders. *Offender Rehabilitation*, 3; 171-179.

Kogan, L. (1980). A family systems perspective on status offenders. *Juvenile and Family Court Journal*, 31; 49-54.

Maskin, M.B. (1976). The differential impact of work-oriented vs. communication-oriented juvenile corrections programs upon recidivism rates in delinquent males. *Journal of Clinical Psychology*, 32; 431-433.

Millard, J., & McLogan, J.R. (1972). Multifamily group work: A hopeful approach to the institutionalized delinquent and his family. *Comparative Group Studies*, 3; 117-127.

Parsons, B.V., & Alexander, J.F. (1972). Short term family intervention: A therapy outcome study. *Journal of Consulting and Clinical Psychology*, 41; 195-201.

Rodick, J., Henggeler, S.W., & Hanson, C. (1986). An evaluation of family adaptability and cohesion evaluation scales (FACES) and the circumplex model. *Journal of Abnormal Child Psychology*, 14; 77-87.

Romig, D.A. (1978). *Justice for our children*. Lexington, MA: Heath.

Tolan, P., Cromwell, R., & Braswell, M. (1986). Family therapy with delinquents: A critical review of the literature. *Family Process*, 25; 619-649.

Travisiono, A.P., & O'Neill, C.F. (1969). Understanding the family of the delinquent child. *Juvenile Court Judges' Journal, 19*; 147-154.

Visher, E., & Visher, J. (1979). *Step-families*. New York: Brunner/Mazel.

School-Family Intervention and the Circumplex Model

Don-David Lusterman

SUMMARY. The use of the Circumplex model to evaluate and to track change in an ecosystem is discussed. A case study illustrates the model's utility in describing stages in the treatment of a school-family problem. The model's heuristic value in organizing data, and particularly in visualizing and conceptualizing shifts in the interaction between two subsystems is considered.

When a child is functioning poorly at school, a member of the school staff may refer the family for therapy on the assumption that the family interaction is contributing to the problem. When is it appropriate to accept this hypothesis and to engage the family as the unit of treatment? When, on the other hand, is it of value to include the school in the treatment plan? If school personnel are to be included, how is the determination of whom to include made?

Olson's Circumplex Model (Olson, 1986) has been used to evaluate family systems and to track change during the therapeutic process. A systemic treatment that intervenes in two or more related systems may be termed an ecosystemic intervention. Olson's model is also of value in ecosystemic intervention. First, it forces the therapist to conceptualize clearly each subsystem along several dimensions. Second, as one examines each of these dimensions, the process of description fulfills a heuristic function, in that the act of organizing the data frequently suggests new courses of action. The model is also of value in supervision, in that it provides both super-

---

Don-David Lusterman, PhD, is a psychologist in independent practice in Baldwin, NY.

Interested parties may address reprint requests to the author at 856 McKinley Street, Baldwin, NY 11510.

visee and supervisor with a common and clearly defined method of tracking complex interactions.

DEFINING THE TREATMENT SYSTEM

In deciding whom to include in a given family session the therapist must take into account many factors. These include such information as who lives at home, whether there is a stepfamily situation, the degree of differentiation already achieved by the identified patient, and other relevant factors. The therapist may at times see only one member of the family, sometimes a dyad (parents, siblings, mother-daughter, etc.) and may at other times enlarge the meeting to include relevant others beyond the family circle, such as grandparents or live-in help. It should be pointed out that beyond the information derived from direct observation in session, the therapist's map of the family is determined as well by history provided by family members present, and by ancillary contacts by telephone or by letter. This constantly developing map enables the therapist to make decisions about whom it is appropriate to include in a given intervention.

In determining whether it is necessary to involve school personnel directly in the treatment of a family presenting with a child with a school problem, it is important to take into account the amount and quality of interaction between the school and the family, and its impact on the dysfunctional child. In some instances, it is evident from the outset that the family welcomes and responds appropriately to the school's directives. In such instances it is appropriate to begin therapy with the assumption that family intervention alone may be sufficient to re-empower the family system. In other instances the situation is less clear, and it is necessary to evaluate the school's contribution to the problem.

The term "school system" is generally understood to mean the entire political entity of the schooling offered in a given district. In the meaning assigned here, however, the term is analogous to "family system," and is defined as the cluster of individuals involved in significant interactions with the dysfunctional child and/or with the child's parents. Such a system, or team, may include the school counselor, social worker, nurse, one or more teachers, the building principal, and, on occasion, even the school superintendent. District school committees, such as those that designate children as "labeled" for special education may also be a significant part of the school system.

ECOSYSTEMIC CIRCUMPLEX MAPPING

In order to describe the ecosystemic relationship between two or more subsystems using the Circumplex model, each subsystem must first be rated along the dimensions of *adaptability*, *cohesion* and *communication*. The *family* is rated on the Clinical Rating Scale (CRS) developed by Olson and Killorin (1985) (see Figure 1). The therapist is directed to rate the three dimensions according to a series of criteria. The model diagrammatically maps two of these dimensions, *cohesion* and *adaptability*, while the third, *communication*, is simply assigned a numerical value. The first two variables are curvilinear, so that middle-level values place the system in the more balanced, and generally better-functioning central area of the model. Communication is a linear variable. Thus, the higher the score, the better the level of communication.

Although Olson (1986a) has recently developed a form for the evaluation of organizational styles of work groups (OSW) which requires that the members of the organization give their own ratings on the various dimensions, this does not seem appropriate in the use of the model in the school-family context. Rather, it appears advisable to maintain a consistent evaluative scheme, in which the therapist who has observed and rated the family system does the same for the school system. This is called a modified OSW. The object of this evaluation is twofold: to assess the team members' interaction with one another, and their interaction with the family.

Let us examine the use of the modified OSW with a simple example. A guidance counselor, often the first school contact when troubles arise, may not perceive the child's problem in the same light as the classroom teacher. This dissonance might be of value in that through collaboration, the teacher and counselor could exploit their discrepant ideas to arrive at a clear picture and then to devise a good intervention (possibility *a*). On the other hand, these differences might remain unresolved, leading to frequent and conflicting com-

Figure 1: Circumplex Model: Sixteen Types of Marital and Family Systems

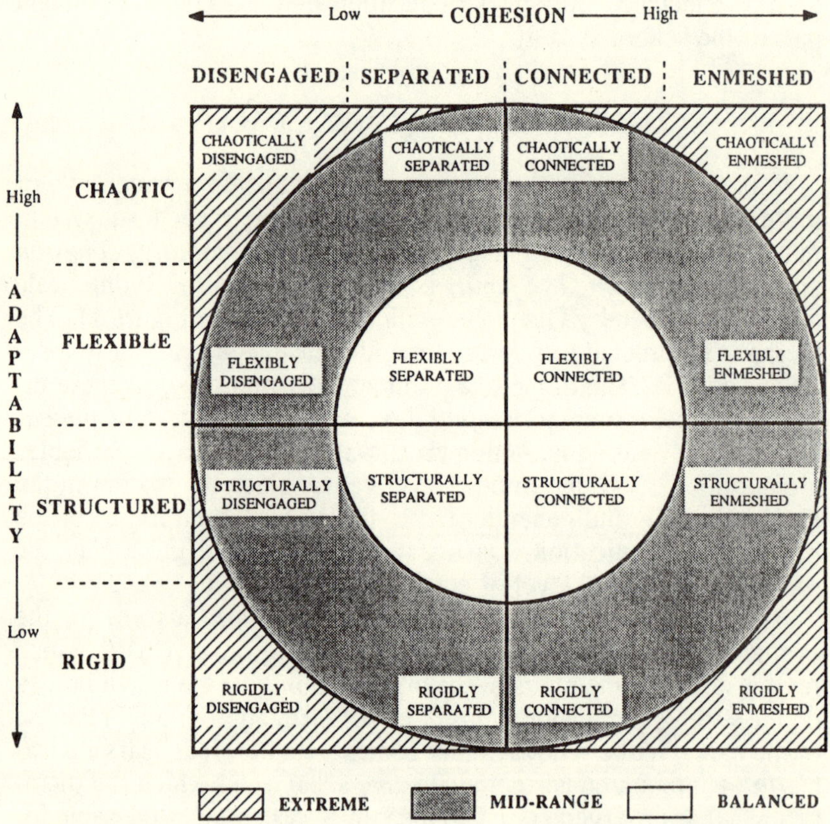

munications among teacher, counselor, and the family (possibility *b*).

In order to illustrate the modified OSW, we will examine possibility *b*, the dyad holding discrepant views which each expresses directly to the family. The first dimension evaluated is *Group Cohesion*, consisting of five factors, each rated on a four-point scale. Question 1 relates to work-group commitment. Since each team member feels free to confront the parents without regard to the other's position, the evaluation would rate a 1. Question 2, relating to the team's sharing of their personal life and feelings with each other, would generally be information unavailable to the external rater, and so would be excluded. Question 3, relating to how often the individuals work alone, rather than together, could be ascertained by questioning. For example, the counselor might report that the teacher regards involvement of the counselor as an unwarranted intrusion, so the counselor tends to work outside of the teacher's awareness. This would yield a rating of 1. Question 4, cooperation vs. competition, would likewise yield a 1. Question 5, "How close do you feel to your work group?" is, like Question 2, information generally unavailable to the external rater. Of the three applicable questions, the total score of 3 represents a very low level of cohesion. Since the lowest value listed for the cohesion factor is a 5, any number lower than 5 will be coded as 5. It should be noted that, through contact with the members of the work group, the evaluator may develop information relevant to Questions 2 and 5 as well, and in that event, those factors would be included. It should also be noted that each question yields useful information, as well as contributing to a global score.

The second dimension is *Group Adaptability*. Question 1 refers to the kind of leadership. In this instance, a rating of 4, (no clear leader) seems most accurate. Question 2, how often members do the same thing, would yield a 4 (seldom). Question 3 refers to the degree of flexibility of policies. Since there is no rule forbidding teacher and counselor from cooperating on a strategy to help the student, a rating of 3 (generally flexible) would seem appropriate. Question 4 refers to the degree of organization of the work group. Questioning of the counselor and teacher would reveal that there is no clear structure of organizational time provided for cooperative effort, and a score of 1 would be appropriate (not well organized). Question 5 refers to flexibility in making change. Discussion with the teacher and the counselor might reveal that while there is little structure encouraging flexibility, with informal consultation, they can alter their roles to a degree. This would be scored as a 2 (sometimes flexible). Thus, the total score for Adaptability would be 14, denoting a flexible system. By fixing these two points on the Circumplex map for work groups, a description of *flexibly disengaged* is obtained. In the usual OSW scoring, each factor is rated on a scale of 1 to 4, producing a summed score with a range of 5 to 20.

For the sake of comparability to the CRS, the modified OSW is compressed to a global score of 1 to 8.

For the *Communication* dimension, a somewhat different approach than either the CRS or the OSW is needed. Once again, the problem is that obtaining the team members' subjective appraisal is not appropriate, nor is it possible for the evaluator to directly observe the team in action. The school-family communication form, patterned after the CRS communication form, uses two of the CRS criteria, namely respect and regard and clarity, and adds a third, frequency and intensity (see Table 1). Current functioning of this team would place it in the very low range of communication, a score of 1. It is marked by little respect and regard for one another's views, poor clarity, especially in view of the frequent incongruences between the members, and a low rating for intensity and frequency, due to frequent contacts and a negative, blaming approach.

The task of creating a *Circumplex Ecomap* should begin with the family telephone intake. If it becomes apparent that the presenting problem is school related, the therapist should question the caller about the nature of the interaction between the family and the school, in addition to collecting other relevant information. If the referral was made by the school, permission should be requested to contact relevant school personnel. As a result of these calls, the therapist should begin to map a hypothetical description of the home and school systems and how they interact.

The Olson model's utility lies in the ease with which one may visualize the interfacing elements of the ecosystem in order to chart change and reevaluate shifts in strategy as shifts in one or another element in the ecosystem occur.

The following case example illustrates how the model may be used in this process. The reader may follow shifts in the ecosystem during the course of treatment by following Figure 2.

CASE EXAMPLE

Phase I: Initial Evaluation

The Y family consists of Anne, a 39-year-old professional woman, and her husband Bill, a 42-year-old businessman. They describe

TABLE 1. School-Family Communication*

	School Team Score	Low- - - - - - - - F a c i l i t a t i n g - - - - - - - - High		
		1 2	3 4	5 6
Respect and Regard		Lack of respect for feelings or message of other(s); possibly overtly disrespectful or belittling attitude	Somewhat respectful of others but not consistent across time or across all members;	Consistently appears respectful of others' feelings and message
Clarity		Inconsistent and/or unclear verbal message;	Some degree of clarity; but not consistent across time or across all members;	Verbal messages very clear;
		Frequent incongruencies between or among team members' messages;	Some incongruent messages;	Generally congruent messages;
Intensity and Frequency		No contact whatsoever or constant calling about minor problems; a parent-blaming approach	Frequent contacts about both inconsequential and important problems; both parent-blaming and problem-solving approaches;	Judicious contact about important issues; a problem-solving approach
Global Family-School Communication Rating (1-6)				

*After Olson and Killorin, 1985

Figure 2: Circumplex Model - Phases of Ecosystemic Treatment

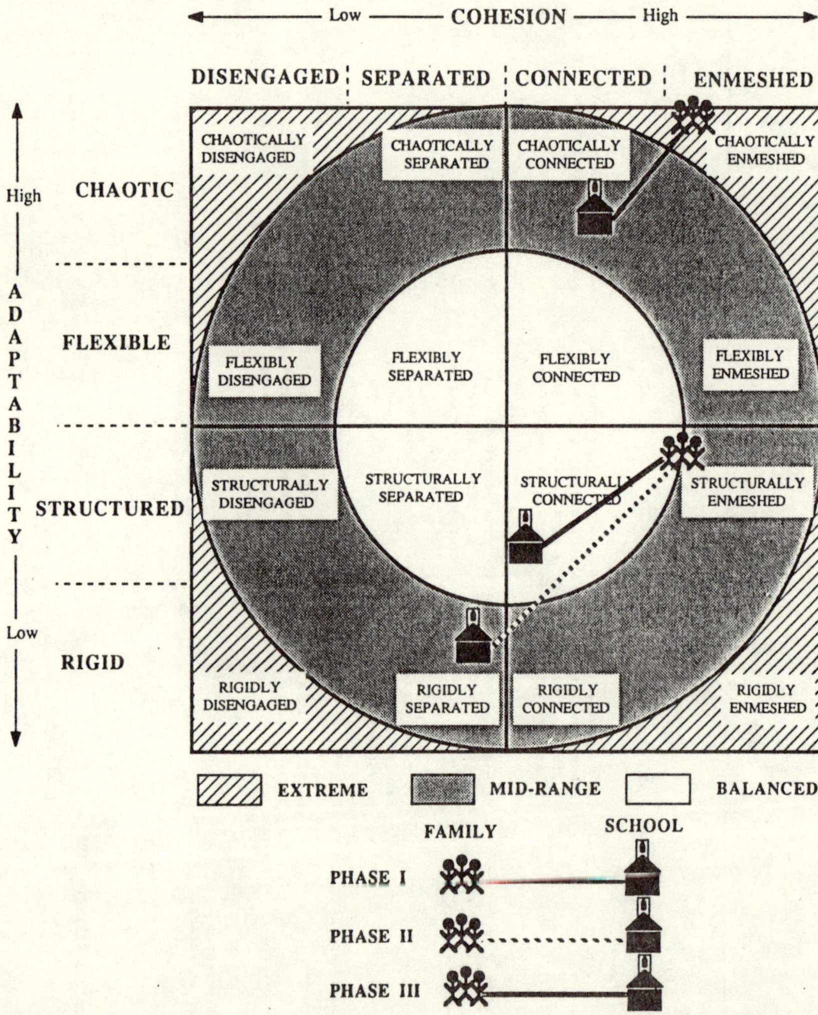

their three children, 9, 12 and 15, as "all on the difficult side." Jennie, the identified patient, is the oldest. She has a history of school avoidance, poor performance and poor impulse control. Both parents readily admit that they have been very lax with the children, and that they have difficulty agreeing on how to handle them. Jennie had transferred from another school about one year before therapy began. She was referred to this therapist by the school social worker.

Evaluation of the Family

An initial interview with the family resulted in an evaluation of chaotic enmeshment. On the cohesion scale, emotional bonding was very high, with great demands placed on the children for family loyalty. Family involvement was very high. The siblings continually bickered, often to the point of physical violence, at which point they vied for parental support. The marital relationship was characterized by extreme separateness. In fact, emotional "heat" was shown only when they disagreed about childrearing. Parent-child coalitions were very high. Jennie frequently took a parental child position. Father often took sides with Jennie against Mother. Internal boundaries showed a lack of personal separateness and privacy. In addition, decision-making was almost impossible, because while consensus was desired, it could almost never be achieved. External boundaries were very high, mainly focussed inside the family. The global rating was 7, very high enmeshment.

On the adaptability scale, leadership was limited and erratic, with parental control frequently unsuccessful or rebuffed, unless Mr. Y outshouted or sometimes hit the children. Mrs. Y was generally discounted. Discipline was inconsistent and generally ineffective. Negotiation was endless and decisions were arbitrary and impulsive. Roles were poorly defined. The children bickered about who should do which chores, while the parents argued over who was to exert discipline. Rules were characterized by frequent changes and inconsistent enforcement. The global rating was 8, or chaotic.

Communication was generally poor. Continuity tracking was low, with frequent asides and little continuity of content. Respect and regard were low, with overt disrespect and cross-generational belittling behavior. Clarity was low, with frequent incongruences between verbal and nonverbal messages. Freedom of expression was moderate, with some discussions of self, feelings and relationships. In terms of communication skills, empathy and attentive listening were sometimes evident, as were speaking for self and speaking for others. Intrusions, interruptions and premature closure were often evident.

In summary, the family was rated as chaotically enmeshed, with generally poor communication. The family's greatest strengths at this point lay in the areas of listeners' skills and some speakers' skills.

Evaluation of the School Team

The school system to which Jennie transferred included a school psychologist, a counselor, social worker, and several interested teachers. At first, as a newcomer, she seemed to fall through the cracks. However, within a few months' time, the school became most concerned with her acting-out behavior, and many contacts were made with the parents by the counselor and social worker, as well as by several teachers. Different messages were given, ranging from the thought that she was simply a stubborn, arrogant student, to the possibility that she was "severely disturbed." An initial evaluation was obtained through telephone interviews with several staff members, incidental to collecting information about Jennie and her family. They were rated at this point as a chaotically connected system. On the cohesion dimension, they were very committed, in that there was frequent conferring among staff about this case, as part of a generally good working relationship. They worked more together than alone on this particular case. Although they differed as to what to do, at this point they shared a problem-solving approach. A global rating of 6 was assigned for cohesion.

In terms of adaptability they were seen as chaotic. There was no clear leader. There was frequent overlap of tasks, in that the teachers, as well as the mental health staff, took a general position that Jennie was a "disturbed" person, and was to be treated as such. Policies were seen as flexible, in that members were able to overlap functions without much monitoring. For example, teachers, counselors, psychologist and social worker all had contact with the parents as a result of their interactions with Jennie. In short, the level of adaptability leaned toward the chaotic side, with a global rating of 7.

Communication was poor. The disagreement about how she

should be handled conveyed a lack of respect and regard among team members, both towards one another and towards Jennie and her family. Clarity was likewise low, because of the incongruence of messages. Intensity and frequency were characterized by constant calling, which conveyed a blaming approach. The global rating for communication was 2.

Strategy

It can be seen from the above that there was a great deal of similarity between the level of functioning of the two subsystems. Placed on the Circumplex Model (see Figure 2), they occupy adjacent regions. When two subsystems are very close in functioning in any extreme or high mid-range region, ecosystemic problems are most likely to require intense therapeutic interventions. Because they share so many negative qualities, they have entered into an escalating behavioral cycle, where the school's frequent and conflicting contacts with the family intensify the family's already poorly functioning system, at the same time further straining the school's function. Viewed in its own context, the interaction of the two systems is chaotic, enmeshed, and characterized by poor communication.

Such an impasse can sometimes be broken by an interdiction strategy (Lusterman, 1985). Direct contact between family and school is at first radically reduced. While the interdiction is in effect, information about the child is reported not to the family, but to the therapist, who helps to develop problem-solving strategies with the staff as problems arise. The therapist is available for frequent telephone communication during this phase. The school is thus freed to concentrate on more effective educational interventions, while the family can focus on its own issues, relieved to an extent of the additional stress imposed by the school. Such a strategy was initiated, thus ending Phase I, and preparing the way for the second phase, which consisted of several months during which the effects of the interdiction on both family and school could be observed, and a next strategy developed. Table 2 indicates the shifts in the school-family interaction from phase to phase.

TABLE 2. Shifts in School-Family Interaction

	Family			School		
Phase	Cohesion	Adaptabilty	Communication	Cohesion	Adaptability	Communication
I	7	8	2	6	7	2
II	6	4	3	4	2	4
III	6	4	4	5	3	5

Phase II: Managing the Interdiction

During the following three months, most communication about Jennie's school problems was between school staff and the therapist. Family meetings continued, but their focus was on issues other than school.

Evaluation of the Family

Both Jennie and her parents expressed relief at the reduction in pressure from school authorities. This is not to say that there were not further incidents, but simply that the family was not as disturbed by them. On the cohesion dimension, family involvement moved to the high moderate range, as parents gained greater control over sibling interaction. Parent-child coalitions declined to the low end of the enmeshed range as the parents became more aware of how the children manipulated them, and took a more united stand. The marital relationship improved slightly as they joined together on the parental level. The global rating was now 6.

On the adaptability dimension, the parents focussed their energy on leadership and discipline. A good example of this was the family's ability to complete a long vacation without serious incident for the first time in many years. Building on the reasonably good listener and speaker skills discussed in the Phase I evaluation, it was possible to develop their empathic skills to the point where they could see how their actions affected one another. Leadership moved into the structured range. Discipline improved somewhat, with less yelling and no hitting. Negotiation improved greatly. Roles were more clearly defined, and there was an improved ability to state rules clearly. The global adaptability rating was now 4.

Communication also improved, particularly in the areas of continuity tracking, respect and regard, and clarity, with a global rating of 3.

In summary, the family was now rated as structurally connected, with low moderate communication.

Evaluation of the School Team

During this phase, the school made considerable shifts. Through frequent consultation, teachers took a more definite stance with Jennie, tolerating little misbehavior. Jennie continued to test and was a frequent visitor to the counselor's office. There were still some differences of opinion among the remaining personnel, with the counselor taking the most rigid stand, and assuming a position of leadership. A fairly serious problem arose when, toward year's end, the counselor insisted that Jennie could not be assigned to an age-appropriate homeroom for the following year since it was clear that she was failing major subjects. Jennie became very angry and abusive, feeling that she was now trying, and getting little back for it. There was some disagreement among the mental health staff about this, but it was agreed that this would have to be negotiated between the parents and the counselor. The counselor remained adamant in this first meaningful encounter between home and school in several months. The parents were able to remain reasonably calm, and not overprotect Jennie. Nonetheless, they too felt that this was a very rigid stance. It was later discovered that the counselor was unsure of how much authority she indeed had to negotiate on this point, and, feeling backed into a corner by Jennie's anger, made no move to clarify this issue.

There was a reduction in the cohesion score as the teachers took a more disinterested approach and therefore conferred less frequently with the mental health staff. The mental health staff, which had mobilized so much energy around her, was also less absorbed with her. The global rating was now 4.

Adaptability showed a radical downward shift, as policies became more rigid, and a clear leader, in this case the counselor, emerged. Adaptability was now rated in the separated range, with a score of 2.

Communication was now in the moderate range, as messages became more consistent, and the frequency of contact declined radically.

In summary, the school was now viewed as rigidly separated, with moderate communication.

Strategy

It can be seen that there was a radical shift in both systems during this phase. Also, there was a general shift away from the extreme range, and towards the mid-range and the balanced range. Communication had improved sufficiently that, in a first return to school-family contact, there was no blowup, although an agreement could not be obtained. This meeting signalled the ending of Phase II, and paved the way for the next phase, during which an attempt would be made to reengage family and school in more direct contact.

Phase III: Reengagement

Although school and family were now back in communication, Jennie still was doing some acting out in school. The family reported great improvement at home, including better control of the children. Jennie had one remaining serious problem, they reported, and that was staying up very late at night, and not being able to get up on time in the morning. This was a cause of distress to both parents and school. She was sometimes so late now that she missed most of her morning classes, a serious violation of school rules.

The therapist presented to Mr. and Mrs. Y the idea of involving the family court by declaring Jennie what is called in New York State a PINS—that is, a "person in need of supervision." Under this procedure, if the court accepts the petition, then the child is so designated, and a probation officer is assigned to evaluate adherence to a set of rules laid down by the family court judge.

The rules may include obedience to parental directive, no physical fighting, compliance with an educational plan, attendance at therapy, and other similar strictures. In the absence of compliance, the court may impose meaningful sanctions, going so far as to place the child in a residential treatment center. One advantage of such a strategy is that pressure is increased on the parents and the school to produce results, in that the designation PINS implies that the family and the school are not supplying satisfactory guidance for the child. Everyone, including the parents, siblings, school and therapist, as well as the child, are reduced in the hierarchy, in that all must meet the standards imposed by the court if they are not to lose all autonomy to the court. This tactic frequently mobilizes the school, perhaps because it is now under scrutiny by an external agency. Just as the interdiction strategy was designed to separate the two subsystems, this strategy was designed to bring them closer together.

It is interesting to note that after the PINS petition was instituted, the building principal became directly involved for the first time. He took a somewhat autocratic position, in that he assumed responsibility for bending rules that lower echelon staff felt unable to undertake. This enabled Mr. and Mrs. Y to negotiate with the school a set of rules that both they and the school were willing to live with. Jennie was now under increased pressure from the court, and both family and school could present themselves to her as allies in her attempt to avoid court penalties.

Evaluation of the Family

Cohesion and adaptability remained stable in this phase. There was some improvement in communication, with continued growth in continuity tracking, respect and regard, and clarity. The global rating was now 4. In summary, the family continued to function as structurally connected, with high moderate communication.

Evaluation of the School Team

It should be noted that, at this point, the makeup of the team had changed to some degree. The teaching staff was no longer making much contact with the family. The principal was now a part of the team, providing some new direction, and sanctioning a somewhat more flexible approach.

There was an improvement in the cohesion score, in that the group was working together more now, and there was an increase in cooperation. The global rating was now 5.

An increase in flexibility caused a rise in adaptability to a global score of 3.

Communication continued to improve, attaining a global rating of 5.

In summary, the school team was now evaluated as structurally connected, with communication moderately high.

At this point, both school and family had achieved greatly improved ratings. Both now lay in the balanced region and were structurally connected, with improved communication. Therapeutic intervention is now very occasional. Family and school report an increasing ability to approach difficulties with Jennie on the basis of a problem-solving approach.

DISCUSSION

Olson (1985) has discussed the advantages of both the "insider's" and the "outsider's" perspectives. The rationale for the decision to limit all information in the ecosystemic evaluation to the outsider's perspective was discussed earlier, both in terms of the impracticality and lack of consistent methodology in attempting to gather OSW information directly from the school team. Nonetheless, the modified OSW presents several problems. Although an attempt was made to clearly define variables and to maintain a close match between cohesion, adaptability and communication as defined for the CRS and for the modified OSW, a perfect match is not attained. A complicating factor is the need for the OSW to perform double duty, in that it must describe both the workings of the team internally, and also its interaction with the family. Further refinement may also require a more careful description of the reciprocity of the school-family interaction, with more emphasis on the family's contribution.

Nonetheless, even in this very early form, the ecosystem mapping on the Circumplex Model is a rich source of hypotheses for treatment, and a valuable aid in describing school-family interaction.

What has been presented here is a single case study. It is hoped that future research will deal with refining the modified OSW and determining its reliability, validity, and especially, the orthogonality of the three dimensions.

REFERENCES

Lusterman, D-D. (1985). An ecosystemic approach to family-school problems. *American Journal of Family Therapy, 13*, 22-30.

Olson, D. & Killorin, E. (1985). *Clinical Rating Scale for the Circumplex Model of Marital and Family Systems*. St. Paul, MN: Family Social Science, University of Minnesota.

Olson, D. (1986). Circumplex model VII: Validation studies and FACES III. *Family Process, 25*, 337-351.

Olson, D. (1986a). *Organization Styles for Work Groups*. St. Paul, MN: Family Social Science, University of Minnesota.

Index

